THE TEACHER

First published 1908
This edition published by Lector House in 2024

ISBN: 978-93-6138-443-1

Lector House LLP
Registered Office: H. No. 96, Block C, Tomar Colony,
Burari, Delhi – 110084, India
info@lectorhouse.com
www.lectorhouse.com

THE TEACHER

ALICE FREEMAN PALMER,
GEORGE HERBERT PALMER

2024

LECTOR HOUSE LLP

THE TEACHER

ESSAYS AND ADDRESSES ON EDUCATION

BY

GEORGE HERBERT PALMER
AND
ALICE FREEMAN PALMER

PREFACE

The papers of this volume fall into three groups, two of the three being written by myself. From my writings on education I have selected only those which may have some claim to permanent interest, and all but two have been tested by previous publication. Those of the first group deal with questions about which we teachers, eager about our immeasurable art beyond most professional persons, never cease to wonder and debate: What is teaching? How far may it influence character? Can it be practiced on persons too busy or too poor to come to our classrooms? To subjects of what scope should it be applied? And how shall we content ourselves with its necessary limitations? Under these diverse headings a kind of philosophy of education is outlined. The last two papers, having been given as lectures and stenographically reported, I have left in their original colloquial form. A group of papers on Harvard follows, preceded by an explanatory note, and the volume closes with a few papers by Mrs. Palmer. She and I often talked of preparing together a book on education. Now, alone, I gather up these fragments.

CONTENTS

Page

I
PROBLEMS OF SCHOOL AND COLLEGE

I

THE IDEAL TEACHER

In America, a land of idealism, the profession of teaching has become one of the greatest of human employments. In 1903-04 half a million teachers were in charge of sixteen million pupils. Stating the same facts differently, we may say that a fifth of our entire population is constantly at school; and that wherever one hundred and sixty men, women, and children are gathered, a teacher is sure to be among them.

But figures fail to express the importance of the work. If each year an equal number of persons should come in contact with as many lawyers, no such social consequences would follow. The touch of the teacher, like that of no other person, is formative. Our young people are for long periods associated with those who are expected to fashion them into men and women of an approved type. A charge so influential is committed to nobody else in the community, not even to the ministers; for though these have a more searching aim, they are directly occupied with it but one day instead of six, but one hour instead of five. Accordingly, as the tract of knowledge has widened, and the creative opportunities involved in conducting a young person over it have correspondingly become apparent, the profession of teaching has risen to a notable height of dignity and attractiveness. It has moved from a subordinate to a central place in social influence, and now undertakes much of the work which formerly fell to the church. Each year divinity schools attract fewer students, graduate and normal schools more. On school and college instruction the community now bestows its choicest minds, its highest hopes, and its largest sums. During the year 1903-04 the United States spent for teaching not less than $350,000,000.

Such weighty work is ill adapted for amateurs. Those who take it up for brief times and to make money usually find it unsatisfactory. Success is rare, the hours are fixed and long, there is repetition and monotony, and the teacher passes his days among inferiors. Nor are the pecuniary gains considerable. There are few prizes, and neither in school nor in college will a teacher's ordinary income carry him much above want. College teaching is falling more and more into the hands of men of independent means. The poor can hardly afford to engage in it. Private schools, it is true, often show large incomes; but they are earned by the proprietors, not the teachers. On the whole, teaching as a trade is poor and disappointing business.

When, however, it is entered as a profession, as a serious and difficult fine art, there are few employments more satisfying. All over the country thousands of men and women are following it with a passionate devotion which takes little account of the income received. A trade aims primarily at personal gain; a profession at the exercise of powers beneficial to mankind. This prime aim of the one, it is true, often properly becomes a subordinate aim of the other. Professional men may even be said to offer wares of their own—cures, conversions, court victories, learning—much as traders do, and to receive in return a kind of reward. But the business of the lawyer, doctor, preacher, and teacher never squares itself by equivalent exchange. These men do not give so much for so much. They give in lump and they get in lump, without precise balance. The whole notion of bargain is inapplicable in a sphere where the gains of him who serves and him who is served coincide; and that is largely the case with the professions. Each of them furnishes its special opportunity for the use of powers which the possessor takes delight in exercising. Harvard College pays me for doing what I would gladly pay it for allowing me to do. No professional man, then, thinks of giving according to measure. Once engaged, he gives his best, gives his personal interest, himself. His heart is in his work, and for this no equivalent is possible; what is accepted is in the nature of a fee, gratuity, or consideration, which enables him who receives it to maintain a certain expected mode of life. The real payment is the work itself, this and the chance to join with other members of the profession in guiding and enlarging the sphere of its activities.

The idea, sometimes advanced, that the professions might be ennobled by paying them powerfully, is fantastic. Their great attraction is their removal from sordid aims. More money should certainly be spent on several of them. Their members should be better protected against want, anxiety, neglect, and bad conditions of labor. To do his best work one needs not merely to live, but to live well. Yet in that increase of salaries which is urgently needed, care should be used not to allow the attention of the professional man to be diverted from what is important,—the outgo of his work,—and become fixed on what is merely incidental,—his income. When a professor in one of our large universities, angered by the refusal of the president to raise his salary on his being called elsewhere, impatiently exclaimed, "Mr. President, you are banking on the devotion of us teachers, knowing that we do not willingly leave this place," the president properly replied, "Certainly, and no college can be managed on any other principle." Professional men are not so silly as to despise money; but after all, it is interest in their work, and not the thought of salary, which predominantly holds them.

Accordingly in this paper I address those only who are drawn to teaching by the love of it, who regard it as the most vital of the Fine Arts, who intend to give their lives to mastering its subtleties, and who are ready to meet some hardships and to put up with moderate fare if they may win its rich opportunities.

But supposing such a temper, what special qualifications will the work require? The question asked thus broadly admits no precise answer; for in reality there is no human excellence which is not useful for us teachers. No good quality can be thought of which we can afford to drop. Some day we shall discover a disturbing vacuum in the spot which it left. But I propose a more limited problem: what are those characteristics of the teacher without which he must fail, and what those which, once his, will almost certainly insure him success? Are there any such essentials, and how many? On this matter I have pondered long; for, teaching thirty-nine years in Harvard College, I have each year found out a little more fully my own incompetence. I have thus been forced to ask myself the double question, through what lacks do I fail, and in what direction lie the roots of my small successes? Of late years I think I have hit on these roots of success and have come to believe that there are four of them,—four characteristics which every teacher must possess. Of course he may possess as many more as he likes,—indeed, the more the better. But these four appear fundamental. I will briefly name them.

First, a teacher must have an aptitude for vicariousness; and second, an already accumulated wealth; and third, an ability to invigorate life through knowledge; and fourth, a readiness to be forgotten. Having these, any teacher is secure. Lacking them, lacking even one, he is liable to serious failure. But as here stated they have a curiously cabalistic sound and show little relation to the needs of any profession. They have been stated with too much condensation, and have become unintelligible through being too exact. Let me repair the error by successively expanding them.

The teacher's art takes its rise in what I call an aptitude for vicariousness. As year by year my college boys prepare to go forth into life, some laggard is sure to come to me and say, "I want a little advice. Most of my classmates have their minds made up about what they are going to do. I am still uncertain. I rather incline to be a teacher, because I am fond of books and suspect that in any other profession I can give them but little time. Business men do not read. Lawyers only consult books. And I am by no means sure that ministers have read all the books they quote. On the whole it seems safest to choose a profession in which books will be my daily companions. So I turn toward teaching. But before settling the matter I thought I would ask how you regard the profession." "A noble profession," I answer, "but quite unfit for you. I would advise you to become a lawyer, a car conductor, or something equally harmless. Do not turn to anything so perilous as teaching. You would ruin both it and yourself; for you are looking in exactly the wrong direction."

Such an inquirer is under a common misconception. The teacher's task is not primarily the acquisition of knowledge, but the impartation of it,—an entirely different matter. We teachers are forever taking thoughts out of our minds and putting them elsewhere. So long as we are content to keep them in our possession, we are not teachers at all. One who is interested in laying hold on wisdom is likely to become a scholar. And while no doubt it is well for a teacher to be a fair scholar,—I have known several such,—that is not the main thing. What constitutes the teacher is the passion to make scholars; and again and again it happens that the great scholar has no such passion whatever.

But even that passion is useless without aid from imagination. At every instant of the teacher's life he must be controlled by this mighty power. Most human beings are contented with living one life and delighted if they can pass that agreeably. But this is far from enough for us teachers. We incessantly go outside ourselves and enter into the many lives about us,—lives dull, dark, and unintelligible to any but an eye like ours. And this is imagination, the sympathetic creation in ourselves of conditions which belong to others. Our profession is therefore a double-ended one. We inspect truth as it rises fresh and interesting before our eager sight. But that is only the beginning of our task. Swiftly we then seize the lines of least intellectual resistance in alien minds and, with perpetual reference to these, follow our truth till it is safely lodged beyond ourselves. Each mind has its peculiar set of frictions. Those of our pupils can never be the same as ours. We have passed far on and know all about our subject. For us it wears an altogether different look from that which it has for beginners. It is their perplexities which we must reproduce and—as if a rose should shut and be a bud again—we must reassume in our developed and accustomed souls something of the innocence of childhood. Such is the exquisite business of the teacher, to carry himself back with all his wealth of knowledge and understand how his subject should appear to the meagre mind of one glancing at it for the first time.

And what absurd blunders we make in the process! Becoming immersed in our own side of the affair, we blind ourselves and readily attribute to our pupils modes of thought which are not in the least theirs. I remember a lesson I had on this point, I who had been teaching ethics half a lifetime. My nephew, five years old, was fond of stories from the Odyssey. He would creep into bed with me in the morning and beg for them. One Sunday, after I had given him a pretty stiff bit of adventure, it occurred to me that it was an appropriate day for a moral. "Ulysses was a very brave man," I remarked. "Yes," he said, "and I am very brave." I saw my opportunity and seized it. "That is true," said I. "You have been gaining courage lately. You used to cry easily, but you don't do that nowadays. When you want to cry now, you think how like a baby it would be to cry, or how you would disturb mother and upset the house; and so you conclude not to cry." The little fellow seemed hopelessly puzzled. He lay silent a minute or two and then said, "Well no, Uncle, I don't do that. I just go sh-sh-sh, and I don't." There the moral crisis is stated in its simplicity; and I had been putting off on that holy little nature sophistications borrowed from my own battered life.

But while I am explaining the blunders caused by self-engrossment and lack of imagination, let me show what slight adjustments will sometimes carry us past depressing difficulties. One year when I was lecturing on some intricate problems of obligation, I began to doubt whether my class was following me, and I determined that I would make them talk. So the next day I constructed an ingenious ethical case and, after stating it to the class, I said, "Supposing now the state of affairs were thus and thus, and the interests of the persons involved were such and such, how would you decide the question of right,—Mr. Jones." Poor Jones rose in confusion. "You mean," he said, "if the case were as you have stated it? Well, hm, hm, hm,—yes,—I don't think I know, sir." And he sat down. I called on one and another with the same result. A panic was upon them, and all their minds were alike empty. I went home disgusted, wondering whether they had comprehended anything I had said during the previous fortnight, and hoping I might never have such a stupid lot of students again. Suddenly it flashed upon me that it was I who was stupid. That is usually the case when a class fails; it is the teacher's fault. The next day I went back prepared to begin at the right end. I began, "Oh, Mr. Jones." He rose, and I proceeded to state the situation as before. By the time I paused he had collected his wits, had worked off his superfluous flurry, and was ready to give me an admirable answer. Indeed in a few minutes the whole class was engaged in an eager discussion. My previous error had been in not remembering that they, I, and everybody, when suddenly attacked with a big question, are not in the best condition for answering. Occupied as I was with my end of the story, the questioning end, I had not worked in that double-ended fashion which alone can bring the teacher success; in short, I was deficient in vicariousness,—in swiftly putting myself in the weak one's place and bearing his burden.

Now it is in this chief business of the artistic teacher, to labor imaginatively himself in order to diminish the labors of his slender pupil, that most of our failures occur. Instead of lamenting the imperviousness of our pupils, we had better ask ourselves more frequently whether we have neatly adjusted our teachings to the conditions of their minds. We have no right to tumble out in a mass whatever comes into our heads, leaving to that feeble folk the work of finding in it what order they may. Ours it should be to see that every beginning, middle, and end of what we say is helpfully shaped for readiest access to those less intelligent and interested than we. But this is vicariousness. *Noblesse oblige.* In this profession any one who will be great must be a nimble servant, his head full of others' needs.

Some discouraged teacher, glad to discover that his past failures have been due to the absence of sympathetic imagination, may resolve that he will not commit that blunder again. On going to his class to-morrow he will look out upon his subject with his pupils' eyes, not with his own. Let him attempt it, and his pupils will surely say to one another, "What is the matter to-day with teacher?" They will get nothing from that exercise. No, what is wanted is not a resolve, but an aptitude. The time for using vicariousness is not the time for acquiring it. Rather it is the time for dismissing all thoughts of it from the mind. On entering the classroom we should leave every consideration of method outside the door, and talk simply as interested men and women in whatever way comes most natural to us. But into that nature vicariousness should long ago have been wrought. It should be already on hand. Fortunate we if our great-grandmother supplied us with it before we were born. There are persons who, with all good will, can never be teachers. They are not made in that way. Their business it is to pry into knowledge, to engage in action, to make money, or to pursue whatever other aim their powers dictate; but they do not readily think in terms of the other person. They should not, then, be teachers.

The teacher's habit is well summed in the Apostle's rule, "Look not every man on his own things, but every man also"—it is double—"on the things of others." And this habit should become as nearly as possible an instinct. Until it is rendered instinctive and passes beyond conscious direction, it will be of little worth. Let us then, as we go into society, as we walk the streets, as we sit at table, practice altruistic limberness and learn to escape from ourselves. A true teacher is always meditating his work, disciplining himself for his profession, probing the problems of his glorious art, and seeing illustration of them everywhere. In only one place is he freed from such criticism, and that is in his classroom. Here in the moment of action he lets himself go, unhampered by theory, using the nature acquired elsewhere, and uttering as simply as possible the fulness of his mind and heart. Direct human intercourse requires instinctive aptitudes. Till altruistic vicariousness has become our second nature, we shall not deeply influence anybody.

But sympathetic imagination is not all a teacher needs. Exclusive altruism is absurd. On this point too I once got instruction from the mouths of babes and sucklings. The children of a friend of mine, children of six and four, had just gone to bed. Their mother overheard them talking when they should have been asleep. Wondering what they might need, she stepped into the entry and listened. They were discussing what they were here in the world for. That is about the size of problems commonly found in infant minds. The little girl suggested that we are probably in the world to help others. "Why, no indeed, Mabel," said her big brother, "for then what would others be here for?" Precisely! If anything is only fit to give away, it is not fit for that. We must know and prize its goodness in ourselves before generosity is even possible.

Plainly, then, beside his aptitude for vicariousness, our ideal teacher will need the second qualification of an already accumulated wealth. These hungry pupils are drawing all their nourishment from us, and have we got it to give? They will be poor, if we are poor; rich if we are wealthy. We are their source of supply. Every time we cut ourselves off from nutrition, we enfeeble them. And how frequently devoted teachers make this mistake! dedicating themselves so to the immediate needs of those about them that they themselves grow thinner each year. We all know the "teacher's face." It is meagre, worn, sacrificial, anxious, powerless. That is exactly the opposite of what it should be. The teacher should be the big bounteous being of the community. Other people may get along tolerably by holding whatever small knowledge comes their way. A moderate stock will pretty well serve their private turn. But that is not our case. Supplying a multitude, we need wealth sufficient for a multitude. We should then be clutching at knowledge on every side. Nothing must escape us. It is a mistake to reject a bit of truth because it lies outside our province. Some day we shall need it. All knowledge is our province.

In preparing a lecture I find I always have to work hardest on the things I do not say. The things I am sure to say I can easily get up. They are obvious and generally accessible. But they, I find, are not enough. I must have a broad background of knowledge which does not appear in speech. I have to go over my entire subject and see how the things I am to say look in their various relations, tracing out connections which I shall not present to my class. One might ask what is the use of this? Why prepare more matter than can be used? Every successful teacher knows. I cannot teach right up to the edge of my knowledge without a fear of falling off. My pupils discover this fear, and my words are ineffective. They feel the influence of what I do not say. One cannot precisely explain it; but when I move freely across my subject as if it mattered little on what part of it I rest, they get a sense of assured power which is compulsive and fructifying. The subject acquires consequence, their minds swell, and they are eager to enter regions of which they had not previously thought.

Even, then, to teach a small thing well we must be large. I asked a teacher what her subject was, and she answered, "Arithmetic in the third grade." But where is the third grade found? In knowledge, or in the schools? Unhappily it is in the schools. But if one would be a teacher of arithmetic, it must be arithmetic she teaches and not third grade at all. We cannot accept these artificial bounds without damage. Instead of accumulated wealth they will bring us accumulated poverty, and increase it every day. Years ago at Harvard we began to discuss the establishment of a Graduate School; and I, a young instructor, steadily voted against it. My thought was this: Harvard College, in spite of what the public imagines, is a place of slender resources. Our means are inadequate for teaching even undergraduates. But graduate instruction is vastly more expensive; courses composed of half a dozen students take the time of the ablest professors. I thought we could not afford this. Why not leave graduate instruction to a university which gives itself entirely to that task? Would it not be wiser to spend ourselves on the lower ranges of learning, covering these adequately, than to try to spread ourselves over the entire field?

Doubting so, I for some time opposed the coming of a Graduate School. But a luminous remark of our great President showed me the error of my ways. In the course of debate he said one evening, "It is not primarily for the graduates that I care for this school; it is for the undergraduates. We shall never get good teaching here so long as our instructors set a limit to their subjects. When they are called on to follow these throughout, tracing them far off toward the unknown, they may become good teachers; but not before."

I went home meditating. I saw that the President was right, and that I was myself in danger of the stagnation he deprecated. I changed my vote, as did others. The Graduate School was established; and of all the influences which have contributed to raise the standard of scholarship at Harvard, both for teachers and taught, that graduate work seems to me the greatest. Every professor now must be the master of a field of knowledge, and not of a few paths running through it.

But the ideal teacher will accumulate wealth, not merely for his pupils' sake, but for his own. To be a great teacher one must be a great personality, and without ardent and individual tastes the roots of our being are not fed. For developing personal power it is well, therefore, for each teacher to cultivate interests unconnected with his official work. Let the mathematician turn to the English poets, the teacher of classics to the study of birds and flowers, and each will gain a lightness, a freedom from exhaustion, a mental hospitality, which can only be acquired in some disinterested pursuit. Such a private subject becomes doubly dear because it is just our own. We pursue it as we will; we let it call out our irresponsible thoughts; and from it we ordinarily carry off a note of distinction lacking in those whose lives are too tightly organized.

To this second qualification of the teacher, however, I have been obliged to prefix a condition similar to that which was added to the first. We need not merely wealth, but an already accumulated wealth. At the moment when wealth is wanted it cannot be acquired. It should have been gathered and stored before the occasion arose. What is more pitiable than when a person who desires to be a benefactor looks in his chest and finds it empty? Special knowledge is wanted, or trained insight, or professional skill, or sound practical judgment; and the teacher who is called on has gone through no such discipline as assures these resources. I am inclined to think that women are more liable to this sort of bankruptcy than men. Their sex is more sympathetic than ours and they spend more hastily. They will drop what they are doing and run if a baby cries. Excellence requires a certain hardihood of heart, while quick responsiveness is destructive of the larger giving. He who would be greatly generous must train himself long and tenaciously, without much attention to momentary calls. The plan of the Great Teacher, by which he took thirty years for acquisition and three for bestowal, is not unwise, provided that we too can say, "For their sakes I sanctify myself."

But the two qualifications of the teacher already named will not alone suffice. I have known persons who were sympathetically imaginative, and who could not be denied to possess large intellectual wealth, who still failed as teachers. One needs a third something, the power to invigorate life through learning. We do not always notice how knowledge naturally buffets. It is offensive stuff, and makes young and wholesome minds rebel. And well it may; for when we learn anything, we are obliged to break up the world, inspect it piecemeal, and let our minds seize it bit by bit. Now about a fragment there is always something repulsive. Any one who is normally constituted must draw back in horror, feeling that what is brought him has little to do with the beautiful world he has known. Where was there ever a healthy child who did not hate the multiplication table? A boy who did not detest such abstractions as seven times eight would hardly be worth educating. By no ingenuity can we relieve knowledge of this unfortunate peculiarity. It must be taken in disjointed portions. That is the way attention is made. In consequence each of us must be to some extent a specialist, devoting himself to certain sides of the world and neglecting others quite as important. These are the conditions under which we imperfect creatures work. Our sight is not worldwide. When we give our attention to one object, by that very act we withdraw it from others. In this way our children must learn and have their expansive natures subdued to pedagogic exigencies.

Because this belittlement through the method of approach is inevitable, it is all-important that the teacher should possess a supplemental dignity, replacing the oppressive sense of pettiness with stimulating intimations of high things in store. Partly on this account a book is an imperfect instructor. Truth there, being impersonal, seems untrue, abstract, and insignificant. It needs to shine through a human being before it can exert its vital force on a young student. Quite as much for vital transmission as for intellectual elucidation, is a teacher employed. His consolidated character exhibits the gains which come from study. He need not point them out. If he is a scholar, there will appear in him an augustness, accuracy, fulness of knowledge, a buoyant enthusiasm even in drudgery, and an unshakable confidence that others must soon see and enjoy what has enriched himself; and all this will quickly convey itself to his students and create attention in his classroom. Such kindling of interest is the great function of the teacher. People sometimes say, "I should like to teach if only pupils cared to learn." But then there would be little need of teaching. Boys who have made up their minds that knowledge is worth while are pretty sure to get it, without regard to teachers. Our chief concern is with those who are unawakened. In the Sistine Chapel Michael Angelo has depicted the Almighty moving in clouds over the rugged earth where lies the newly created Adam, hardly aware of himself. The tips of the fingers touch, the Lord's and Adam's, and the huge frame loses its inertness and rears itself into action. Such may be the electrifying touch of the teacher.

But it must be confessed that not infrequently, instead of invigorating life through knowledge, we teachers reduce our classes to complete passivity. The blunder is not altogether ours, but is suggested by certain characteristics of knowledge itself: for how can a learner begin without submitting his mind, accepting facts, listening to authority, in short becoming obedient? He is called on to put aside his own notions and take what truth dictates. I have said that knowledge buffets, forcing us into an almost slavish attitude, and that this is resented by vigorous natures. In almost every school some of the most original, aggressive, and independent boys stand low in their classes, while at the top stand "grinds,"—objects of horror to all healthy souls.

Now it is the teacher's business to see that the onslaught of knowledge does not enfeeble. Between the two sides of knowledge, information and intelligence, he is to keep the balance true. While a boy is taking in facts, facts not allowed to be twisted by any fancy or carelessness, he is all the time to be made to feel that these facts offer him a field for critical and constructive action. If they leave him inactive, docile, and plodding, there is something wrong with the teaching. Facts are pernicious when they subjugate and do not quicken the mind that grasps them. Education should unfold us and truth together; and to enable it to do so the learner must never be allowed to sink into a mere recipient. He should be called on to think, to observe, to form his own judgments, even at the risk of error and crudity. Temporary one-sidedness and extravagance is not too high a price to pay for originality. And this development of personal vigor, emphasized in our day by the elective system and independent research, is the great aim of education. It should affect the lower ranges of study as truly as the higher. The mere contemplation of truth is always a deadening affair. Many a dull class in school and college would come to life if simply given something to do. Until the mind reacts for itself on what it receives, its education is hardly begun.

The teacher who leads it so to react may be truly called "productive," productive of human beings. The noble word has recently become Germanized and corrupted, and is now hardly more than a piece of educational slang. According to the judgments of to-day a teacher may be unimaginative, pedantic, dull, and may make his students no less so; he will still deserve a crown of wild olive as a "productive" man if he neglects his classroom for the printing press. But this is to put first things second and second things first. He who is original and fecund, and knows how to beget a similar spirit in his students, will naturally wish to express himself beyond his classroom. By snatching the fragments of time which his arduous work allows, he may accomplish much worthy writing and probably increase too his worth for his college, his students, and himself. But the business of book-making is, after all, collateral with us teachers. Not for this are we employed, desirable though it is for showing the kind of mind we bear. Many of my most productive colleagues have printed little or nothing, though they have left a deep mark on the life and science of our time. I would encourage publication. It keeps the solitary student healthy, enables him to find his place among his fellows, and more distinctly to estimate the contributions he is making to his subject. But let him never neglect his proper work for that which must always have in it an element of advertising.

Too long I have delayed the fourth, the disagreeable, section of my paper. Briefly it is this: a teacher must have a readiness to be forgotten. And what is harder? We may be excellent persons, may be daily doing kindnesses, and yet not be quite willing to have those kindnesses overlooked. Many a man is ready to be generous, if by it he can win praise. The love of praise,—it is almost our last infirmity; but there is no more baffling infirmity for the teacher. If praise and recognition are dear to him, he may as well stop work. Dear to him perhaps they must be, as a human being; but as a teacher, he is called on to rise above ordinary human conditions. Whoever has followed me thus far will perceive the reason. I have shown that a teacher does not live for himself, but for his pupil and for the truth which he imparts. His aim is to be a colorless medium through which that truth may shine on opening minds. How can he be this if he is continually interposing himself and saying, "Instead of looking at the truth, my children, look at me and see how skilfully I do my work. I thought I taught you admirably to-day. I hope you thought so too." No, the teacher must keep himself entirely out of the way, fixing young attention on the proffered knowledge and not on anything so small as the one who brings it. Only so can he be vicarious, whole-hearted in invigorating the lives committed to his charge.

Moreover, any other course is futile. We cannot tell whether those whom we are teaching have taken our best points or not. Those best points, what are they? We shall count them one thing, our pupils another. We gather what seems to us of consequence and pour it out upon our classes. But if their minds are not fitted to receive it, the little creatures have excellent protective arrangements which they draw down, and all we pour is simply shed as if nothing had fallen; while again we say something so slight that we hardly notice it, but, happening to be just the nutritive element which that small life then needs, it is caught up and turned into human fibre. We cannot tell. We work in the dark. Out upon the waters our bread is cast, and if we are wise we do not attempt to trace its return.

On this point I received capital instruction from one of my pupils. In teaching a course on English Empiricism I undertook a line of exposition which I knew was abstruse. Indeed, I doubted if many of the class could follow; but there on the front seat sat one whose bright eyes were ever upon me. It seemed worth while to teach my three or four best men, that man in particular. By the end of the term there were many grumblings. My class did not get much out of me that year. They graduated, and a couple of years later this young fellow appeared at my door to say that he could not pass through Cambridge without thanking me for his work on Locke, Berkeley, and Hume. Pleased to be assured that my questionable methods were justified, and unwilling to drop a subject so agreeable, I asked if he could tell precisely where the value of the course lay. "Certainly," he answered. "It all centred in a single remark of Locke's. Locke said we ought to have clear and distinct ideas. I don't think I got anything else out of the course."

Well, at first I was inclined to think the fellow foolish, so to mistake a bit of commonplace for gospel truth. Why did he not listen to some of the profound things I was saying? But on reflection I saw that he was right and I wrong. That trivial saying had come to him at a critical moment as a word of power; while the deep matters which interested me, and which I had been offering him so confidently day by day, being unsuited to him, had passed him by. He had not heard them.

To such proper unthankfulness we teachers must accustom ourselves. We cannot tell what are our good deeds, and shall only plague ourselves and hinder our classes if we try to find out. Let us display our subjects as lucidly as possible, allow our pupils considerable license in apprehension, and be content ourselves to escape observation. But though what we do remains unknown, its results often awake deep affection. Few in the community receive love more abundantly than we. Wherever we go, we meet a smiling face. Throughout the world, by some good fortune, the period of learning is the period of romance. In those halcyon days of our boys and girls we have a share, and the golden lights which flood the opening years are reflected on us. Though our pupils cannot follow our efforts in their behalf, and indeed ought not,—it being our art to conceal our art,—yet they perceive that in the years when their happy expansion occurred we were their guides. To us, therefore, their blind affections cling as to few beside their parents. It is better to be loved than to be understood.

Perhaps some readers of this paper will begin to suspect that it is impossible to be a good teacher. Certainly it is. Each of the four qualifications I have named is endless. Not one of them can be fully attained. We can always be more imaginative, wealthy, stimulating, disinterested. Each year we creep a little nearer to our goal, only to find that a finished teacher is a contradiction in terms. Our reach will forever exceed our grasp. Yet what a delight in approximation! Even in our failures there is comfort, when we see that they are generally due not to technical but to personal defects. We have been putting ourselves forward, or have taught in mechanical rather than vital fashion, or have not undertaken betimes the labor of preparation, or have declined the trouble of vicariousness.

Evidently, then, as we become better teachers we also become in some sort better persons. Our beautiful art, being so largely personal, will at last be seen to connect itself with nearly all other employments. Every mother is a teacher. Every minister. The lawyer teaches the jury, the doctor his patient. The clever salesman might almost be said to use teaching in dealing with his customer, and all of us to be teachers of one another in daily intercourse. As teaching is the most universal of the professions, those are fortunate who are able to devote their lives to its enriching study.

II

ETHICAL INSTRUCTION IN THE SCHOOLS

Within a few years a strong demand has arisen for ethical teaching in the schools. Teachers themselves have become interested, and wherever they are gathered the question, "What shall this teaching be?" is eagerly discussed. The educational journals are full of it. Within a year there have been published seven books on the subject. Several of them—it would be hardly an exaggeration to say all—are books of marked excellence. Seldom does so large a percentage of books in a single year, in a single country, and on a single subject reach so high a level of merit. I shall not criticise them, however, nor even engage in the popular discussion of which they form a part. That discussion concerns itself chiefly with the methods by which ethics may be taught. I wish to go behind this controversy and to raise the previous question whether ethics should be taught to boys and girls at all.

Evidently there are strong reasons why it should be. Always and everywhere it is important that men should be good. To be a good man!—it is more than half the fulfilment of life. Better to miss fame, wealth, learning, than to miss righteousness. And in America, too, we must demand not the mere trifle that men shall be good for their own sakes, but good in order that the life of the state may be preserved. A widespread righteousness is in a republic a matter of necessity. Where all rule all, each man who falls into evil courses infects his neighbor, corrupting the law and corrupting still more its enforcement. The question of manufacturing moral men becomes, accordingly, in a democracy, urgent to a degree unknown in a country where but a few selected persons guide the state.

There is also special urgency at the present time. The ancient and accredited means of training youth in goodness are becoming, I will not say broken, but enfeebled and distrusted. Hitherto a large part of the moral instruction of mankind has been superintended by the clergy. In every civilized state the expensive machinery of the Church has been set up and placed in the hands of men of dignity, because it has been believed that by no other engine can we so effectively render people upright. I still believe this, and I am pretty confident that a good many years will pass before we shall dispense with the ennobling services of our ministers. And yet it is plain that much of the work which formerly was exclusively theirs is so no longer. Much of it is performed by books, newspapers, and facilitated human intercourse. Ministers do not now speak with their old authority; they speak merely as other men speak; and we are all asking whether in the immense readjustment of faith now going on something of their peculiar power of moral as well as of intellectual guidance may not slip away.

The home too, which has hitherto been the fundamental agency for fostering morality in the young, is just now in sore need of repair. We can no longer depend upon it alone for moral guardianship. It must be supplemented, possibly reconstructed. New dangers to it have arisen. In the complex civilization of city life, in the huge influx of untutored foreigners, in the substitution of the apartment for the house, in the greater ease of divorce, in the larger freedom now given to children, to women, in the breaking down of class distinctions and the readier accessibility of man to man, there are perils for boy and girl which did not exist before. And while these changes in the outward form of domestic life are advancing, certain protections against moral peril which the home formerly afforded have decayed. It would be curious to ascertain in how many families of our immediate time daily prayers are used, and to compare the number with that of those in which the holy practice was common fifty years ago. It would be interesting to know how frequently parents to-day converse with their children on subjects serious, pious, or personal. The hurry of modern life has swept away many uplifting intimacies. Even in families which prize them most, a few minutes only can be had each day for such fortifying things. Domestic training has shrunk, while the training of haphazard companions, the training of the streets, the training of the newspapers, have acquired a potency hitherto unknown.

It is no wonder, then, that in such a moral crisis the community turns to that agency whose power is already felt beneficently in a multitude of other directions, the school. The cry comes to us teachers, "We established you at first to make our children wiser; we want you now for a profounder service. Can you not unite moral culture with intellectual?" It may be; though discipline of the passions is enormously more difficult than discipline of the mind. But at any rate we must acknowledge that our success in the mental field is largely staked on our success in the moral. Our pupils will not learn their lessons in arithmetic if they have not already made some progress in concentration, in self-forgetfulness, in acceptance of duty. Nor can we touch them in a single section of their nature and hope for results. Instruction must go all through. We are obliged to treat each little human being as a whole if we would have our treatment wholesome. And then too we have had such successes elsewhere that we may well feel emboldened for the new task. Nearly the whole of life is now advantageously surveyed in one form or another in our schools and colleges; and we have usually found that advance in instruction develops swiftly into betterment of practice. We teach, for example, social science and analyze the customs of the past; but soon we find bands of young men and women in all the important cities criticising the government of those cities, suggesting better modes of voting, wiser forms of charity; and before we know it the community is transformed. We cannot teach the science of electricity without improving our street-cars, or at least without raising hopes that they may some day be improved. Each science claims its brother art. Theory creeps over into action. It will not stay by itself; it is pervasive, diffusive. And as this pervasive character of knowledge in the lower ranges is perceived, we teachers are urged to press forward its operation in the higher also. Why have we no school-books on human character, the highest of all themes? Once direct the attention of our pupils to this great topic, and may we not ultimately bring about that moral enlargement for which the time waits?

I have stated somewhat at length the considerations in behalf of ethical instruction in the schools because those considerations on the whole appear to me illusory. I cannot believe such instruction feasible. Were it so, of course it would have my eager support. But I see in it grave difficulties, difficulties imperfectly understood; and a difficulty disregarded becomes a danger, possibly a catastrophe. Let me explain in a few words where the danger lies.

Between morals and ethics there is a sharp distinction, frequently as the two words are confused. Usage, however, shows the meaning. If I call a man a man of bad morals, I evidently mean to assert that his conduct is corrupt; he does things which the majority of mankind believe he ought not to do. It is his practice I denounce, not his intellectual formulation. In the same way we speak of the petty morals of society, referring in the phrase to the small practices of mankind, the unnumbered actions which disclose good or bad principles unconsciously hidden within. It is entirely different when I call a man's ethics bad. I then declare that I do not agree with his comprehension of moral principles. His practice may be entirely correct. I do not speak of that; it is his understanding that is at fault. For ethics, as was long ago remarked, is related to morals as geometry to carpentry: the one is a science, the other its practical embodiment. In the former, consciousness is a prime factor; from the latter it often is absent altogether.

Now what is asked of us teachers is that we invite our pupils to direct study of the principles of right conduct, that we awaken their consciousness about their modes of life, and so by degrees impart to them a science of righteousness. This is theory, ethics; not morals, practice; and in my judgment it is dangerous business, with the slenderest chance of success. Useless is it to say that the aim of such instruction need not be ethical, but moral. Whatever the ultimate aim, the procedure of instruction is of necessity scientific. It operates through intelligence, and only gets into life so far as the instructed intelligence afterward becomes a director. This is the work of books and teachers everywhere: they discipline the knowing act, and so bring within its influence that multitude of matters which depend for excellent adjustment on clear and ordered knowledge. Such a work, however, is evidently but partial. Many matters do not take their rise in knowledge at all. Morality does not. The boy as soon as born is adopted unconsciously into some sort of moral world. While he is growing up and is thinking of other things, habits of character are seizing him. By the time he comes to school he is incrusted with customs. The idea that his moral education can be fashioned by his teacher in the same way as his education in geography is fantastic. It is only his ethical training which may now begin. The attention of such a boy may be called to habits already formed; he may be led to dissect those habits, to pass judgment on them as right or wrong, and to inquire why and how they may be bettered. This is the only power teaching professes: it critically inquires, it awakens interest, it inspects facts, it discovers laws. And this process applied in the field of character yields ethics, the systematized knowledge of human conduct. It does not primarily yield morals, improved performance.

Nor indeed is performance likely to be improved by ethical enlightenment if, as I maintain, the whole business of self-criticism in the child is unwholesome. By a course of ethical training a young person will, in my view, much more probably become demoralized than invigorated. What we ought to desire, if we would have a boy grow morally sturdy, is that introspection should not set in early and that he should not become accustomed to watch his conduct. And the reason is obvious. Much as we incline to laud our prerogative of consciousness and to assert that it is precisely what distinguishes us from our poor relations, the brutes, we still must acknowledge that consciousness has certain grave defects when exalted into the position of a guide. Large tracts of life lie altogether beyond its control, and the conduct which can be affected by it is apt—especially in the initial stages—to be rendered vague, slow, vacillating, and distorted. Only instinctive action is swift, sure, and firm. For this reason we distrust the man who calculates his goodness. We find him vulgar and repellent. We are far from sure that he will keep that goodness long. If I offer to shake hands with a man with precisely that degree of warmth which I have decided it is well to express, will he willingly take my hand? A few years ago there were some nonsense verses on this subject going the rounds of the English newspapers. They seemed to me capitally to express the morbid influence of consciousness in a complex organism. They ran somewhat as follows:

> The centipede was happy, quite,
> Until the toad for fun
> Said, "Pray which leg comes after which?"
> This worked her mind to such a pitch
> She lay distracted in a ditch.
> Considering how to run.

And well she might! Imagine the hundred legs steered consciously—now it is time to move this one, now to move that! The creature would never move at all, but would be as incapable of action as Hamlet himself. And are the young less complex than centipedes? Shall their little lives be suddenly turned over to a fumbling guide? Shall they not rather be stimulated to unconscious rectitude, gently led into those blind but holy habits which make goodness easy, and so be saved from the perilous perplexities of marking out their own way? So thought the sagacious Aristotle. To the crude early opinion of Socrates that virtue is knowledge, he opposed the ripened doctrine that it is practice and habit.

This, then, is the inexpugnable objection to the ethical instruction of children: the end which should be sought is performance, not knowledge, and we cannot by supplying the latter induce the former. But do not these considerations cut the ground from under practical teaching of every kind? Instruction is given in other subjects in the hope that it may finally issue in strengthened action, and I have acknowledged that as a fact this hope is repeatedly justified. Why may not a similar result appear in ethics? What puts a difference between that study and electricity, social science, or manual training? This: according as the work studied includes a creative element and is intended to give expression to a personal life, consciousness becomes an increasingly dangerous dependence. Why are there no classes and text-books for the study of deportment? Is it because manners are unimportant? No, but because they make the man, and to be of any worth must be an expression of his very nature. Conscious study would tend to distort rather than to fashion them. Their practice cannot be learned in the same way as carpentry.

But an analogy more enlightening for showing the inaptitude of the child for direct study of the laws of conduct is found in the case of speech. Between speech and morals the analogies are subtle and wide. So minute are they that speech might almost be called a kind of vocal morality. Like morality, it is something possessed long before we are aware of it, and it becomes perfect or debased with our growth. We employ it to express ourselves and to come into ordered contact with our neighbor. By it we confer benefits and by it receive benefits in turn. Rigid as are its laws, we still feel ourselves free in its use, though obliged to give to our spontaneous feelings forms constructed by men of the past. Ease, accuracy, and scope are here confessedly of vast consequence. It has consequently been found a matter of extreme difficulty to bring a young person's attention helpfully to bear upon his speech. Indirect methods seem to be the only profitable ones. Philology, grammar, rhetoric, systematic study of the laws of language, are dangerous tools for a boy below his teens. The child who is to acquire excellent speech must be encouraged to keep attention away from the words he uses and to fix it upon that which he is to express. Abstract grammar will either confound the tongue which it should ease, or else it will seem to have no connection with living reality, but to be an ingenious contrivance invented by some Dry-as-dust for the torture of schoolboys.

And a similar pair of dangers await the young student of the laws of conduct. On the one hand, it is highly probable that he will not understand what his teacher is talking about. He may learn his lesson; he may answer questions correctly; but he will assume that these things have nothing to do with him. He becomes dulled to moral distinctions, and it is the teaching of ethics that dulls him. We see the disastrous process in full operation in a neighboring field. There are countries which have regular public instruction in religion. The argument runs that schools are established to teach what is of consequence to citizens, and religion is of more consequence than anything else. Therefore introduce it, is the conclusion. Therefore keep it out, is the sound conclusion. It lies too near the life to be announced in official propositions and still to retain a recognizable meaning. I have known a large number of German young men. I have yet to meet one whose religious nature has been deepened by his instruction in school. And the lack of influence is noticeable not merely in those who have failed in the study, but quite as much in those who have ranked highest. In neither case has the august discipline meant anything. The danger would be wider, the disaster from the benumbing influence more serious, if ethical instruction should be organized; wider, because morality underlies religion, and insensitiveness to the moral claim is more immediately and concretely destructive. Yet here, as in the case of religion, of manners, or of speech, the child will probably take to heart very little of what is said. At most he will assume that the text-book statement of the rules of righteousness represents the way in which the game of life is played by some people; but he will prefer to play it in his own way still. Young people are constructed with happy protective arrangements; they are enviably impervious. So in expounding moral principles in the schoolroom, I believe we shall touch the child in very few moral spots. Nevertheless, it becomes dulled and hardened if it listens long to sacred words untouched.

But the benumbing influence is not the gravest danger; analogies of speech suggest a graver still. If we try to teach speech too early and really succeed in fixing the child's attention upon its tongue, we enfeeble its power of utterance. Consciousness once awakened, the child is perpetually inquiring whether the word is the right word, and suspecting that it is not quite sufficiently right to be allowed free passage. Just so a momentous trouble appears when the moral consciousness has been too early stirred. That self-questioning spirit springs up which impels its tortured possessor to be continually fingering his motives in unwholesome preoccupation with himself. Instead of entering heartily into outward interests, the watchful little moralist is "questioning about himself whether he has been as good as he should have been, and whether a better man would not have acted otherwise." No part of us is more susceptible of morbidness than the moral sense; none demoralizes more thoroughly when morbid. The trouble, too, affects chiefly those of the finer fibre. The majority of healthy children, as has been said, harden themselves against theoretic talk, and it passes over them like the wind. Here and there a sensitive soul absorbs the poison and sets itself seriously to work installing duty as the mainspring of its life. We all know the unwholesome result: the person from whom spontaneity is gone, who criticises everything he does, who has lost his sense of proportion, who teases himself endlessly and teases his friends—so far as they remain his friends—about the right and wrong of each petty act. It is a disease, a moral disease, and takes the place in the spiritual life of that which the doctors are fond of calling "nervous prostration" in the physical. Few countries have been so desolated by it as New England. It is our special scourge. Many here carry a conscience about with them which makes us say, "How much better off they would be with none!" I declare, at times when I see the ravages which conscientiousness works in our New England stock, I wish these New Englanders had never heard moral distinctions mentioned. Better their vices than their virtues. The wise teacher will extirpate the first sproutings of the weed; for a weed more difficult to extirpate when grown there is not. We run a serious risk of implanting it in our children when we undertake their class instruction in ethics.

Such, then, are some of the considerations which should give us pause when the public is clamoring at our schoolhouse doors and saying to us teachers, "We cannot bring up our children so as to make them righteous citizens. Undertake the work for us. You have done so much already that we turn to you again and entreat your help." I think we must sadly reply, "There are limits to what we can do. If you respect us, you will not urge us to do the thing that is not ours. By pressing into certain regions we shall bring upon you more disaster than benefit."

Fully, however, as the dangers here pointed out may be acknowledged, much of a different sort remains also true. Have we not all received a large measure of moral culture at school? And are we quite content to say that the greatest of subjects is unteachable? I would not say this; on the contrary, I hold that no college is properly organized where the teaching of ethics does not occupy a position of honor. The college, not the school, is the place for the study. It would be absurd to maintain that all other subjects of study are nutritious to man except that of his own nature; but it is far from absurd to ask that a young man first possess a nature before he undertakes to analyze it. A study useless for developing initial power may still be highly profitable for doctrine, for reproof, for correction, for instruction in righteousness. Youth should be spontaneous, instinctive, ebullient; reflection whispers to the growing man. Many of the evils that I have thus far traced are brought about by projecting upon a young mind problems which it has not yet encountered in itself. Such problems abound in the later teens and twenties, and then is the time to set about their discussion.

But even in college I would have ethical study more guarded than the rest. Had I the power, I would never allow it to be required of all. It should be offered only as an elective and in the later years of the course. When I entered college I was put in my freshman year into a prescribed study of this sort. Happily I received no influence from it whatever. It passed over and left me untouched; and I think it had no more effect on the majority of my classmates. Possibly some of the more reflective took it to heart and were harmed; but in general it was a mere wasting of precious ointment which might have soothed our wounds if elected in the senior year. Of course great teachers defy all rules; and under a Hopkins, a Garman, or a Hyde, the distinctions of elective and prescribed become unimportant. Yet the principle is clear: wait till the young man is confronted with the problems before you invite him to their solution. Has he grown up unquestioning? Has he accepted the moral code inherited from honored parents? Can he rest in wise habits? Then let him be thankful and go his way untaught. But has he, on the other hand, felt that the moral mechanism by which he was early guided does not fit all cases? Has he found one class of duties in conflict with another? Has he discovered that the moral standards obtaining in different sections of society, in different parts of the world, are irreconcilable? In short, is he puzzled and desirous of working his way through his puzzles, of facing them and tracking them to their beginnings? Then is he ripe for the study of ethics.

Yet when it is so undertaken, when those only are invited to partake of it who in their own hearts have heard its painful call, even then I would hedge it about with two conditions. First, it should be pursued as a science, critically, and the student should be informed at the outset that the aim of the course is knowledge, not the endeavor to make better men. And, secondly, I would insist that the students themselves do the work; that they do not passively listen to opinions set forth by their instructor, but that they address themselves to research and learn to construct moral judgments which will bear critical inspection. Some teachers, no doubt, will think it wisest to accomplish these things by tracing the course of ethics in the past, treating it as a historical science. Others will prefer, by announcing their own beliefs, to stimulate their students to criticise those beliefs and to venture on their own little constructions. The method is unimportant; it is only of consequence that the students themselves do the ethicizing, that they trace the logic of their own beliefs and do not rest in dogmatic statement. Yet such an undertaking may well sober a teacher. I never see my class in ethics come to their first lecture that I do not tremble and say to myself that I am set for the downfall of some of them. In every such studious company there must be unprepared persons whom the teacher will damage. He cannot help it. He must move calmly forward, confident in his subject, but knowing that because it is living it is dangerous.

III

MORAL INSTRUCTION IN THE SCHOOLS

The preceding paper has discussed sufficiently the negative side of moral education. It has shown how children should not be approached. But few readers will be willing to leave the matter here. Are there no positive measures to be taken? Is there no room in our schools for any teaching of morality, or must the most important of subjects be altogether banished from their doors? There is much which might lead us to think so. If a teacher may not instruct his pupils in morality, what other concern with it he should have is not at once apparent. One may even suspect that attention to it will distract him from his proper work. Every human undertaking has some central aim and succeeds by loyalty to it. Each profession, for example, singles out one of our many needs and to this devotes itself whole-heartedly. Such a restriction is wise. No profession could be strong which attempted to meet the requirements of man as a whole. The physician accordingly selects his little aim of extirpating suffering and disease. His studies, his occupation, his aptitudes, his hopes of gain, his dignity as a public character, all have reference to this. Whatever is incompatible with it, of however great worth in itself, is rightly ignored. To save the soul of a patient may be of larger consequence than to invigorate his body. But the faithful physician attends to spiritual matters only so far as he thinks them conducive to bodily health. Or again the painter, because he is setting ocular beauty before us, concerns himself with harmonies of color, balance of masses, rhythms of line, rather than with history, anecdote, or incitements to noble living. I once heard a painter say, "There is religion enough for me in seeing how half a dozen figures can be made to go together," and I honored him for the saying. So too I should hold that the proper aim of the merchant is money-making and that only so much of charity or public usefulness can fairly be demanded of him as does not conflict with his profits. It is true that there are large ways and petty ways of acquiring gain, and one's own advantage cannot for long be separated from that of others. Still, the merchant rightly desists from any course which he finds in the long run commercially unprofitable.

What, then, is the central aim of teaching? Confessedly it is the impartation of knowledge. Whatever furthers this should be eagerly pursued; and all that hinders it, rejected. When schoolmasters understand their business it will be useless for the public to call to them, "We want our children to be patriotic. Drop for a time your multiplication table while you rouse enthusiasm for the old flag." They would properly reply, "We are ready to teach American history. As a part of human knowledge, it belongs to our province. But though the politicians fail to stir patriotism, do not put their neglected work upon us. We have more than we can attend to already."

Now in my previous paper I showed how a theoretic knowledge of good conduct had better not be given to children. By exposition of holy laws they are not nourished, but enfeebled. What they need is right habits, not an understanding of them: to become good persons rather than to acquire a critical acquaintance with goodness. What moral function then remains for the schools? To furnish knowledge of morality has been proved dangerous. For teachers to turn away from imparting knowledge and devote their scanty time to fashioning character is to abandon work which they alone are fitted to perform. Yet to let them send forth boys and girls alert in mind and loose in character is something which no community will long endure.

Until one has clearly faced these alternative perplexities he is in no condition to advise about grafting morality into a school curriculum; for until then he will be pretty sure to be misled by the popular notion of morality as a thing apart, demanding separate study, a topic like geography or English literature. But the morality nutritious for school-children is nothing of this kind. No additional hour need be provided for its teaching. In teaching anything, we teach it. A false antithesis was therefore set up just now when we suggested that a teacher's business was to impart knowledge rather than to fashion character. He cannot do the one without the other. Let him be altogether true to his scientific aims and refuse to accommodate them to anything else; he will be all the better teacher of morality. Carlyle tells of a carpenter who broke all the ten commandments with every stroke of his hammer. A scholar breaks or keeps them with every lesson learned. So conditioned on morality is the process of knowing, so inwrought is it in the very structure of the school, that a school might well be called an ethical instrument and its daily sessions hours for the manufacture of character. Only the species of character manufactured will largely depend on the teacher's acquaintance with the instrument he is using. To increase that acquaintance and give greater deftness in the use of so exquisite an instrument is the object of this paper. Once mastered, the tools of his own trade will be more prized by the earnest teacher than any additional handbook of ethics.

It will be easiest to point out the kind of moral instruction a school is fitted to give, if we distinguish with somewhat exaggerated sharpness its several lines of activity. A school is primarily a place of learning; it is unavoidably a social unit, and it is incidentally a dependent fellowship. No one of these aspects is ever absent from it. Each affords its own opportunity for moral training. The combination of them gives a school its power. Yet each is so detachable that it may well become the subject of independent study.

I. A school is primarily a place of learning, and to this purpose all else in it is rightfully subordinated. But learning is itself an act, and one more dependent than most on moral guidance. It occurs, too, at a period of life whose chief business is the transformation of a thing of nature into a spiritual being. Several stages in this spiritual transformation through which the process of learning takes us I will point out.

A school generally gives a child his first acquaintance with an authoritatively organized world and reveals his dependence upon it. By nature, impulses and appetites rule him. A child is charmingly self-centred. The world and all its ordered goings he notices merely as ministering to his desires. Nothing but what he wishes, and wishes just now, is important. He relates all this but little to the wishes of other people, to the inherent fixities of things, to his own future states, to whether one wish is compatible with another. His immediate mood is everything. Of any difference between what is whimsical or momentary and what is rational or permanent he is oblivious. To him dreams and fancies are as substantial as stars, hills, or moving creatures. He has, in short, no idea of law nor any standards of reality.

Now it is the first business of instruction to impart such ideas and standards; but no less is this a work of moralization. The two accordingly go on together. Whether we call the chaotic conditions of nature in which we begin life ignorance or deficient morality, it is equally the work of education to abolish them. Both education and morality set themselves to rationalize the moody, lawless, transient, isolated, self-assertive, and impatient aspects of things, introducing the wondering scholar to the inherent necessities which surround him. "Schoolmasters," says George Herbert, "deliver us to laws." And probably most of us make our earliest acquaintance with these impalpable and controlling entities when we take our places in the school. There our primary lesson is submission. We are bidden to put away personal likings and see how in themselves things really are. Eight times nine does not permit itself to be seventy-three or sixty-four, but exactly and forever seventy-two. Cincinnati lies obstinately on the Ohio, not on the Mississippi, and it is nonsense to speak of Daniel Webster as a President of the United States. The agreement of verbs and nouns, the reactions of chemical elements were, it seems, settled some time before we appeared. They pay little attention to our humors. We must accept an already constituted world and adjust our little self to its august realities. Of course the process is not completed at school. Begun there, it continues throughout life; its extent, tenacity, and instantaneous application marking the degree which we reach in scientific and moral culture. Let a teacher attempt to lighten the task of himself or his pupil by accepting an inexact observation, a slipshod remembrance, a careless statement, or a distorted truth, and he will corrupt the child's character no less than his intelligence. He confirms the child's habit of intruding himself into reality and of remaining listless when ordained facts are calling. Education may well be defined as the banishment of moods at the bidding of the permanently real.

But to acquire such obedient alertness persistence is necessary, and in gaining it a child wins a second victory over disorderly nature. By this he becomes acquainted not merely with an outer world, but with a still stranger object, himself. I have spoken already of the eagerness of young desires. They are blind and disruptive things. One of them pays small heed to another, but each blocks the other's way, preventing anything like a coherent and united life. A child is notoriously a creature of the moment, looking little before and after. He must be taught to do so before he can know anything or be anybody. A school matures him by connecting his doings of to-day with those of to-morrow. Here he begins to estimate the worth of the present by noticing what it contributes to an organic plan. Each hour of study brings precious discipline in preferring what is distantly important to what is momentarily agreeable. A personal being, in some degree emancipated from time, consequently emerges, and a selfhood appears, built up through enduring interests. The whole process is in the teacher's charge. It is his to enforce diligence and so to assist the vague little life to knit itself solidly together.

Nor should it be forgotten that to become each day the possessor of increasing stores of novel and interesting truths normally brings dignity and pleasure. This honorable delight reacts, too, on the process of learning, quickening its pace, sharpening its observation, and confirming its persistence. It is of no less importance for the character, to which it imparts ease, courage, beauty, and resourcefulness. But on the teacher it will depend whether such pleasure is found. A teacher who has entered deeply into his subject, and is not afraid of allowing enthusiasm to appear, will make the densest subject and the densest pupil glow; while a dull teacher can in a few minutes strip the most engrossing subject of interest and make the diligence exacted in its pursuit deadening. It is dangerous to dissociate toil and delight. The school is the place to initiate their genial union. Whoever learns there to love knowledge, will be pretty secure of becoming an educated and useful man and of finding satisfaction in whatever employment may afterwards be his.

One more contribution to character which comes from the school as a place of learning I will mention: it should create a sense of freedom. Without this both learning and the learner are distorted. It is not enough that the child become submissive to an already constituted world, obedient to its authoritative organization; not enough that he find pleasure in it, or even discover himself emerging, as one day's diligence is bound up with that of another. All these influences may easily make him think of himself as a passive creature, and consequently leave him half formed. There is something more. Rightly does the Psalmist call the fear of the Lord the beginning of wisdom rather than its end; for that education is defective which fashions a docile and slavish learner. As the child introduces order into his previously capricious acts, thoughts, and feelings, he should feel in himself a power of control unknown before, and be encouraged to find an honorable use for his very peculiarities. He should be brought to see that the world is unfinished and needs his joyful coöperation, that it has room for individual activity and admits rationally constructed purposes. From his earliest years a child should be encouraged to criticise, to have preferences, and to busy himself with imaginative constructions; for all this development of orderly freedom and of rejoicing in its exercise is building up at once both knowledge and character.

II. Yet a school becomes an ethical instrument not merely through being a place of learning but because it is also a social unit. It is a coöperative group, or company of persons pledged every instant to consider one another, their common purpose being jarred by the obtrusion of any one's dissenting will. Accordingly much that is proper elsewhere becomes improper here. As soon as a child enters a schoolroom he is impressed by the unaccustomed silence. A happy idea springs in his mind and clamors for the same outgo it would have at home, but it is restrained in deference to the assembled company. In crossing the room he is taught to tread lightly, though for himself a joyous dash might be agreeable; but might it not distract the attention of those who are studying? The school begins at nine o'clock and each recitation at its fixed hour, these times being no better than others except as facilitating common corporate action. To this each one's private ways become adjusted. The subordination of each to all is written large on every arrangement of school life; and it needs must be so if there is to be moral advance. For morality itself is nothing but the acceptance of such habits as express the helpful relations of society and the individual. Punctuality, order, quiet, are signs that the child's life is beginning to be socialized. A teacher who fails to impress their elementary righteousness on his pupils brutalizes every child in his charge.

Such relations between the social whole and the part assume a variety of forms, and the school is the best place for introducing a child to their niceties. Those other persons whom a schoolboy is called on continually to regard may be either his superiors, equals, or inferiors. To each we have specific duties, expressed in an appropriate type of manners. Our teachers are above us,—above us in age, experience, wisdom, and authority. To treat them as comrades is unseemly. Confession of their superiority colors all our approaches. They are to be listened to as others are not. Their will has the right of way. Our bearing toward them, however trustful or even affectionate, shows a respectfulness somewhat removed from familiarity. On the other hand schoolmates are comrades, at least those of the same sex, class, strength, and intelligence. Among them we assert ourselves freely, yet with constant care to secure no less freedom for them, and we guard them against any damage or annoyance which our hasty assertiveness might cause. In case of clash between their interest and our own, ours is withdrawn. And then toward those who are below us, either in rank or powers, helpfulness springs forth. We are eager to bridge over the separating chasm and by our will to abolish hindering defects. These three types of personal adjustment—respect, courtesy, and helpfulness, with their wide variety of combination—form the groundwork of all good manners. In their beginnings they need prompting and oversight from some one who is already mature. A school which neglects to cultivate them works almost irreparable injury to its pupils. For if these possibilities of refined human intercourse are not opened in the school years, it is with great difficulty they are arrived at afterwards.

The spiritualizing influence of the school as a social unit is, however, not confined to the classroom. It is quite as active on the playground. There a boy learns to play fair, accustoms himself to that greatest of social ties, *l'esprit du corps*. Throughout life a man needs continually to merge his own interests in those of a group. He must act as the father of a family, an operative in a factory, a voter of Boston, an American citizen, a member of an engine company, union, church, or business firm. His own small concerns are taken up into these larger ones, and devotion to them is not felt as self-sacrifice. A preparation for such moral ennoblement is laid in the sports of childhood. What does a member of the football team care for battered shins or earth-scraped hands? His side has won, and his own gains and losses are forgotten. Soon his team goes forth against an outside team, and now the honor of the whole school is in his keeping. What pride is his! As he puts on his uniform, he strips off his isolated personality and stands forth as the trusted champion of an institution. Nor does this august supersession of the private consciousness by the public arise in connection with sports alone. As a member of the school, a boy acts differently from what he otherwise would. There is a standard of conduct recognized as suitable for a Washington School boy, and from it his own does not widely depart. For good or for ill each school has its ideals of "good form" which are compulsive over its members and are handed on from class to class. To assist in moulding, refining, and maintaining these is the weightiest work of a schoolmaster. For these ideals have about them the sacredness of what is traditional, institutional, and are of an unseen, august, and penetrative power, comparable to nothing else in character-formation. To modify them ever so slightly a teacher should be content to work for years.

III. A third aspect of the school I have called its character as a Dependent Fellowship, and I have said that this is merely incidental. A highly important incident it is, however, and one that never fails to recur. What I would indicate by the dark phrase is this: in every school an imperfect life is associated with one similar but more advanced, one from which it perpetually receives influences that are not official nor measurable in money payment. A teacher is hired primarily to teach, and with a view also to his ability to keep order throughout his little society and to make his authority respected there. But side by side with these public duties runs the expression of his personality. This is his own, something which he hides or discloses at his pleasure. To his pupils, however, he must always appear in the threefold character of teacher, master, and developed human being; while they correspondingly present themselves to him as pupils, members of the school, and elementary human beings. Of these pairs of relationships two are contrasted and supplemental,—teacher and pupil, master and scholar, having nothing in common, each being precisely what the other is not. As human beings, however, pupil and teacher are akin and removed from one another merely by the degree of progress made by the elder along a common path. Here then the relation is one of fellowship, but a fellowship where the younger is largely dependent on the older for an understanding of what he should be. By example, friendship, and personal influence a teacher is certain to affect for good or ill every member of his school. In any account of the school as an ethical instrument this subtlest of its moral agencies deserves careful analysis.

There are different sorts of example. I may observe how the shopman does up a package, and do one so myself the next morning. A companion may have a special inflection of voice, which I may catch. I may be drawn to industry by seeing how steadily my classmate studies. I may adopt a phrase, a smile, or a polite gesture, which was originally my teacher's. All these are cases of direct imitation. Some one possesses a trait or an act which is passed over entire to another person, by whom it is substituted for one of his own. Though the adoption of such alien ways is dangerous, society could hardly go on without it. It is its mode of transmitting what is supposed to be already tested and of lodging it in the lives of persons of less experience, with the least cost to the receivers. Most teachers will have habits which their pupils may advantageously copy. Yet supposing the imitated ways altogether good, which they seldom are, direct imitation is questionable as disregarding the particular character of him in whom the ways are found and in assuming that they will be equally appropriate if engrafted on anybody. But this is far from true, and consequently he who imitates much is, or soon will be, a weakling. On the whole, a teacher needs to guard his pupils against his imitable peculiarities. If sensible, he will snub whoever is disposed to repeat them.

Still, there is a noble sort of imitation, and that school is a poor place where it does not go on. Certain persons have a strange power of invigorating us by their presence. When with them, we can do what seems impossible alone. They are our examples rather as wholes, and in their strength and spirit, than in their single traits or acts; and so whatever is most distinctive of ourselves becomes renewed through contact with them. It was said of the late Dr. Jowett that he sent out more pupils who were widely unlike himself than any Oxford teacher of his time. That is enviable praise; for the wholesomeness of example is tested by inquiring whether it develops differences or has only the power of duplicating the original. Every teacher knows how easy it is to send out cheap editions of himself, and in his weaker moments he inclines to issue them. But it is ignoble business. Our manners and tones and phrases and the ways we have of doing this and that are after all valuable only as expressions of ourselves. For anybody else they are rubbish. What we should like to impart is that earnestness, accuracy, unselfishness, candor, reverence for God's laws, and sturdiness through hardship, toward which we aspire—matters in reality only half ours and which spring up with fresh and original beauty in every soul where they once take root. The Dependent Fellowship of a school makes these larger, enkindling, and diversifying influences peculiarly possible. It should be a teacher's highest ambition to exercise them. And though we might naturally expect that such inspiring teachers would be rare, I seldom enter a school without finding indications of the presence of at least one of them.

But for those who would acquire this larger influence a strange caution is necessary: Examples do not work that are not real. We sometimes try to "set an example," that is, to put on a type of character for the benefit of a beholder; and are usually disappointed. Personal influence is not an affair of acting, but of being. Those about us are strangely affected by what we veritably are, only slightly by what we would have them see. If we are indisposed to study, yet, knowing that industry is good for our scholars, assume a bustling diligence, they are more likely to feel the real portion of the affair, our laziness, than the activity which was designed for their copying. Astonishingly shrewd are the young at scenting humbug and being unaffected by its pretensions. There is consequently no method to be learned for gaining personal influence. Almost everything else requires plan and effort. This precious power needs little attention. It will not come in one way better than another. A fair measure of sympathetic tact is useful for starting it; but in the long run persons rude and suave, talkative and silent, handsome and ugly, stalwart and slight, possess it in about equal degree, the very characteristics which we should be disposed to count disadvantageous often seeming to confirm its hold. Since it generally comes about that our individual interests become in some measure those of our pupils too, the only safe rule for personal influence is to go heartily about our own affairs, with a friendly spirit, and let our usual nature have whatever effect it may.

Still, there is one important mode of preparation: seeing that personal influence springs from what we are, we can really be a good deal. In a former paper, on The Ideal Teacher, I pointed this out and insisted that to be of any use in the classroom we teachers must bring there an already accumulated wealth. I will not repeat what I have said already, for a little reflection will convince any one that when he lacks personal influence he lacks much besides. A great example comes from a great nature, and we who live in fellowship with dependent and imitative youth should acquire natures large enough to serve both their needs and our own. Let teachers be big, bounteous, and unconventional, and they will have few backward pupils.

Personal influence is often assumed to be greater the closer the intimacy. I believe the contrary to be the case. Familiarity, says the shrewd proverb, breeds contempt. And certainly the young, who are little trained in estimating values, when brought into close association with their elders are apt to fix their attention on petty points and so to miss the larger lines of character. These they see best across an interval where, though visible only in outline, they are clear, unconfused with anything else, and so productive of their best effect. For the immature, distance is a considerable help in inducing enchantment, and nothing is so destructive of high influence as a slap-on-the-back acquaintance. One who is to help us much must be above us. A teacher should carefully respect his own dignity and no less carefully that of his pupil. In our eagerness to help, we may easily cheapen a fine nature by intruding too frequently into its reserves; and on the other hand I have observed that the boy who comes oftenest for advice is he who profits by it least. It is safest not to meddle much with the insides of our pupils. An occasional weighty word is more compulsive than frequent talk.

Within the limits then here marked out we who live in these Dependent Fellowships must submit to be admired. We must allow our pupils to idealize us and even offer ourselves for imitation. It is not pleasant. Usually nobody knows his weaknesses better than the one who is mistaken for an example. But what a helpful mistake! What ennobling influences come to schoolboys when once they can think their teacher is the sort of person they would like to be! Perhaps at the very moment that teacher is thinking they are the sort of person he would like to be. No matter. What they admire is worthy, even if not embodied precisely where they imagine. In humility we accept their admiration, knowing that nothing else can so enlarge their lives. As I recall my college days, there rise before me two teachers. As I entered the lecture rooms of those two men, I said to myself, "Oh, if some day I could be like that!" And always afterwards as I went to those respective rooms, the impression of dignity deepened. I have forgotten the lessons I learned from those instructors. I never can discharge my debt to the instructors themselves.

Such are the moral resources of our schools. Without turning aside in the slightest from their proper aim of imparting knowledge, teachers are able,—almost compelled—to supply their pupils with an intellectual, social, and personal righteousness. What more is wanted? When such opportunities for moral instruction are already within their grasp, is it worth while to incur the grave dangers of ethical instruction too? I think not, and I even fear that the establishment of courses in moral theory might weaken the sense of responsibility among the other teachers and lead them to attach less importance to the moralization of their pupils by themselves. This is burdensome business, no doubt, but we must not shift it to a single pair of shoulders. Rather let us insist, when bad boys and girls continue in a school, that the blame belongs to the teachers as a whole, and not to some ethical coach. It is from the management and temper of a school that its formative influence proceeds. We cannot safely turn over anything so all-pervading to the instructors of a single department. That school where neatness, courtesy, simplicity, obtain; where enthusiasm goes with mental exactitude, thoroughness of work with interest, and absence of artificiality with refinement; where sneaks, liars, loafers, pretenders, rough persons are despised, while teachers who refuse to be mechanical hold sway—that school is engaged in moral training all day long.

Yet while I hold that the systematic study of ethics had on the whole better be left to the colleges, I confess that the line which I have attempted to draw between consciousness and unconsciousness, between the age which is best directed by instinct and the age when the questioning faculties put forward their inexorable demands, is a wavering one and cannot be sharply drawn. By one child it is crossed at one period, by another at another. Seldom is the crossing noticed. Before we are aware we find ourselves in sorrow on the farther side. Happy the youth who during the transition time has a wise friend at hand to answer a question, to speak a steadying word, to open up the vista which at the moment needs to be cleared. Only one in close personal touch is serviceable here. But in defect of home guidance, to us teachers falls much of the charge of developing the youthful consciousness of moral matters naturally, smoothly, and without jar. This has always been a part of the teacher's office. So far as I can ascertain schools of the olden time had in them a large amount of wholesome ethical training. Schools were unsystematic then; there lay no examination paper ahead of them; there was time for pause and talk. If a subject arose which the teacher deemed important for his pupils' personal lives, he could lead them on to question about it, so far as he believed discussion useful. This sort of ethical training the hurry of our time has largely exterminated; and now that wholesome incidental instruction is gone, we demand in the modern way that a clear-cut department of ethics be introduced into the curriculum. But such things do not let themselves be treated in departmental fashion. The teacher must still work as a friend. He cannot be discharged from knowing when and how to stimulate a question, from discerning which boy or girl would be helped by consciousness and which would be harmed. In these high regions our pupils cannot be approached in classes. They require individual attention. And not because we are teachers merely, but because we and they are human beings, we must be ready with spiritual aid.

IV

SELF-CULTIVATION IN ENGLISH

English study has four aims: the mastery of our language as a science, as a history, as a joy, and as a tool. I am concerned with but one, the mastery of it as a tool. Philology and grammar present it as a science; the one attempting to follow its words, the other its sentences, through all the intricacies of their growth, and so to manifest laws which lie hidden in these airy products no less than in the moving stars or the myriad flowers of spring. Fascinating and important as all this is, I do not recommend it here. For I want to call attention only to that sort of English study which can be carried on without any large apparatus of books. For a reason similar, though less cogent, I do not urge historical study. Probably the current of English literature is more attractive through its continuity than that of any other nation. Notable works in verse and prose have appeared in long succession, and without gaps intervening, in a way that would be hard to parallel in any other language known to man. A bounteous endowment this for every English speaker, and one which should stimulate us to trace the marvellous and close-linked progress from the times of the Saxons to those of Tennyson and Kipling. Literature too has this advantage over every other species of art study, that everybody can examine the original masterpieces and not depend on reproductions, as in the cases of painting, sculpture, and architecture; or on intermediate interpretation, as in the case of music. To-day most of these masterpieces can be bought for a trifle, and even a poor man can follow through centuries the thoughts of his ancestors. But even so, ready of access as it is, English can be studied as a history only at the cost of solid time and continuous attention, much more time than the majority of those for whom I am writing can afford. By most of us our mighty literature cannot be taken in its continuous current, the later stretches proving interesting through relation with the earlier. It must be taken fragmentarily, if at all, the attention delaying on those parts only which offer the greatest beauty or promise the best exhilaration. In other words, English may be possible as a joy where it is not possible as a history. In the endless wealth which our poetry, story, essay, and drama afford, every disposition may find its appropriate nutriment, correction, or solace. He is unwise, however busy, who does not have his loved authors, veritable friends with whom he takes refuge in the intervals of work and by whose intimacy he enlarges, refines, sweetens, and emboldens his own limited existence. Yet the fact that English as a joy must largely be conditioned by individual taste prevents me from offering general rules for its pursuit. The road which leads one man straight to this joy leads another to tedium. In all literary enjoyment there is something incalculable, something wayward, eluding the precision of rule, and rendering inexact the precepts of him who would point out the path to it. While I believe that many suggestions may be made, useful to the young enjoyer and promotive of his wise vagrancy, I shall not undertake here the complicated task of offering them. Let enjoyment go, let history go, let science go, and still English remains—English as a tool. Every hour our language is an engine for communicating with others, every instant for fashioning the thoughts of our own minds. I want to call attention to the means of mastering this curious and essential tool, and to lead every one who reads me to become discontented with his employment of it.

The importance of literary power needs no long argument. Everybody acknowledges it, and sees that without it all other human faculties are maimed. Shakespeare says that death-bringing time "insults o'er dull and speechless tribes." It and all who live in it insult over the speechless person. So mutually dependent are we that on our swift and full communication with one another is staked the success of almost every scheme we form. He who can explain himself may command what he wants. He who cannot is left to the poverty of individual resource; for men do what we desire only when persuaded. The persuasive and explanatory tongue is, therefore, one of the chief levers of life. Its leverage is felt within us as well as without, for expression and thought are integrally bound together. We do not first possess completed thoughts and then express them. The very formation of the outward product extends, sharpens, enriches the mind which produces, so that he who gives forth little after a time is likely enough to discover that he has little to give forth. By expression too we may carry our benefits and our names to a far generation. This durable character of fragile language puts a wide difference of worth between it and some of the other great objects of desire,—health, wealth, and beauty, for example. These are notoriously liable to accident. We tremble while we have them. But literary power, once ours, is more likely than any other possession to be ours always. It perpetuates and enlarges itself by the very fact of its existence and perishes only with the decay of the man himself. For this reason, because more than health, wealth, and beauty, literary style may be called the man, good judges have found in it the final test of culture and have said that he, and he alone, is a well-educated person who uses his language with power and beauty. The supreme and ultimate product of civilization, it has well been said, is two or three persons talking together in a room. Between ourselves and our language there accordingly springs up an association peculiarly close. We are as sensitive to criticism of our speech as of our manners. The young man looks up with awe to him who has written a book, as already half divine; and the graceful speaker is a universal object of envy.

But the very fact that literary endowment is immediately recognized and eagerly envied has induced a strange illusion in regard to it. It is supposed to be something mysterious, innate in him who possesses it and quite out of the reach of him who has it not. The very contrary is the fact. No human employment is more free and calculable than the winning of language. Undoubtedly there are natural aptitudes for it, as there are for farming, seamanship, or being a good husband. But nowhere is straight work more effective. Persistence, care, discriminating observation, ingenuity, refusal to lose heart,—traits which in every other occupation tend toward excellence,—tend toward it here with special security. Whoever goes to his grave with bad English in his mouth has no one to blame but himself for the disagreeable taste; for if faulty speech can be inherited, it can be exterminated too. I hope to point out some of the methods of substituting good English for bad. And since my space is brief, and I wish to be remembered, I throw what I have to say into the form of four simple precepts which, if pertinaciously obeyed, will, I believe, give anybody effective mastery of English as a tool.

First then, "Look well to your speech." It is commonly supposed that when a man seeks literary power he goes to his room and plans an article for the press. But this is to begin literary culture at the wrong end. We speak a hundred times for every once we write. The busiest writer produces little more than a volume a year, not so much as his talk would amount to in a week. Consequently through speech it is usually decided whether a man is to have command of his language or not. If he is slovenly in his ninety-nine cases of talking, he can seldom pull himself up to strength and exactitude in the hundredth case of writing. A person is made in one piece, and the same being runs through a multitude of performances. Whether words are uttered on paper or to the air, the effect on the utterer is the same. Vigor or feebleness results according as energy or slackness has been in command. I know that certain adaptations to a new field are often necessary. A good speaker may find awkwardnesses in himself when he comes to write, a good writer when he speaks. And certainly cases occur where a man exhibits distinct strength in one of the two, speaking or writing, and not in the other. But such cases are rare. As a rule, language once within our control can be employed for oral or for written purposes. And since the opportunities for oral practice enormously outbalance those for written, it is the oral which are chiefly significant in the development of literary power. We rightly say of the accomplished writer that he shows a mastery of his own tongue.

This predominant influence of speech marks nearly all great epochs of literature. The Homeric poems are addressed to the ear, not to the eye. It is doubtful if Homer knew writing, certain that he knew profoundly every quality of the tongue,—veracity, vividness, shortness of sentence, simplicity of thought, obligation to insure swift apprehension. Writing and rigidity are apt to go together. In Homer's smooth-slipping verses one catches everywhere the voice. So too the aphorisms of Hesiod might naturally pass from mouth to mouth, and the stories of Herodotus be told by an old man at the fireside. Early Greek literature is plastic and garrulous. Its distinctive glory is that it contains no literary note; that it gives forth human feeling not in conventional arrangement, but with apparent spontaneity—in short, that it is speech literature, not book literature. And the same tendency continued long among the Greeks. At the culmination of their power the drama was their chief literary form,—the drama, which is but speech ennobled, connected, clarified. Plato too, following the dramatic precedent and the precedent of his talking master, accepted conversation as his medium for philosophy and imparted to it the vivacity, ease, waywardness even, which the best conversation exhibits. Nor was the experience of the Greeks peculiar. Our literature shows a similar tendency. Its bookish times are its decadent times, its talking times its glory. Chaucer, like Herodotus, is a story-teller, and follows the lead of those who on the Continent entertained courtly circles with pleasant tales. Shakespeare and his fellows in the spacious times of great Elizabeth did not concern themselves with publication. Marston in one of his prefaces thinks it necessary to apologize for putting his piece in print, and says he would not have done such a thing if unscrupulous persons, hearing the play at the theatre, had not already printed corrupt versions of it. Even the Queen Anne's men, far removed though they are from anything dramatic, still shape their ideals of literature by demands of speech. The essays of the Spectator, the poems of Pope, are the remarks of a cultivated gentleman at an evening party. Here is the brevity, the good taste, the light touch, the neat epigram, the avoidance of whatever might stir passion, controversy, or laborious thought, which characterize the conversation of a well-bred man. Indeed it is hard to see how any literature can be long vital which is based on the thought of a book and not on that of living utterance. Unless the speech notion is uppermost, words will not run swiftly to their mark. They delay in delicate phrasings while naturalness and a sense of reality disappear. Women are the best talkers. I sometimes please myself with noticing that three of the greatest periods of English literature coincide with the reigns of the three English queens.

Fortunate it is, then, that self-cultivation in the use of English must chiefly come through speech; because we are always speaking, whatever else we do. In opportunities for acquiring a mastery of language the poorest and busiest are at no large disadvantage as compared with the leisured rich. It is true the strong impulse which comes from the suggestion and approval of society may in some cases be absent, but this can be compensated by the sturdy purpose of the learner. A recognition of the beauty of well-ordered words, a strong desire, patience under discouragements, and promptness in counting every occasion as of consequence,—these are the simple agencies which sweep one on to power. Watch your speech then. That is all which is needed. Only it is desirable to know what qualities of speech to watch for. I find three,—accuracy, audacity, and range,—and I will say a few words about each.

Obviously, good English is exact English. Our words should fit our thoughts like a glove and be neither too wide nor too tight. If too wide, they will include much vacuity beside the intended matter. If too tight, they will check the strong grasp. Of the two dangers, looseness is by far the greater. There are people who say what they mean with such a naked precision that nobody not familiar with the subject can quickly catch the sense. George Herbert and Emerson strain the attention of many. But niggardly and angular speakers are rare. Too frequently words signify nothing in particular. They are merely thrown out in a certain direction to report a vague and undetermined meaning or even a general emotion. The first business of every one who would train himself in language is to articulate his thought, to know definitely what he wishes to say, and then to pick those words which compel the hearer to think of this and only this. For such a purpose two words are often better than three. The fewer the words, the more pungent the impression. Brevity is the soul, not simply of a jest, but of wit in its finer sense where it is identical with wisdom. He who can put a great deal into a little is the master. Since firm texture is what is wanted, not embroidery or superposed ornament, beauty has been well defined as the purgation of superfluities. And certainly many a paragraph might have its beauty brightened by letting quiet words take the place of its loud words, omitting its "verys," and striking out its purple patches of fine writing. Here is Ben Jonson's description of Bacon's language: "There happened in my time one noble speaker who was full of gravity in his speech. No man ever spoke more neatly, more pressly, more weightily, or suffered less emptiness, less idleness, in what he uttered. No member of his speech but consisted of his own graces. His hearers could not cough or look aside without loss. He commanded when he spoke, and had his judges angry or pleased at his discretion." Such are the men who command, men who speak "neatly and pressly." But to gain such precision is toilsome business. While we are in training for it, no word must unpermittedly pass the portal of the teeth. Something like what we mean must never be counted equivalent to what we mean. And if we are not sure of our meaning or of our word, we must pause until we are sure. Accuracy does not come of itself. For persons who can use several languages, capital practice in acquiring it can be had by translating from one language to another and seeing that the entire sense is carried over. Those who have only their native speech will find it profitable often to attempt definitions of the common words they use. Inaccuracy will not stand up against the habit of definition. Dante boasted that no rhythmic exigency had ever made him say what he did not mean. We heedless and unintending speakers, under no exigency of rhyme or reason, say what we mean but seldom, and still more seldom mean what we say. To hold our thoughts and words in significant adjustment requires unceasing consciousness, a perpetual determination not to tell lies; for of course every inaccuracy is a bit of untruthfulness. We have something in mind, yet convey something else to our hearer. And no moral purpose will save us from this untruthfulness unless that purpose is sufficient to inspire the daily drill which brings the power to be true. Again and again we are shut up to evil because we have not acquired the ability of goodness.

But after all, I hope that nobody who hears me will quite agree. There is something enervating in conscious care. Necessary as it is in shaping our purposes, if allowed too direct and exclusive control consciousness breeds hesitation and feebleness. Action is not excellent, at least, until spontaneous. In piano-playing we begin by picking out each separate note; but we do not call the result music until we play our notes by the handful, heedless how each is formed. And so it is everywhere. Consciously selective conduct is elementary and inferior. People distrust it, or rather they distrust him who exhibits it. If anybody talking to us visibly studies his words, we turn away. What he says may be well enough as school exercise, but it is not conversation. Accordingly, if we would have our speech forcible, we shall need to put into it quite as much of audacity as we do of precision, terseness, or simplicity. Accuracy alone is not a thing to be sought, but accuracy and dash. It was said of Fox, the English orator and statesman, that he was accustomed to throw himself headlong into the middle of a sentence, trusting to God Almighty to get him out. So must we speak. We must not before beginning a sentence decide what the end shall be; for if we do, nobody will care to hear that end. At the beginning, it is the beginning which claims the attention of both speaker and listener, and trepidation about going on will mar all. We must give our thought its head, and not drive it with too tight a rein, nor grow timid when it begins to prance a bit. Of course we must retain coolness in courage, applying the results of our previous discipline in accuracy; but we need not move so slowly as to become formal. Pedantry is worse than blundering. If we care for grace and flexible beauty of language, we must learn to let our thought run. Would it, then, be too much of an Irish bull to say that in acquiring English we need to cultivate spontaneity? The uncultivated kind is not worth much; it is wild and haphazard stuff, unadjusted to its uses. On the other hand no speech is of much account, however just, which lacks the element of courage. Accuracy and dash, then, the combination of the two, must be our difficult aim; and we must not rest satisfied so long as either dwells with us alone.

But are the two so hostile as they at first appear? Or can, indeed, the first be obtained without the aid of the second? Supposing we are convinced that words possess no value in themselves, and are correct or incorrect only as they truly report experience, we shall feel ourselves impelled in the mere interest of accuracy to choose them freshly and to put them together in ways in which they never coöperated before, so as to set forth with distinctness that which just we, not other people, have seen or felt. The reason why we do not naturally have this daring exactitude is probably twofold. We let our experiences be blurred, not observing sharply, nor knowing with any minuteness what we are thinking about; and so there is no individuality in our language. And then, besides, we are terrorized by custom and inclined to adjust what we would say to what others have said before. The cure for the first of these troubles is to keep our eye on our object, instead of on our listener or ourselves; and for the second, to learn to rate the expressiveness of language more highly than its correctness. The opposite of this, the disposition to set correctness above expressiveness, produces that peculiarly vulgar diction known as "school-ma'am English," in which for the sake of a dull accord with usage all the picturesque, imaginative and forceful employment of words is sacrificed. Of course we must use words so that people can understand them, and understand them too with ease; but this once granted, let our language be our own, obedient to our special needs. "Whenever," says Thomas Jefferson, "by small grammatical negligences the energy of an idea can be condensed, or a word be made to stand for a sentence, I hold grammatical rigor in contempt." "Young man," said Henry Ward Beecher to one who was pointing out grammatical errors in a sermon of his, "when the English language gets in my way, it doesn't stand a chance." No man can be convincing, writer or speaker, who is afraid to send his words wherever they may best follow his meaning, and this with but little regard to whether any other person's words have ever been there before. In assessing merit let us not stupefy ourselves with using negative standards. What stamps a man as great is not freedom from faults, but abundance of powers.

Such audacious accuracy, however, distinguishing as it does noble speech from commonplace speech, can be practised only by him who has a wide range of words. Our ordinary range is absurdly narrow. It is important, therefore, for anybody who would cultivate himself in English to make strenuous and systematic efforts to enlarge his vocabulary. Our dictionaries contain more than a hundred thousand words. The average speaker employs about three thousand. Is this because ordinary people have only three or four thousand things to say? Not at all. It is simply due to dulness. Listen to the average schoolboy. He has a dozen or two nouns, half a dozen verbs, three or four adjectives, and enough conjunctions and prepositions to stick the conglomerate together. This ordinary speech deserves the description which Hobbes gave to his "State of Nature," that "it is solitary, poor, nasty, brutish and short." The fact is, we fall into the way of thinking that the wealthy words are for others and that they do not belong to us. We are like those who have received a vast inheritance, but who persist in the inconveniences of hard beds, scanty food, rude clothing, who never travel, and who limit their purchases to the bleak necessities of life. Ask such people why they endure niggardly living while wealth in plenty is lying in the bank, and they can only answer that they have never learned how to spend. But this is worth learning. Milton used eight thousand words, Shakespeare fifteen thousand. We have all the subjects to talk about that these early speakers had; and in addition we have bicycles and sciences and strikes and political combinations and all the complicated living of the modern world.

Why then do we hesitate to swell our words to meet our needs? It is a nonsense question. There is no reason. We are simply lazy, too lazy to make ourselves comfortable. We let our vocabularies be limited and get along rawly without the refinements of human intercourse, without refinements in our own thoughts; for thoughts are almost as dependent on words as words on thoughts. For example, all exasperations we lump together as "aggravating," not considering whether they may not rather be displeasing, annoying, offensive, disgusting, irritating, or even maddening; and without observing too that in our reckless usage we have burned up a word which might be convenient when we should need to mark some shading of the word "increase." Like the bad cook, we seize the frying-pan whenever we need to fry, broil, roast, or stew, and then we wonder why all our dishes taste alike while in the next house the food is appetizing. It is all unnecessary. Enlarge the vocabulary. Let any one who wants to see himself grow resolve to adopt two new words each week. It will not be long before the endless and enchanting variety of the world will begin to reflect itself in his speech, and in his mind as well. I know that when we use a word for the first time we are startled, as if a fire-cracker went off in our neighborhood. We look about hastily to see if any one has noticed. But finding that no one has, we may be emboldened. A word used three times slips off the tongue with entire naturalness. Then it is ours forever, and with it some phase of life which had been lacking hitherto. For each word presents its own point of view, discloses a special aspect of things, reports some little importance not otherwise conveyed, and so contributes its small emancipation to our tied-up minds and tongues.

But a brief warning may be necessary to make my meaning clear. In urging the addition of new words to our present poverty-stricken stock I am far from suggesting that we should seek out strange, technical or inflated expressions, which do not appear in ordinary conversation. The very opposite is my aim. I would put every man who is now employing a diction merely local and personal in command of the approved resources of the English language. Our poverty usually comes through provinciality, through accepting without criticism the habits of our special set. My family, my immediate friends, have a diction of their own. Plenty of other words, recognized as sound, are known to be current in books and to be employed by modest and intelligent speakers, only we do not use them. Our set has never said "diction," or "current," or "scope," or "scanty," or "hitherto," or "convey," or "lack." Far from unusual as these words are, to adopt them might seem to set me apart from those whose intellectual habits I share. From this I shrink. I do not like to wear clothes suitable enough for others, but not in the style of my own plain circle. Yet if each one of that circle does the same, the general shabbiness is increased. The talk of all is made narrow enough to fit the thinnest there. What we should seek is to contribute to each of the little companies with which our life is bound up a gently enlarging influence, such impulses as will not startle or create detachment, but which may save from humdrum, routine and dreary usualness. We cannot be really kind without being a little venturesome. The small shocks of our increasing vocabulary will in all probability be as helpful to our friends as to ourselves.

Such then are the excellences of speech. If we would cultivate ourselves in the use of English, we must make our daily talk accurate, daring and full. I have insisted on these points the more because in my judgment all literary power, especially that of busy men, is rooted in sound speech. But though the roots are here, the growth is also elsewhere. And I pass to my later precepts, which, if the earlier one has been laid well to heart, will require only brief discussion.

Secondly, "Welcome every opportunity for writing." Important as I have shown speech to be, there is much that it cannot do. Seldom can it teach structure. Its space is too small. Talking moves in sentences, and rarely demands a paragraph. I make my little remark,—a dozen or two words,—then wait for my friend to hand me back as many more. This gentle exchange continues by the hour; but either of us would feel himself unmannerly if he should grasp an entire five minutes and make it uninterruptedly his. That would not be speaking, but rather speech-making. The brief groupings of words which make up our talk furnish capital practice in precision, boldness and variety; but they do not contain room enough for exercising our constructive faculties. Considerable length is necessary if we are to learn how to set forth *B* in right relation to *A* on the one hand and to *C* on the other; and while keeping each a distinct part, are to be able through their smooth progression to weld all the parts together into a compacted whole. Such wholeness is what we mean by literary form. Lacking it, any piece of writing is a failure; because in truth it is not a piece, but pieces. For ease of reading, or for the attainment of an intended effect, unity is essential—the multitude of statements, anecdotes; quotations, arguings, gay sportings and appeals, all "bending one way their gracious influence." And this dominant unity of the entire piece obliges unity also in the subordinate parts. Not enough has been done when we have huddled together a lot of wandering sentences and penned them in a paragraph, or even when we have linked them together by the frail ties of "and, and." A sentence must be compelled to say a single thing; a paragraph, a single thing; an essay, a single thing. Each part is to be a preliminary whole and the total a finished whole. But the ability to construct one thing out of many does not come by nature. It implies fecundity, restraint, an eye for effects, the forecast of finish while we are still working in the rough, obedience to the demands of development and a deaf ear to whatever calls us into the by-paths of caprice; in short it implies that the good writer is to be an artist.

Now something of this large requirement which composition makes, the young writer instinctively feels, and he is terrified. He knows how ill-fitted he is to direct "toil coöperant to an end"; and when he sits down to the desk and sees the white sheet of paper before him, he shivers. Let him know that the shiver is a suitable part of the performance. I well remember the pleasure with which, as a young man, I heard my venerable and practised professor of rhetoric say that he supposed there was no work known to man more difficult than writing. Up to that time I had supposed its severities peculiar to myself. It cheered me, and gave me courage to try again, to learn that I had all mankind for my fellow sufferers. Where this is not understood, writing is avoided. From such avoidance I would save the young writer by my precept to seek every opportunity to write. For most of us this is a new way of confronting composition—treating it as an opportunity, a chance, and not as a burden or compulsion. It saves from slavishness and takes away the drudgery of writing, to view each piece of it as a precious and necessary step in the pathway to power. To those engaged in bread-winning employments these opportunities will be few. Spring forward to them, then, using them to the full. Severe they will be because so few, for only practice breeds ease; but on that very account let no one of them pass with merely a second-best performance. If a letter is to be written to a friend, a report to an employer, a communication to a newspaper, see that it has a beginning, a middle and an end. The majority of writings are without these pleasing adornments. Only the great pieces possess them. Bear this in mind and win the way to artistic composition by noticing what should be said first, what second and what third.

I cannot leave this subject, however, without congratulating the present generation on its advantages over mine. Children are brought up to-day, in happy contrast with my compeers, to feel that the pencil is no instrument of torture, hardly indeed to distinguish it from the tongue. About the time they leave their mother's arms they take their pen in hand. On paper they are encouraged to describe their interesting birds, friends, adventures. Their written lessons are almost as frequent as their oral, and they learn to write compositions while not yet quite understanding what they are about. Some of these fortunate ones will, I hope, find the language I have sadly used about the difficulty of writing extravagant. And let me say too that since frequency has more to do with ease of writing than anything else, I count the newspaper men lucky because they are writing all the time, and I do not think so meanly of their product as the present popular disparagement would seem to require. It is hasty work undoubtedly and bears the marks of haste. But in my judgment, at no period of the English language has there been so high an average of sensible, vivacious and informing sentences written as appears in our daily press. With both good and evil results, the distinction between book literature and speech literature is breaking down. Everybody is writing, apparently in verse and prose; and if the higher graces of style do not often appear, neither on the other hand do the ruder awkwardnesses and obscurities. A certain straightforward English is becoming established. A whole nation is learning the use of its mother tongue. Under such circumstances it is doubly necessary that any one who is conscious of feebleness in his command of English should promptly and earnestly begin the cultivation of it.

My third precept shall be, "Remember the other person." I have been urging self-cultivation in English as if it concerned one person alone, ourself. But every utterance really concerns two. Its aim is social. Its object is communication; and while unquestionably prompted halfway by the desire to ease our mind through self-expression, it still finds its only justification in the advantage somebody else will draw from what is said. Speaking or writing is, therefore, everywhere a double-ended process. It springs from me, it penetrates him; and both of these ends need watching. Is what I say precisely what I mean? That is an important question. Is what I say so shaped that it can readily be assimilated by him who hears? This is a question of quite as great consequence and much more likely to be forgotten. We are so full of ourselves that we do not remember the other person. Helter-skelter we pour forth our unaimed words merely for our personal relief, heedless whether they help or hinder him whom they still purport to address. For most of us are grievously lacking in imagination, which is the ability to go outside ourselves and take on the conditions of another mind. Yet this is what the literary artist is always doing. He has at once the ability to see for himself and the ability to see himself as others see him. He can lead two lives as easily as one life; or rather, he has trained himself to consider that other life as of more importance than his, and to reckon his comfort, likings and labors as quite subordinated to the service of that other. All serious literary work contains within it this readiness to bear another's burden. I must write with pains, that he may read with ease. I must

> Find out men's wants and wills,
> And meet them *there.*

As I write, I must unceasingly study what is the line of least intellectual resistance along which my thought may enter the differently constituted mind; and to that line I must subtly adjust, without enfeebling, my meaning. Will this combination of words or that make the meaning clear? Will this order of presentation facilitate swiftness of apprehension, or will it clog the movement? What temperamental perversities in me must be set aside in order to render my reader's approach to what I would tell him pleasant? What temperamental perversities in him must be accepted by me as fixed facts, conditioning all I say? These are the questions the skilful writer is always asking.

And these questions, as will have been perceived already, are moral questions no less than literary. That golden rule of generous service by which we do for others what we would have them do for us is a rule of writing too. Every writer who knows his trade perceives that he is a servant, that it is his business to endure hardship if only his reader may win freedom from toil, that no impediment to that reader's understanding is too slight to deserve diligent attention, that he has consequently no right to let a single sentence slip from him unsocialized—I mean, a sentence which cannot become as naturally another's possession as his own. In the very act of asserting himself he lays aside what is distinctively his. And because these qualifications of the writer are moral qualifications they can never be completely fulfilled so long as we live and write. We may continually approximate them more nearly, but there will still always be possible an alluring refinement of exercise beyond. The world of the literary artist and the moral man is interesting through its inexhaustibility; and he who serves his fellows by writing or by speech is artist and moral man in one. Writing a letter is a simple matter, but it is a moral matter and an artistic; for it may be done either with imagination or with raw self-centredness. What things will my correspondent wish to know? How can I transport him out of his properly alien surroundings into the vivid impressions which now are mine? How can I tell all I long to tell and still be sure the telling will be for him as lucid and delightful as for me? Remember the other person, I say. Do not become absorbed in yourself. Your interests cover only the half of any piece of writing; the other man's less visible half is necessary to complete yours. And if I have here discussed writing more than speech, that is merely because when we speak we utter our first thoughts, but when we write, our second,—or better still, our fourth; and in the greater deliberation which writing affords I have felt that the demands of morality and art, which are universally imbedded in language, could be more distinctly perceived. Yet none the less truly do we need to talk for the other person than to write for him.

But there remains a fourth weighty precept, and one not altogether detachable from the third. It is this: "Lean upon the subject." We have seen how the user of language, whether in writing or in speaking, works for himself; how he works for another individual too; but there is one more for whom his work is performed, one of greater consequence than any person, and that is his subject. From this comes his primary call. Those who in their utterance fix their thoughts on themselves, or on other selves, never reach power. That resides in the subject. There we must dwell with it and be content to have no other strength than its. When the frightened schoolboy sits down to write about Spring, he cannot imagine where the thoughts which are to make up his piece are to come from. He cudgels his brain for ideas. He examines his pen-point, the curtains, his inkstand, to see if perhaps ideas may not be had from these. He wonders what his teacher will wish him to say and he tries to recall how the passage sounded in the Third Reader. In every direction but one he turns, and that is the direction where lies the prime mover of his toil, his subject. Of that he is afraid. Now, what I want to make evident is that this subject is not in reality the foe, but the friend. It is his only helper. His composition is not to be, as he seems to suppose, a mass of his laborious inventions, but it is to be made up exclusively of what the subject dictates. He has only to attend. At present he stands in his own way, making such a din with his private anxieties that he cannot hear the rich suggestions of the subject. He is bothered with considering how he feels, or what he or somebody else will like to see on his paper. This is debilitating business. He must lean on his subject, if he would have his writing strong, and busy himself with what it says rather than with what he would say. Matthew Arnold, in the important preface to his poems of 1853, contrasting the artistic methods of Greek poetry and modern poetry, sums up the teaching of the Greeks in these words: "All depends upon the subject; choose a fitting action, penetrate yourself with the feeling of its situations; this done, everything else will follow." And he calls attention to the self-assertive and scatter-brained habits of our time. "How different a way of thinking from this is ours! We can hardly at the present day understand what Menander meant when he told a man who inquired as to the progress of his comedy that he had finished it, not having yet written a single line, because he had constructed the action of it in his mind. A modern critic would have assured him that the merit of his piece depended on the brilliant things which arose under his pen as he went along. I verily think that the majority of us do not in our hearts believe that there is such a thing as a total-impression to be derived from a poem or to be demanded from a poet. We permit the poet to select any action he pleases and to suffer that action to go as it will, provided he gratifies us with occasional bursts of fine writing and with a shower of isolated thoughts and images." Great writers put themselves and their personal imaginings out of sight. Their writing becomes a kind of transparent window on which reality is reflected, and through which people see, not them, but that of which they write. How much we know of Shakespeare's characters! How little of Shakespeare! Of him that might almost be said which Isaiah said of God, "He hideth himself." The best writer is the best mental listener, the one who peers farthest into his matter and most fully heeds its behests. Preëminently obedient is such a writer,—refinedly, energetically obedient. I once spent a day with a great novelist when the book which subsequently proved his masterpiece was only half written. I praised his mighty hero, but said I should think the life of an author would be miserable who, having created a character so huge, now had him in hand and must find something for him to do. My friend seemed puzzled by my remark, but after a moment's pause said, "I don't think you know how we work. I have nothing to do with the character. Now that he is created he will act as he will."

And such docility must be cultivated by every one who would write well, such strenuous docility. Of course there must be energy in plenty; the imagination which I described in my third section, the passion for solid form as in my second, the disciplined and daring powers as in my first; but all these must be ready at a moment's notice to move where the matter calls and to acknowledge that all their worth is to be drawn from it. Religion is only enlarged good sense, and the words of Jesus apply as well to the things of earth as of heaven. I do not know where we could find a more compendious statement of what is most important for one to learn who would cultivate himself in English than the saying in which Jesus announces the source of his power, "The word which ye hear is not mine, but the Father's which sent me." Whoever can use such words will be a noble speaker indeed.

These then are the fundamental precepts which every one must heed who would command our beautiful English language. There is of course a fifth. I hardly need name it; for it always follows after, whatever others precede. It is that we should do the work, and not think about it; do it day after day and not grow weary in bad doing. Early and often we must be busy and be satisfied to have a great deal of labor produce but a small result. I am told that early in life John Morley, wishing to engage in journalism, wrote an editorial and sent it to a paper every day for nearly a year before he succeeded in getting one accepted. We all know what a power he became in London journalism. I will not vouch for the truth of this story, but I am sure an ambitious author is wise who writes a weekly essay for his stove. Publication is of little consequence so long as one is getting one's self hammered into shape.

But before I close this paper let me acknowledge that in it I have neglected a whole class of helpful influences, probably quite as important as any I have discussed. Purposely I have passed them by. Because I wished to show what we can do for ourselves, I have everywhere assumed that our cultivation in English is to be effected by naked volition and a kind of dead lift. These are mighty agencies, but seldom in this interlocked world do they work well alone. They are strongest when backed by social suggestion and unconscious custom. Ordinarily the good speaker is he who keeps good company, but increases the helpful influence of that company by constant watchfulness along the lines I have marked out. So supplemented, my teaching is true. By itself it is not true. It needs the supplementation of others. Let him who would speak or write well seek out good speakers and writers. Let him live in their society,—for the society of the greatest writers is open to the most secluded,—let him feel the ease of their excellence, the ingenuity, grace and scope of their diction, and he will soon find in himself capacities whose development may be aided by the precepts I have given. Most of us catch better than we learn. We take up unconsciously from our surroundings what we cannot altogether create. All this should be remembered, and we should keep ourselves exposed to the wholesome words of our fellow men. Yet our own exertions will not on that account be rendered less important. We may largely choose the influences to which we submit; we may exercise a selective attention among these influences; we may enjoy, oppose, modify, or diligently ingraft what is conveyed to us,—and for doing any one of these things rationally we must be guided by some clear aim. Such aims, altogether essential even if subsidiary, I have sought to supply; and I would reiterate that he who holds them fast may become superior to linguistic fortune and be the wise director of his sluggish and obstinate tongue. It is as certain as anything can be that faithful endeavor will bring expertness in the use of English. If we are watchful of our speech, making our words continually more minutely true, free and resourceful; if we look upon our occasions of writing as opportunities for the deliberate work of unified construction; if in all our utterances we think of him who hears as well as of him who speaks; and above all, if we fix the attention of ourselves and our hearers on the matter we talk about and so let ourselves be supported by our subject—we shall make a daily advance not only in English study, but in personal power, in general serviceableness and in consequent delight.

V

DOUBTS ABOUT UNIVERSITY EXTENSION[1]

A step has lately been taken in American education which excites the interest and hopes of us all. England has been our teacher,—England and a persuasive apostle from that country. A few years ago the English universities became discontented with their isolation. For generations they had been devoting themselves to a single class in the community, and that too a class which needed least to be brought to intelligence and power. The mass of the nation, those by whom its labor and commerce were conducted, had little access to Oxford and Cambridge. Poverty first, then social distinctions, and, until recent days, sectarian haughtiness barred them out. Their exclusion reacted on the training of the universities themselves. Conservatism flourished. The worth of an intellectual interest was rated rather by its traditional character than by its closeness to life. The sciences, latter-day things, were pursued hardly at all. The modern literatures, English included, had no place. Plato and Aristotle furnished most of the philosophy. While the rest of the world was deriving from Germany methods of study, from France methods of exposition, and from America methods of treating all men alike as rational, English scholarship, based on no gymnasia, lycées, or high schools, went its way, little regarding the life of its nation or that of the world at large.

But there has come a change. Reformers have been endeavoring to go out and find the common man, and, in connection with him, to develop those subjects which before, according to university tradition, were looked at somewhat askance. English literature, political economy, modern history, have been put in the foreground of this popularized education. Far and wide throughout England an enthusiastic band of young teachers, under the guidance of officers of the universities, have been giving instruction in these subjects to companies in which social grades are for the time forgotten. And since public libraries are rare in England, and among the poorer classes the reading habit is but slightly formed, an ambitious few among the hearers have prized their opportunities sufficiently to undertake a certain amount of study and to hand in papers for the lecturer to inspect and to mark. In exceptional cases as many as one third of the audience have thus written exercises and passed examinations. The great majority of those in attendance during the three months' term of course do nothing more than listen to the weekly lecture.

This is the very successful English movement which for some years has been exciting admiration the world over, and which it is proposed to introduce into

[1] Printed in 1892.

the United States. Rightly to estimate its worth those aspects of it to which attention has just been directed should carefully be borne in mind. They are these: the movement is as much social as scholarly and accompanies a general democratic upheaval of an aristocratic nation; it springs up in the neighborhood of universities to which the common people do not resort, and in which those subjects which most concern the minds of modern men are little taught; in its country other facilities for enabling the average man to capture knowledge—public libraries, reading clubs, illustrated magazines, free high schools—are not yet general; it flourishes in a small and compact land, where a multitude of populous towns are in such immediate neighborhood and so connected by a network of railroads that he who is busied in one place to-day can, with the slightest fatigue and expense, appear in five other towns during the remaining days of the week.

These conditions, and others as gravely distinctive, do not exist in America. From the first the American college has been organized by the people and for the people. It has been about as much resorted to by the poor as by the rich. Through a widely developed system of free public schools it has kept itself closely in touch with popular ideals. Its graduates go into commercial life as often as into medicine, the ministry, or the law. It has shown itself capable of expansion too in adjusting itself to the modern enlargement of knowledge. The rigid curriculum, which suited well enough the needs of our fathers, has been discarded, and every college, in proportion to the resources at its command, now offers elective studies and seeks to meet the needs of differing men. To all who can afford four years (soon it may be three), and who are masters of about half as much capital as would support them during the same time elsewhere, the four hundred colleges of our country offer an education far too good to be superseded, duplicated, or weakened. In these colleges excellent provision has been made, and has been made once for all, for everybody who has a little time and a little money to devote to systematic education of the higher sort.

But our educational scheme has one serious limitation, and during the last fifty years there have been many earnest efforts to surmount it. Not every man is free to seek a systematic training. Multitudes are tied to daily toil and only in the evening can they consider their own enlargement. Many grow old before the craving for knowledge arises. Many also, with more or less profit, have attended a college, but are glad subsequently to supply those defects of education which the experiences of life relentlessly bring to view. To all these classes, caught in the whirl of affairs, the college does not minister. It is true that much that such people want they get from the public library, especially as our librarians of the modern type energetically accept their duties as facilitators of the public reading. Much is also obtainable from the cheap issues of the press and from such endowed courses of higher instruction as those of the Lowell, Cooper, Brooklyn, Peabody, and Drexel institutes. But, after all, these supplementary aids, though valuable, are deficient in guiding power. Most persons, especially if novices, work best under inspection. To learners teachers are generally important. There seems to be still a place in our well-supplied country for an organization which shall arouse a more general desire for knowledge; which shall stand ready to satisfy this desire more cheaply, with less interruption to daily occupation, and consequently in ways more fragmentary than the colleges can; and yet one which shall not leave its pupils alone with books, but shall supply them with the impulse of the living word and through writing, discussion and directed reading, shall economize and render effective the costly hours of learning. Unquestionably there is a field here which the colleges cannot till, a field whose harvest would enrich us all. Can any other agency till it? To every experiment thus far it has yielded only meagre, brief and expensive returns. A capital thing it would be to give to the busy that which normally requires time and attention; but how to do it is the question,—how to do it in reality, and not in mere outward seeming.

Chautauqua has not done it, impassioned though that rough and generous institution has been for wide and fragmentary culture. Its work, indeed, has had a different aim; and, amusing as that work often appears, it ought to be understood and acknowledged as of fundamental consequence in our hastily settled and heterogeneous land. Chautauqua sends its little books and papers into stagnant homes from Maine to California and gives the silent occupants something to think about. Conversation springs up; and with it fresh interests, fresh hopes. A new tie is formed between young and old, as together they persue the same studies and in the same graduating class walk through the Golden Gate. Any man who loves knowledge and his native land must be glad at heart when he visits a summer assembly of Chautauqua: there listens to the Orator's Recognition Address; attends the swiftly successive Round Tables upon Milton, Temperance, Geology, the American Constitution, the Relations of Science and Religion, and the Doctrine of Rent; perhaps assists at the Cooking School, the Prayer Meeting, the Concert and the Gymnastic Drill; or wanders under the trees among the piazzaed cottages and sees the Hall of Philosophy and the wooden Doric Temple shining on their little eminences; and, best of all, perceives in what throngs have gathered here the butcher, the baker, and the candlestick-maker,—a throng themselves, their wives and daughters a throng—all heated in body, but none the less aglow for learning and a good time. The comic aspects of this mixture of science, fresh air, flirtation, Greek reminiscence, and devoutness are patent enough; but the way in which the multitude is being won to discard distrust of knowledge, and to think of it rather as the desirable goal for all, is not so generally remarked by scholarly observers. Yet that is the weighty fact. The actual product in education may not be large; enthusiasm and the memory may be more stimulated than the rational intelligence. But minds are set in motion; an intellectual world, beyond the domestic and personal, begins to appear; studious thought forms its fit friendship with piety, gladness and the sense of a common humanity; a groundwork of civilization is prepared. To find a popular movement so composite and aspiring, we must go back to the mediæval Crusades or the Greek Mysteries. In these alone do we observe anything so ideal, so bizarre, so expressive of the combined intellectual and religious hopes of a people. In many Chautauqua homes pathetic sacrifices will be made in the next generation to send the boys and girls to a real college.

Now, in proposing to transport to this country English extension methods the managers have had in mind nothing so elementarily important as Chautauqua.

They have felt the pity we all feel for persons of good parts who, through poverty or occupation, are debarred from a college training. They seek to reach minds already somewhat prepared, and to such they undertake to supply solid instruction of the higher grades. It is this more ambitious design which calls for criticism. Professor R. G. Moulton speaks of extension education as "distinguished from school education, being moulded to meet the wants of adults." And again, "So far as method is concerned, we have considered that we are bound to be not less thorough, but more thorough, if possible, than the universities themselves." If, in the general educational campaign, we liken Chautauqua to a guerrilla high school, university extension will be a guerrilla college. Both move with light armor, have roving commissions, attack individuals, and themselves appear in the garb of ordinary life; but they are equipped for a service in which the more cumbrous organizations of school and college have thus far proved ineffective. It is a fortunate circumstance that, with fields of operation so distinct, no jealousy can exist between the two bands of volunteers, or between them both and the regular army. The success of either would increase the success of the other two. To Chautauqua we are all indebted for lessening the popular suspicion of expert knowledge; and if the plans of the extension committee could be carried out, college methods would have a vogue, and a consequent respect, which they have never yet enjoyed.

Every one, accordingly, civilian or professional, wishes the movement well, and recognizes that the work it proposes to do in our country is not at present performed. Its aims are excellent. Are they also practicable? We cannot with certainty say that they are not, but it is here that doubts arise,—doubts of three sorts: those which suspect a fundamental difference in the two countries which try the experiment; those which are incredulous about the permanent response which our people will make to the education offered; and those which question the possibility of securing a stable body of extension teachers. The first set of these doubts has been briefly but sufficiently indicated at the beginning of this paper; the second may with still greater brevity be summed up here in the following connected series of inquiries:—

With the multitude of other opportunities for education which American life affords, will any large body of men and women attend extension lectures? Will they attend after the novelty is worn off, say during the third year? Will they do anything more than attend? Will they follow courses of study, write essays, and pass examinations? Will the extension system, any better than its decayed predecessor, the old lyceum system, resist the demands of popular audiences and keep itself from slipping out of serious instruction into lively and eloquent entertainment? If the lectures are kept true to their aim of furnishing solid instruction, can they in the long run be paid for? Will it be possible to find in our country clusters of half a dozen towns so grouped and so ready to subscribe to a course of lectures on each day of the week that out of the entire six a living salary can be obtained? Will the new teachers be obliged to confine themselves to the suburbs of large cities, abandoning the scattered dwellers in the country, that portion of our population which is almost the only one at present cut off from tolerable means of culture? If in order to pursue these destitute ones, correspondence methods are employed, in addition to the already approved methods of lecture instruction, will lowering of the standard follow? In England three or four years of extension lectures are counted equivalent to one year of regular study, and a person who has attended extension courses for this time may be admitted without further examination to the second year of university residence. Will anything of the sort be generally attempted here?

These grave questions are as yet insusceptible of answer. Affirmative, desirable answers do not seem probable; but experience alone can make the matter plain. Of course the managers are watchfully bearing such questions in mind, and critical watchfulness may greatly aid the better answer and hinder the less desirable. Accordingly anything like a discussion of this class of practical doubts would be inappropriate here. Data for the formation of a confident opinion do not exist. All that can be done by way of warning is to indicate certain large improbabilities, leaving them to be confirmed or thwarted by time and human ingenuity.

But with the third class of doubts the case is different. These relate to the constitution of the staff of teachers, and here sufficient facts are at hand to permit a few points to be demonstrated with considerable certainty. When, for example, we ask from what source teachers are to be drawn, we are usually told that they must come from college faculties. If the method of the extension lecturer is to be as thorough as that of the universities themselves, the lecturers must be experts, not amateurs; and where except at the colleges does a body of experts exist? No doubt many well-trained men are scattered throughout the community as merchants, doctors, school-teachers, and lawyers. But these men, when of proved power, have more than they properly can attend to in their own affairs. It seems to be the colleges, therefore, to which the movement must look for its teachers; and in the experiments thus far made in this country the extension lecturing has been done for the most part by college officers. A professor of history, political economy, or literature has, in addition to his college teaching, also given a course of instruction elsewhere. This feature of the American system, one may say with confidence, must prove a constant damage to the work of the colleges and, if persisted in, must ultimately destroy the extension scheme itself.

In England the extension teachers are not university teachers. To have no independent staff for extension work is a novelty of the American undertaking. The very name, university extension, besides being barbaric, is in its English employment largely misleading; since neither the agencies for extending nor indeed, for the most part, the studies extended, are found at the universities at all. A small syndicate or committee, appointed from among the university officers, is the only share the university has in the business. The impression, so general in this country, that English university teachers are roaming about the island, lecturing to mixed audiences, is an entire error. The university teachers stay at home and send other people, their own graduates chiefly, to instruct the multitude. A committee of them decides on the qualifications for the work of such persons as care to devote themselves to itinerant teaching as a profession. For those so selected they arrange times, places, and subjects; but they themselves do not move from their own lecture rooms. Nor is there occasion for their doing so. In the slender development of popular education in England, many more persons of the upper classes become trained as specialists than can find places as university teachers. There thus arises a learned and leisured accumulation which capitally serves the country in case of a new educational need. On this accumulated stock of cultured men—men who otherwise could not easily bring their culture to market—the extension movement draws. These men are its teachers, its permanent teachers, since there are not competing places striving to draw them away. In the two countries the educational situation is exactly reversed: in England there are more trained men than positions; in America, more positions than trained men. It seems probable too that this condition of things will continue long, so far as we are concerned; at least there is no present prospect of our reaching a limit in the demand for competent men. Whenever a college has a chair to fill, it is necessary to hunt far and wide for a suitable person to fill it. The demand is not from the old places alone. Almost every year a new college is founded. Every year the old ones grow. In twenty-five years Harvard has quadrupled its staff. Columbia, Cornell, Princeton, Yale, the University of Michigan, the University of Pennsylvania,—indeed almost every strong college in the country,—shows an immense advance. A Western state is no sooner settled than it establishes a state university, and each of the sects starts from one to three colleges besides. No such perpetual expansion goes on in England. The number of learned positions there is measurably fixed. If more experts than can fill them, or than care to enter political life, the liberal professions, and the civil service, are manufactured in the course of a year, the surplus stock is at the disposal of the extension syndicate. Many of these men too are persons of means, to whom a position of dignity is of more consequence than a large salary. The problem, accordingly, of organizing popular instruction out of such a body of waiting experts is a comparatively simple one; but it is not so simple here. In our country any man who has a fair acquaintance with a special subject and moderate skill in imparting it, especially if he will be contented with a small salary, can be pretty sure of college appointment.

Naturally enough, therefore, the organizers of the extension movement, despairing of finding among us competent unattached teachers, have turned at once to the colleges; but the colleges are a very unsafe support to lean upon. A professor in a university where the studies are elective has no more superfluous time than a busy lawyer, or doctor, or business man. Merely to keep up with the literature of a subject, to say nothing of that research and writing which should enlarge its limits, is an enormous task. Teaching too is no longer an affair of text-books and recitations. Leisurely days of routine ease belong to the past. A professor nowadays must prepare lectures incessantly; must perpetually revise them; must arrange examinations; direct the reading of his students; receive their theses; himself read a large part of their voluminous written work; personally oversee his advanced men; gather them about him in laboratory, seminary and conference; attend innumerable committee and faculty meetings; devise legislation for the further development of his college and department; correspond with schools and colleges where his students, after taking their higher degree, may suitably be placed; and if at the end of a hard-worked day he can find an hour's leisure, he must still keep his door open for students or fellow-officers to enter. So laborious have become the duties of a university teacher that few large staffs now go through a year without one or two of their members breaking down. With the growing complexity of work it often seems as if the proper business of college officers, study and teaching, must some day cease altogether, crowded out by the multifarious tasks with which they are only indirectly connected. It is useless to say that these things are not necessary. Whoever neglects them will cease to make his college, his subject and his influence grow. It is because professors now see that they cannot safely neglect them that the modern college differs fundamentally from its humdrum predecessor of a quarter of a century ago. Any movement which seeks to withdraw a professor's attention from these things, and induces him to put his soul elsewhere, inflicts on the community a serious damage. No amount of intellectual stimulus furnished to little companies here and there can atone for the loss that must fall on education when college teachers pledge themselves to do serious work in other places than in their own libraries and lecture rooms. To be an explorer and a guide in a department of human knowledge is an arduous profession. It admits no half-hearted service.

Of course if the work demanded elsewhere is not serious, the case is different. Rather with benefit than with damage a college teacher may on occasion recast the instruction that was intended for professionals and offer it to a popular audience. In this way a professor makes himself known and makes his college known. Many of the small colleges are now engaging in university extension as an inexpensive means of advertising themselves. But such lecturing is incidental, voluntary and perpetually liable to interruption. Beyond the immediate series of lectures it cannot be depended on. There is nothing institutional about it. The men who undertake it are owned elsewhere, and a second mortgage is not usually a very valuable piece of property. A movement which places its reliance on the casual teaching of overworked men is condemned from the start. University extension can never pass beyond the stage of amateurism and temporary expedient until, like its English namesake, it has a permanent staff of instructors exclusively devoted to its service.

Where, then, is such a staff to be obtained? In view of the conditions of education in this country already described, it is improbable that it can be obtained at all. But something may still be done,—something, however, of a more modest sort than enthusiasts at present have in mind. There issue from our great universities every year a number of men who have had two or three years' training beyond their bachelor's degree. Some of them have had a year or two of foreign study. They frequently wish to teach. Places do not immediately open to them. If the extension movement would set them to work, it might have all their time at a moderate salary for two or three years. Such men, it is true, would be inexperienced, and their connection with itinerant teaching could not be rendered lasting. As soon as one of them proved his power as a teacher, some college would call him; and he would seldom prefer the nomadic and fragmentary life to an established one. Plainly too under the charge of such men the grade of instruction could not be the highest; but it might be sound, inspiriting even, and it is in any case all that present circumstances render possible. We may mourn that those who are masters in their several provinces are already fully employed. We may wish there were a multitude of masters sitting about, ready for enlistment in a missionary undertaking. But there are no such masters. The facts are evident enough; and if the extension movement aims at a durable existence, it will respect these facts. The men it wants it cannot have without damaging them; and damaging them, it damages the higher education of which they are the guardians. Teachers of a lower grade are at hand, ready to be experimented with. The few experiments already tried have been fairly successful. Let the extension leaders give up all thought of doing here what has been done in England. The principal part of that work is performed for us by other means. The wisest guidance, accordingly, may not lead the movement to any long success. If, however, university extension will keep itself clearly detached from other educational agencies and make a quiet offer of humble yet serviceable instruction, there is a fair prospect that by somewhat slow degrees a permanent new power may be added to the appliances for rendering busy Americans intelligent.

VI

SPECIALIZATION[2]

Ladies and gentlemen of the graduating class, this afternoon belongs to you. This morning we dedicated a chime of bells to the memory of Mrs. Palmer, and in those moving exercises you had but a slender share. Probably not half a dozen of you ever saw her who, once seen, was loved with romantic ardor. Undoubtedly many of you are different from what you would have been had she not lived, and lived here; for her influence so passed into the structure of this University that she will shape successive generations of you for a long time to come. But enough of her. Let us dismiss her from our thoughts. Too much praise we have already lavished on one who was ever simple and self-forgetting. She would chide our profusion. If we would think as she would wish us to think, let us turn rather to the common matters of the day, reflecting on those joys and perplexities which have attended you throughout these formative years. One especially among these perplexities, perhaps the greatest of all, I would invite you to consider now. Let me set it clearly before you.

This morning I sat down to breakfast with about a hundred of you who had entered on the attainment of the highest degree which this University offers. You were advanced specialists. You had each chosen some single line of endeavor. But even then I remembered that you were not the only specialists here. Before me this afternoon I see candidates in medicine, men and women who have taken for their specialty the warfare with pain and disease. They have said, "All that I can ever know, I will bring to bear on this urgent problem." Here also are the lawyers, impassioned for justice, for the quelling of human strife. That is their specialty. They too restrict themselves to a single point of view. Beside them sit the scientific men, who looking over the vast expanse of nature have accepted the task of tracing the physical aspects of this marvellous machine. Nor can I stop here. Throughout the undergraduate department, as we all know, run dominant interests. I should be ashamed of a young man who in his four years had not found some compulsive interest; for it is only when an interest compels that we can say that education has begun. So long as we are simply learning what is set before us, taking the routine mass of academic subjects, we may be faithful students, but we are not scholars. No, it is when with a free heart we give ourselves to a subject, bidding it take of us all it demands and feeling that we had rather attend to it than to anything else,

[2] On the morning of June 9, 1908, a chime of bells was dedicated at the University of Chicago in honor of Alice Freeman Palmer. At the Convocation Exercises in the afternoon the following address was delivered.

because it expresses our personal desires—then it is that its quickening influence takes hold. But this is specialization. We might think of the University of Chicago then as a great specializing machine.

But why has each of you set himself this task of specialization? Because the world needs leaders, and you have chosen yourselves to be those leaders. Are you aware how exceptional is your condition? The last census shows that at present hardly one per cent of our population is in our colleges. You are of that one per cent, and you are here in order that you may enlighten the other ninety-nine per cent. If through ignorance you fail, you will cause others to fail and you had better never have come to this University. To some sort of leadership you have dedicated yourselves, and to this aim you should be true. But do not at times doubts cross your mind? Have you not occasionally asked yourselves whether you can attain such leadership and make the most of your lives by shutting yourselves up to a specialty? Multitudes of interesting things are calling; shall you turn away from them and follow a single line? It will be worth while to-day to consider these fundamental questions and inquire how far we are justified in specializing, what dangers there are in it, and in what degree those dangers may be avoided.

Let me say, then, at the start, that I regard specialization as absolutely essential to scholarship. There is no scholarship without it, for it is involved in the very process of knowing. When I look at this desk I am specializing; that is, I am detaching this piece of furniture from all else in the room. I am limiting myself, and I cannot see without it. I can gaze without specialization, but I cannot see without specialization. If I am to know anything by sight, that knowledge must come through the limitation of sight. I seize this object, cast away all others, and thus fix my attention. Or if I am carefully to observe, I even put my eye on a single point of the desk. There is no other way. Clear knowledge becomes possible only through precise observation. Now specialization is nothing but this necessary limitation of attention; and we, as specialists, are merely carrying out on a large scale what every human being must practise in some degree whenever he knows. We employ the process persistently, and for the sake of science are willing to hold ourselves steadily to a single line of observation. And we cannot do otherwise. The principles involved in the specialization of the senses run throughout all science. If we would know, we must hold the attention long on a given subject.

But there is an unfortunate side to specialization. It obliges us to discard other important interests. To discard merely unimportant ones is easy. But every evening when I sit down to devote myself to my ethics I am aware that there are persons starving in Boston who might be saved if I should drop my work and go to them. Yet I sit calmly there and say, "Let them starve; I am going to study ethics." I do not see how I could be a suitable professor of ethics unless I were willing thus to limit myself. That is the hard part, as I understand it, of specialization,—the cutting off of things that are worth while. I am sure you have already found it out. Many of you have come from places of narrow opportunity and here find a welcome abundance. Remembering how you have longed to obtain such privileges, you will be tempted to scatter yourselves over a wide field, gathering a little here and a little there. At the end of the year you will have nothing, if you do that. The only possibility of gain is to choose your field, devote serious time to it, count yourself a specialist, and propose to live like one. Goethe admirably announces the principle: "Wer grosses will muss sich beschränken können." You must accept limitations if you will go on to power, for in limitation the very process of knowledge is rooted.

Furthermore, not only is specialization forced upon us by the nature of knowledge, but without it our own powers cannot receive appropriate discipline. It is difficult business to fashion a sound observer. Each province of science has its special modes of observation, its own modes of reasoning even. So long as we are unfamiliar with these and obliged to hold ourselves to them through conscious control, our work is poor. It is slow, inaccurate, and exhausting. Only when we have trained ourselves to such aptitudes that within a certain field our observations and reasonings are instinctive do we become swift, sure, and unfatigued in research. To train our powers then we must begin to specialize early and hold ourselves steadily within bounds. As one looks over the names of those who have accomplished much, one is surprised at the number who were early specialists. Take my own department: Berkeley writes his great work when he is twenty-five; Hume publishes his masterpiece at twenty-seven. Or again, Keats had brought his wonderful results to accomplishment and died at twenty-five; Shelley at thirty; Marlowe, the greatest loss English letters ever met, at twenty-seven. It is just the same in other fields: Alexander dies at thirty-six, Jesus at thirty-three. Yes, let us look nearer home: the most forcible leader American education has ever had became president of Harvard University at thirty-five; President Hyde of Bowdoin took his position at twenty-seven; my own wife, Alice Freeman, was president of Wellesley at twenty-six. These are early specialists; and because they specialized early they acquired an aptitude, a smoothness of work, a precision of insight, and width of power which could not have been theirs had they begun later. I would not deny that there have been geniuses who seemed to begin late: Kant was such; Locke was such. You will recall many within your own fields. But I think when you search the career of those who come to power in comparatively late years, you will find that there has usually been a train of covert specialization running through their lives. They may not have definitely named their field to themselves, or produced work within that field in early years, but everything had been converging toward that issue. I believe, therefore, you ought to respect your specialty, because only through it can your powers be brought to their highest accuracy and service.

One more justification of specialization I will briefly mention, that it is necessary for the organization of society. No motive is good for much until it is socialized. If specialization only developed our individual selves, we could hardly justify it; but it is the means of progress for society. The field of knowledge is vast; no man can master it, and its immensity was never so fully understood as to-day. The only way the whole province can be conquered and brought under subjection to human needs is by parting it out, one man being content to till his little corner while his neighbor is engaged on something widely different. We must part out the field of knowledge and specialize on our allotted work, in order that there may be entirety in science. If we seek to have entirety in ourselves, science will be fragmentary and feeble. That division of labor which has proved efficient everywhere else is no less needful in science.

But I suppose it is hardly necessary to justify specialization to this audience. Most of you have staked heavily on it, putting yourselves to serious inconvenience, many of you heavily mortgaging your future, in order to come here and devote yourselves to some single interest. I might confidently go through this room asking each of you what is your subject? And you would proudly reply, "My subject is this. My subject is this. My subject is this." I think you would feel ashamed if you had not thus specialized. I see no occasion, therefore, to elaborate what I have urged. As I understand it, the three roots of specialization are these: it is grounded in the very nature of the knowing process; it is grounded in the needs of ourselves as individuals, in order that we may attain our maximum efficiency; it is grounded in the needs of society, because only so can society reach that fulness of knowledge which its progress requires.

But, after all, the beliefs which are accepted as matters of course in this room are largely denounced outside it. We must acknowledge that our confidence in specialization encounters many doubts in the community. It may be well, then, to place ourselves where that community stands and ask the general public to tell us why it doubts us, what there is in our specialized attitude which it thinks defective, and what are the complaints which it is disposed to bring against us? I will try to take the position of devil's advocate and plead the cause of the objector to specialization.

Specialization, it is said, leads to ignorance; indeed it rather aims at ignorance than knowledge. When I attend to this desk, it is true I secure a bit of knowledge, but how small is that bit in comparison to all the things in this room which I might know about! It is but a fraction. Yet I have condemned all else in the room to ignorance, reserving only this one little object for knowledge. Now that is what we are all of us doing on a great scale; by specializing, by limiting our attention, we cut off what is not attended to. It is often assumed that attention is mainly a positive affair and occupied with what we are to know. But that is a very small portion of it; really its important part is the negative, the removal of what we do not wish to observe. We cut ourselves off from the great mass of knowledge which is offered. Is it not then true that every specialist has disciplined himself to be an ignoramus? He has drawn a fence around a little portion of the universe and said, "Within that fence I know something." "Yes," the public replies, "but you do not know anything outside." And is not the public right? When we step forward and claim to be learned men, is not the public justified in saying, "I know a great deal more than you do; I know a thousand things and you know only one. You say you know that one through and through, and of course I do not know my thousand things through and through. But it is not necessary. I perceive their relations; I can handle them; I can use them in practice; can you?" "Well, no," we are obliged to say, "we specialists are a little fumbling when we try to take hold of the world. We are not altogether skilful in action, just because we are such specialists." You students here have been devoting yourselves to some one point—I am afraid many of you are going to have sad experience of it—you have been learning to know something nobody else on earth does know, and then you go forth to seek a position. But the world may have no use for you; there are only two or three positions of that sort in the country, and those may happen to be filled. Just because you are such an elaborate scholar you cannot earn your daily bread. You have cut yourself off from everything but that one species of learning, and that does not happen to be wanted. Therefore you are not wanted. Such is the too frequent condition of the specialist. The thousand things he does not know; it is only the one thing he does know. And because he is so ignorant, he is helpless.

Turning then to our second justification of specialization, the case seems equally bad. I said that specialization was needed for the training of our powers. The training of them all? Not that, but the training of only certain ones among them. The others hang slack. In those regions of ourselves we count for little. We are men of weight only within the range of the powers we have trained; and what a large slice of us lies outside these! Accordingly the general public declares that there is no judgment so bad as the judgment of a specialist. Few practical situations exactly coincide with his specialty, and outside his specialty his judgment is worse than that of the novice. He has been training himself in reference to something precise; and the moment he ventures beyond it, the very exactitude of his discipline limits his worth. The man who has not been a specialist, who has dabbled in all things and has acquired a rough and ready common sense, that man's judgment is worth something in many different sections of life, but the judgment of the specialist is painfully poor beyond his usual range. You remember how, in the comic opera, the practice is satirized of appointing a person who has never been at sea to take charge of the navy of a great country. But that is the only sensible course to pursue. Put a specialist there, and the navy will be wretchedly organized, because the administration of the navy requires something more than the specialism of seamanship. It is necessary to coördinate seamanship with many other considerations, and the man trained in the specialty of seamanship is little likely to have that ability. Therefore ordinarily we use our experts best by putting them under the control of those who are not experts. Common sense has the last word. The coördinating power which has not been disciplined in single lines is what ultimately takes the direction of affairs. We need the specialist within his little field; shut him up there, and he is valuable enough; but don't let him escape. That seems to be the view of the public. They keep the specialist confined because they utterly distrust his judgment when he extends himself abroad.

And when we look at the third of our grounds for justification, social need, the public declares that the specialists are intolerably presumptuous. Knowing their own subject, they imagine they can dictate to anybody and do not understand how limited is their importance. Again and again it happens that because a man does know some one thing pretty well he sets himself up as a great man in general. My own province suffers in this respect more than most; for as soon as a man acquires considerable skill in chemistry or biology, he is apt to issue a pronunciamento on philosophy. But philosophy does not suffer alone. Everywhere the friends of the great specialist are telling him he has proved himself a mighty man, quite competent to sit in judgment on the universe; and he, forgetting that the universe and the particular subject he knows something about are two different things, really imagines that his ignorant opinions deserve consideration.

Now I suppose we must acknowledge that in all this blasphemy against our calling, there is a good deal of truth. These certainly are dangers which all of us specialists incur. I agree that they are inevitable dangers. Do not, however, let us on account of them abandon specialization and seek to acquire a mass of miscellaneous information. Bacon said, "I take all knowledge for my province." If we say it, we shall become not Bacons but fools. No, that is the broad road to ignorance. But laying these profound dangers of specialization well to heart, assured that they beset us all, let us search for remedial measures. Let us ask how such dangers may be reduced to a minimum. Is there a certain way in which we may engage in the specialist's research and still save ourselves from some of the evils I have here depicted? I think there is. To find it we will follow the same three avenues which have been leading us thus far.

In regard to the first, the limitation of attention, I understand that, after all, our specialty cannot fill our entire life. We do sometimes sit down to dinner; we occasionally talk with a friend; we now and then take a journey; we permit ourselves from time to time to read some other book than one which refers to our subject. That is, I take it, if we are fully alive to the great danger that in specializing we are cutting off a large part of the universe, we shall be wise in gathering eagerly whatever additional knowledge we may acquire outside our specialty. And I must say that the larger number of eminent specialists whom I have happened to know have been men pretty rich in knowledge outside their specialties. They were men who well apprehended the extreme danger of their limited modes of pursuit and who greedily grasped, therefore, at every bit of knowledge they could obtain which lay beyond their province. They appropriated all the wisdom they could; and merely because it did not exactly fit in with their specialty, they did not turn it away. I do not know how far it is wise to go in this effort to repair the one-sidedness in which most of us are compelled to live. A rather extreme case was once brought to my attention. There was a student at Harvard who had been a high scholar with me, and I found that he was also so specializing in the classics that when he graduated he took classical honors. Some years later I learned that he was one of the highest scholars in the Medical School. Meeting him a few years after he had entered his profession, I asked, "How did it happen that you changed your mind so markedly? You devoted yourself to classics and philosophy in college. What made you finally decide to become a physician?" "Finally decide!" said he. "Why, from childhood up I never intended to be anything else." "But," I persisted, "I cannot be mistaken in recalling that you devoted yourself in college to classics and philosophy." "Yes," he said, "I did, because I knew I should never have another chance at those subjects. I was going to give the rest of my life to medicine, so I took those years for classics and philosophy." I asked, "Wasn't that a great mistake; haven't you now found out your blunder?" "Oh, no," said he, "I am a much better physician on that account; I could not have done half so well if I hadn't had all that training in philosophy and classics." Now I cannot advise such a course for everybody. It takes a big man to do that. If you are big enough, it is worth while laying a very broad foundation; but considering the size on which most of us are planned, it is wiser to begin early and specialize from the very start.

Well, then, here is one mode of making up for the defects of specialization: we may pick up knowledge outside our subject. But it is an imperfect mode; you never can put away your limitations altogether. You can do a great deal. Use your odd quarter-hours wisely and do not merely play in fragmentary times, understanding that these are precious seasons for acquiring the knowledge which lies beyond your province. Then every time you talk with anybody, lead him neatly to what he knows best, keeping an attentive ear, becoming a first-class listener, and seeking to get beyond yourself. By doing so you will undoubtedly much enlarge the narrow bounds to which you have pledged yourself. Yet this policy will not be enough. It will require to be supplemented by something more. Therefore I should say in the second place, that in disciplining our powers we must be careful to conceive our specialty broadly enough. In taking it too narrowly lies our chief danger. There are two types of specialist. There is the man who regards his specialty as a door into which he goes and by which he shuts the world out, hiding himself with his own little interests. That is the petty, poor specialist, the specialist who never becomes a man of power, however much he may be a man of learning. But there is an entirely different sort of specialist from that; it is the man who regards his specialty as a window out of which he may peer upon all the world. His specialty is merely a point of view from which everything is regarded. Consequently without departing from our specialty each of us may escape narrowness. Instead of running over all the earth and contemplating it in a multitude of different aspects, the wise specialist chooses some single point of view and examines the universe as it is related to this. Everything therefore has a meaning for him, everything contributes something to his specialty. Narrowing himself while he is getting his powers disciplined, as those powers become trained he slacks them off and gives them a wider range; for he knows very well that while the world is cut up into little parcels it never can be viewed rightly. It will always be distorted. For, after all, things are what they are through their relations, and if you snap those relations you never truly conceive anything. Accordingly, as soon as we have got our specialty, we should begin to coördinate that specialty with everything else. At first we may fix our attention on some single problem within a given field, but soon we discover that we cannot master that problem without knowing the rest of the field also. As we go on to know the rest of the field and make ourself a fair master of that science, we discover that that science depends on other sciences. Never was there an age of the world in which this interlocking of the sciences was so clearly perceived as in our day. Formerly we seemed able to isolate a particular topic and know something of it, but in our evolutionary time nothing of that kind is possible. Each thing is an epitome of the whole. Have you been training your eye to see a world in a grain of sand? Can you look through your specialty out upon the total universe and say: "I am a specialist merely because I do not want to be a narrow man. My specialty is my telescope. Everything belongs to me. I cannot, it is true, turn to it all at once. Being a feeble person I must advance from point to point, accepting limitations; but just as fast as I can, having mastered those limitations, I shall cast them aside and press on into ever broader regions."

But I said specialization was fundamentally justified through the organization of society, because by its division of toil we contribute our share to the total of human knowledge; and yet the popular objector declares that we are presumptuous, and because we have mastered our own specialty we are apt to assume ourselves capable of pronouncing judgment over the whole field. Undoubtedly there is this danger; but such a result is not inevitable. The danger is one which we are perfectly capable of setting aside. The temper of our mind decides the matter, and this is entirely within our control. What is the use of our going forth presumptuous persons? We certainly shall be unserviceable if we are persons of that type. That is not the type of Charles Darwin in biology, of William James in psychology, of Horace Howard Furness in Shakespeare criticism, of Albert Michelson in physics. These are men as remarkable for modesty and simplicity as for scholarly insight. The true characteristic of a learned specialist is humility. What we want to be training ourselves in is respect for other people and a sense of solidarity with them. Our work would be of little use if there were not somebody at our side who cared nothing for that work of ours and cared immensely for his own. It is our business to respect that other man, whether he respects us or not. We must learn to look upon every specialist as a fellow worker. Without him we cannot be perfect. Let us make ourselves as large as possible, in order that we may contribute our little something to that to which all others are contributing. It is this coöperative spirit which it should be ours to acquire. And it seems to me that you are under peculiarly fortunate circumstances for acquiring it. What strikes me as fatal is to have a group of young specialists taken and trained by themselves, detachedly, shut off from others. Nothing of that sort occurs here. Every day you are rubbing shoulders with persons who have other interests than yours. When you walk to dinner, you fall in with a comrade who has been spending his day over something widely unlike that which has concerned you. Possibly you have been able to lead him to talk about it; possibly you have gained an insight into what he was seeking, and seen how his work largely supplements your own. If you have had proper respect for him and proper humility in regard to yourself, this great society of specialists has filled out your work for you day after day; and in that sense of coöperation, of losing yourselves in the common service of scientific mankind, you have found the veritable glory of these happy years.

VII

THE GLORY OF THE IMPERFECT[3]

A few years ago Matthew Arnold, after travelling in this country and revising the somewhat unfavorable opinion of us which he had formed earlier and at a distance, still wrote in his last paper on Civilization in the United States that America, in spite of its excellences, is an uninteresting land. He thought our institutions remarkable. He pointed out how close a fit exists between them and the character of the citizens, a fit so close as is hardly to be found in other countries. He saw much that is of promise in our future. But after all, he declares that no man will live here if he can live elsewhere, because America is an uninteresting land.

This remark of Mr. Arnold's is one which we may well ponder. As I consider how many of you are preparing to go forth from college and establish yourselves in this country, I ask myself whether you must find your days uninteresting. You certainly have not been finding them uninteresting here. Where were college days ever dull? It is a beautiful circumstance that, the world over, the period of education is the period of romance. No such thing was ever heard of as a college student who did not enjoy himself, a college student who was not full of hope. And if this has been the case with us prosaic males of the past, what must be the experience of your own hopeful sex? I am sure you are looking forward with eagerness to your intended work. Is it to be blighted? Are you to find life dull? It might seem from the remark of Mr. Arnold that it would probably be so, for you must live in an uninteresting land.

When this remark of Mr. Arnold's was first made a multitude of voices in all parts of our country declared that Mr. Arnold did not know what he was talking about. As a stupid Englishman he had come here and had failed to see what our land contains. In reality every corner of it is stuffed with that beauty and distinction which he denied. For that was the offensive feature of his statement: he had said in substance the chief sources of interest are beauty and distinction. America is not beautiful. Its scenery, its people, its past, are not distinguished. It is impossible, therefore, for an intelligent and cultivated man to find permanent interests here.

The ordinary reply to these unpleasant sayings was, "America is beautiful, America is distinguished." But on the face of the matter this reply might well be distrusted. Mr. Arnold is not a man likely to make such a mistake. He is a trained observer. His life has been passed in criticism, and criticism of an extremely del-

[3] Delivered at the first commencement of the Woman's College of Western Reserve University.

icate sort. It seems to me it must be rather his standards than his facts which are at fault. Many of us would be slow to believe our teacher had made an error in observation; for to many of us he has been a very great teacher indeed. Through him we have learned the charm of simplicity, the refinement of exactitude, the strength of finished form; we have learned calmness in trial too, the patience of duty, ability to wait when in doubt; in short, we have learned dignity, and he who teaches us dignity is not a man lightly to be forgotten or disparaged. I say, therefore, that this answer to Mr. Arnold, that he was in error, is one which on its face might prudently be distrusted.

But for other than prudential reasons I incline to agree with Mr. Arnold's opinion. Even though I were not naturally disposed to credit his judgment, I should be obliged to acknowledge that my own observations largely coincide with his. In Europe I think I find beauty more abundant than in America. Certainly the distinguished objects, the distinguished persons, whom I go there to see, are more numerous than those I might by searching find here. I cannot think this portion of Mr. Arnold's statement can be impugned. And must we then accept his conclusion and agree that your lives, while sheltered in this interesting college, are themselves interesting; but that when you go forth the romance is to pass away? I do not believe it, because I question the standard which Mr. Arnold employs. He tells us that the sources of the interesting are beauty and distinction. I doubt it. However much delight and refreshment these may contribute to our lives, I do not believe they predominantly constitute our interests.

Evidently Mr. Arnold cannot have reached his opinion through observation, for the commonest facts of experience confute him. There is in every community a certain class of persons whose business it is to discover what people regard as interesting. These are the newspaper editors; they are paid to find out for us interesting matters every day. There is nothing they like better than to get hold of something interesting which has not been observed before. Are they then searchers for beauty and distinction? I should say not. Here are the subjects which these seekers after interesting things discussed in my morning paper. There is an account of disturbances in South America. There is a statement about Mr. Blaine's health. There is a report of a prize fight. There are speculations about the next general election. There is a description of a fashionable wedding. These things interest me, and I suspect they interest the majority of the readers of that paper; though they can hardly be called beautiful or distinguished. Obviously, therefore, if Mr. Arnold had inspected the actual interests of to-day, he would have been obliged to recognize some other basis for them than beauty and distinction.

Yet I suppose all will feel it would be better if the trivial matters which excite our interest in the morning journal were of a more beautiful, of a more distinguished sort. Our interests would be more honorable then. These things interest merely because they are facts, not because they are beautiful. A fact is interesting through being a fact, and this commonest and most basal of interests Mr. Arnold has overlooked. He has not perceived that life itself is its own unceasing interest.

Before we can decide, however, whether he has overlooked anything more, we must determine what is meant by beauty. Let us analyze the matter a little. Let us see if we can detect why the beautiful and the distinguished are interesting, and still how we can provide a place for the other interests which are omitted in his statement. If we should look at a tree and ask ourselves why this tree is more beautiful than another, we should probably find we had thought it so on some such grounds as these: the total bunch of branches and leaves, that exquisite green mass sunning itself, is no larger than can well be supported on the brown trunk. It is large enough; there is nothing lacking. If it were smaller, the office of the trunk would hardly be fulfilled. If larger, the trunk would be overpowered. Those branches which extend themselves to the right adequately balance those which are extended to the left. Scrutinizing it, we find every leaf in order, each one ready to aërate its little sap and so conduce to the life of the whole. There is no decay, no broken branch. Nothing is deficient, but at the same time there is nothing superfluous. Each part ministers to every part. In all parts the tree is proportionate—beautiful, intrinsically beautiful, because it is unsuperfluous, unlacking.

And when we turn to other larger, more intricately beautiful objects, we find the same principle involved. Fulness of relations among the parts, perfection of organism, absence of incongruity, constitute the beauty of the object. Were you ever in Wiltshire in England, and did you visit the splendid seat of the Earls of Pembroke, Wilton House? It is a magnificent pile, designed by Holbein the painter, erected before Elizabeth began to reign. Its green lawns, prepared ages ago, were adapted to their positions originally and perform their ancient offices to-day. Time has changed its gardens only by making them more lovely than when they were planned. So harmonious with one another are grounds and castle that, looking on the stately dwelling, one imagines that the Creator himself must have had it in mind in his design of the spot. And when you enter, all is equally congruous. Around the central court runs the cloistered statuary gallery, out of which open the several halls. Passing through these, you notice the portraits not only of past members of the family—men who have been among the most distinguished of England's worthies—but also portraits of the eminent friends of the Pembrokes, painted by notable artists who were often themselves also friends of the family. In the library is shown Sidney's "Arcadia," written in this very garden, with a lock of Elizabeth's hair inclosed. In the chief hall a play of Shakespeare's is reported to have been performed by his company. Half a dozen names that shine in literature lend intellectual glory to the place. But as you walk from room to room, amazed at the accumulation of wealth and proud tradition, you perceive how each casual object makes its separate contribution to the general impression of stateliness. A glance from a window discloses an enchanting view: in the distance, past the cedars, rises the spire of Salisbury Cathedral, one of the most peaceful and aspiring in England. All parts—scenery, buildings, rich possessions, historic heritages—minister to parts. Romantic imagination is stirred. It is beautiful, beautiful beyond anything America can show.

And if we turn to that region where beauty is most subtly embodied, if we turn to human character, we find the conditions not dissimilar. The character which impresses us most is that which has fully organized its powers, so that every ability finds its appropriate place without prominence; one with no false humility and without self-assertion; a character which cannot be overthrown by petty circumstance, but, steadfast in itself, no part lacking, no part superfluous, easily lets its ample functions assist one another in all that they are summoned to perform. When we behold a man like this, we say, "This is what I would be. Here is the goal toward which I would tend. This man, like Wilton House, like the beautiful tree, is a finished thing." It is true when we turn our attention back and once more criticise, we see that it is not so. No human character can be finished. It is its glory that it cannot be. It must ever press forward; each step reached is but the vantage-ground for a further step. There is no completeness in human character—in human character save one.

And must we then consider human character uninteresting? According to Mr. Arnold's standard perhaps we ought to do so. But through this very case the narrowness of that standard becomes apparent. Mr. Arnold rightly perceives that beauty is one of our higher interests. It certainly is not our only or our highest, because in that which is most profoundly interesting, human life, the completeness of parts which constitutes beauty is never reached. There must obviously be another and a higher source of interest, one too exalted to be found where awhile ago I sketched it, in the mere occurrence of a fact. We cannot say that all events, simply because they occur, are alike interesting. To find in them an intelligent interest we must rate their worth. I agree, accordingly, with Mr. Arnold in thinking that it is the passion for perfection, the assessment of worths, which is at the root of all enduring interests. But I believe that in the history of the world this passion for perfection, this deepest root of human interests, has presented itself in two forms. The Greek conceived it in one way, the Christian has conceived it in another.

It was the office of that astonishing people, the Greeks, to teach us to honor completeness, the majesty of the rounded whole. We see this in every department of their marvellous life. Whenever we look at a Greek statue, it seems impossible that it should be otherwise without loss; we cannot imagine any portion changed; the thing has reached its completeness. Before it we can only bow and feel at rest. Just so it is when we examine Greek architecture. There too we find the same ordered proportion, the same adjustment of part to part. And if we turn to Greek literature, the stately symmetry is no less remarkable. What page of Sophocles could be stricken out? What page—what sentence? Just enough, not more than enough! The thought has grown, has asserted its entirety; and when that entirety has been reached, it has stopped, delighted with its own perfection. A splendid ideal, an ideal which never can fail, I am sure, to interest man so long as he remains intelligent!

And yet this beautiful Greek work shows only one aspect of the world. It omitted something, it omitted formative life. Joy in birth, delight in beginnings, interest in origins,—these things did not belong to the Greek; they came in with Christianity. It is Jesus Christ who turns our attention toward growth, and so teaches us to delight in the imperfect rather than in the perfect. It is he who, wishing to give to his disciples a model of what they should be, does not select the completed man, but takes the little child and sets him before them and to the supercilious says, "Take heed that ye despise not one of these little ones." He teaches us to reverence the beginning of things. And at first thought it might well seem that this reverence for the imperfect was a retrogression. What! is not a consummate man more admirable than a child? "No," Jesus answered; and because he answered so, pity was born. Before the coming of Jesus Christ, I think we may say that the sick, the afflicted, the child—shall I not say the woman?—were but slightly understood. It is because God has come down from heaven, manifesting even himself in forms of imperfection, it is on this account that our intellectual horizon has been enlarged. We may now delight in the lowly, we may stoop and gather imperfect things and rejoice in them,—rejoice beyond the old Greek rejoicing.

Yet it is easy to mistake the nature of this change of standard, and in doing so to run into grave moral danger. If we content ourselves with the imperfect rather than with the perfect, we are barbarians. We are not Christians nor are we Greeks, we are barbarians. But that is not the spirit of Jesus. He teaches us to catch the future in the instant, to see the infinite in the finite, to watch the growth of the perfect out of the imperfect. And he teaches us that this delight in progress, in growth, in aspiration, in completing, may rightly be greater than our exultation in completeness. In his view the joy of perfecting is beyond the joy of perfection.

Now I want to be sure that you young women, who are preparing yourselves here for larger life and are soon to emerge into the perplexing world, go forth with clear and Christian purpose. For though what I have been discussing may appear dry and abstract, it is an extremely practical matter. Consider a moment in which direction you are to seek the interests of your life. Will you demand that the things about you shall already possess their perfection? Will you ask from life that it be completed, finished, beautiful? If so, you are doomed to dreary days. Or are you to get your intellectual eyes open, see beauty in the making, and come to rejoice in it there rather than after it is made? That is the question I wish to present to-day; and I shall ask you to examine several provinces of life and see how different they appear when surveyed from one point of view or from the other.

Undoubtedly all of you on leaving here will go into some home, either the home of your parents or—less fortunate—some stranger's home. And when you come there, I think I can foretell one thing: it will be a tolerably imperfect place in which you find yourself. You will notice a great many points in which it is improvable; that is to say, a great many respects in which you might properly wish it otherwise. It will seem to you, I dare say, a little plain, a little commonplace, compared with your beautiful college and the college life here. I doubt whether you will find all the members of your family—dear though they may be—so wise, so gentle-mannered, so able to contribute to your intellectual life as are your companions here. Will you feel then, "Ah! home is a dull place; I wish I were back in college again! I think I was made for college life. Possibly enough I was made for a wealthy life. I am sure I was made for a comfortable life. But I do not find these things here. I will sit and wish I had them. Of course I ought not to enjoy a home that is short of perfection; and I recognize that this is a good way from complete." Is this to be your attitude? Or are you going to say, "How interesting this home! What a brave struggle the dear people are making with the resources at their command! What kindness is shown by my tired mother; how swift she is in finding out the many small wants of the household! How diligent my father! Should I, if I had had only their narrow opportunities, be so intelligent, so kind, so self-sacrificing as they? What can I do to show them my gratitude? What can I contribute toward the furtherance, the enlargement, the perfecting, of this home?" That is the wise course. Enter this home not merely as a matter of loving duty, but find in it also your own strong interests, and learn to say, "This home is not a perfect home, happily not a perfect home. I have something here to do. It is far more interesting than if it were already complete."

And again, you will not always live in a place so attractive as Cleveland. There are cities which have not your beautiful lake, your distant views, your charming houses excellently shaded with trees. These things are exceptional and cannot always be yours. You may be obliged to live in an American town which appears to you highly unfinished, a town which constantly suggests that much still remains to be done. And then are you going to say, "This place is not beautiful, and I of course am a lover of the beautiful. How could one so superior as I rest in such surroundings? I could not respect myself were I not discontented." Is that to be your attitude? It is, I am sorry to think, the attitude of many who go from our colleges. They have been taught to reverence perfection, to honor excellence; and instead of making it their work to carry this excellence forth, and to be interested in spreading it far and wide in the world, they sit down and mourn that it has not yet come. How dull the world would be had it come! Perfection, beauty? It constitutes a resting-place for us; it does not constitute our working-place.

I maintain, therefore, in regard to our land as a whole that there is no other so interesting on the face of the earth; and I am led to this conviction by the very reasoning which brought Mr. Arnold to a contrary opinion. I accept his judgment of the beauty of America. His premise is correct, but it should have conducted him to the opposite conclusion. In America we still are in the making. We are not yet beautiful and distinguished; and that is why America, beyond every other country, awakens a noble interest. The beauty which is in the old lands, and which refreshes for a season, is after all a species of death. Those who dwell among such scenes are appeased, they are not quickened. Let them keep their past; we have our future. We may do much. What they can do is largely at an end.

In literature also I wish to bring these distinctions before you, these differences of standard; and perhaps I cannot accomplish this better than by exhibiting them as they are presented in a few verses from the poet of the imperfect. I suppose if we try to mark out with precision the work of Mr. Browning,—I mean not to mark it out as the Browning societies do, but to mark it out with precision,—we might say that its distinctive feature is that he has guided himself by the principle on which I have insisted: he has sought for beauty where there is seeming chaos; he has loved growth, has prized progress, has noted the advance of the spiritual, the pressing on of the finite soul through hindrance to its junction with the infinite. This it is which has inspired his somewhat crabbed verses, and has made men willing to undergo the labor of reading them, that they too may partake of his insight. In one of his poems—one which seems to me to contain some of his sublimest as well as some of his most commonplace lines, the poem on "Old Pictures in Florence,"—he discriminates between Greek and Christian art in much the same way I have done. In "Greek Art," Mr. Browning says:—

You saw yourself as you wished you were,
As you might have been, as you cannot be;
Earth here, rebuked by Olympus there;
And grew content in your poor degree
With your little power, by those statues' godhead,
And your little scope, by their eyes' full sway,
And your little grace, by their grace embodied,
And your little date, by their forms that stay.

You would fain be kinglier, say, than I am?
Even so, you will not sit like Theseus.
You would prove a model? The son of Priam
Has yet the advantage in arms' and knees' use.
You're wroth—can you slay your snake like Apollo?
You're grieved—still Niobe's the grander!
You live—there's the Racers' frieze to follow:
You die—there's the dying Alexander.

So, testing your weakness by their strength,
Your meagre charms by their rounded beauty,
Measured by Art in your breadth and length,
You learned—to submit is a mortal's duty.

Growth came when, looking your last on them all,
You turned your eyes inwardly one fine day
And cried with a start—What if we so small
Be greater and grander the while than they!
Are they perfect of lineament, perfect of stature?
In both, of such lower types are we
Precisely because of our wider nature;
For time, theirs—ours, for eternity.

To-day's brief passion limits their range;
It seethes with the morrow for us and more.
They are perfect—how else? they shall never change:
We are faulty—why not? we have time in store.
The Artificer's hand is not arrested
With us; we are rough-hewn, no-wise polished:
They stand for our copy, and once invested
With all they can teach, we shall see them abolished.

You will notice that in this subtle study Mr. Browning points out how through contact with perfection there may come content with our present lot. This I call the danger of perfection, our possible belittlement through beauty. For in the lives of us all there should be a divine discontent,—not devilish discontent, but divine discontent,—a consciousness that life may be larger than we have yet attained, that we are to press beyond what we have reached, that joy lies in the future, in that which has not been found, rather than in the realized present. And it seems to me if ever a people were called on to understand this glory of the imperfect, it is we of America, it is you of the Middle West; it is especially you who are undertaking here the experiment of a woman's college. You are at the beginning, and that fact should lend an interest to your work which cannot so readily be realized in our older institutions. As you look eastward upon my own huge university, Harvard University, it probably appears to you singularly beautiful, reverend in its age, magnificent in its endowments, equable in its working; perhaps you contemplate it as nearing perfection, and contrast your incipient college with it as hardly deserving the name. You are entirely mistaken. Harvard University, to its glory be it said, is enormously unfinished; it is a great way from perfect; it is full of blemishes. We are tinkering at it all the time; and if it were not so, I for one should decline to be connected with it. Its interest for me would cease. You are to start free from some trammels that we feel. Because we have so large a past laid upon us we have not some freedoms of growth, some opportunities of enlargement, which you possess. Accordingly, in your very experiment here you have a superb illustration of the principle I am trying to explain. This young and imperfect college should interest you who are members of it; it should interest this intelligent city. Wise patrons should find here a germ capable of such broad and interesting growth as may well call out their heartiest enthusiasm.

If then the modes of accepting the passion for perfection are so divergent as I have indicated, is it possible to suggest methods by which we may discipline ourselves in the nobler way of seeking the interests of life?—I mean by taking part with things in their beginnings, learning to reverence them there, and so attaining an interest which will continually be supported and carried forward. You may look with some anxiety upon the doctrine which I have laid down. You may say, "But beauty is seductive; beauty allures me. I know that the imperfect in its struggle toward perfection is the nobler matter. I know that America is, for him who can see all things, a more interesting land than Spain. Yes, I know this, but I find it hard to feel it. My strong temptation is to lie and dream in romance, in ideal perfection. By what means may I discipline myself out of this degraded habit and bring myself into the higher life, so that I shall always be interested in progress, in the future rather than in the past, in the on-going rather than in the completed life?" I cannot give an exact and final receipt for this better mind. A persistently studied experience must be the teacher. To-day you may understand what I say, you may resolve to live according to the methods I approve. But you may be sure that to-morrow you will need to learn it all over again. And yet I think I can mention several forms of discipline, as I may call them. I can direct your attention to certain modes by which you may instruct yourselves how to take an interest in the imperfect thing, and still keep that interest an honorable one.

In my judgment, then, your first care should be to learn to observe. A simple matter—one, I dare say, which it will seem to you difficult to avoid. You have a pair of eyes; how can you fail to observe? Ah! but eyes can only look, and that is not observing. We must not rest in looking, but must penetrate into things, if we would find out what is there. And to find this out is worth while, for everything when observed is of immense interest. There is no object so remote from human life that when we come to study it we may not detect within its narrow compass illuminating and therefore interesting matter. But it makes a great difference whether we do thus really observe, whether we hold attention to the thing in hand, and see what it contains. Once, after puzzling long over the charm of Homer, I applied to a learned friend and said to him, "Can you tell me why Homer is so interesting? Why can't you and I write as he wrote? Why is it that his art is lost, and that to-day it is impossible for us to awaken an interest at all comparable to his?" — "Well," said my friend, "I have often meditated on that, but it seems to come to about this: Homer looked long at a thing. Why," said he, "do you know that if you should hold up your thumb and look at it long enough, you would find it immensely interesting?" Homer looks a great while at his thumb. He sees precisely the thing he is dealing with. He does not confuse it with anything else. It is sharp to him; and because it is sharp to him it stands out sharply for us over thousands of years. Have you acquired this art, or do you hastily glance at insignificant objects? Do you see the thing exactly as it is? Do you strip away from it your own likings and dislikings, your own previous notions of what it ought to be? Do you come face to face with things? If you do, the hardest situation in life may well be to you a delight. For you will not regard hardships, but only opportunities. Possibly you may even feel, "Yes, here are just the difficulties I like to explore. How can one be interested in easy things? The hard things of life are the ones for which we ought to give thanks." So we may feel if we have made the cool and hardy temper of the observer our own, if we have learned to put ourselves into a situation and to understand it on all sides. Why, the things on which we have thus concentrated attention become our permanent interests. For example, unluckily when I was trained I was not disciplined in botany. I cannot, therefore, now observe the rose. Some of you can, for you have been studying botany here. I have to look stupidly on the total beauty of the lovely object; I can see it only as a whole, while you, fine observer, who have trained your powers to pierce it, can comprehend its very structure and see how marvellously the blooming thing is put together. My eyes were dulled to that long ago; I cannot observe it. Beware, do not let yourselves grow dull. Observe, observe, observe in every direction! Keep your eyes open. Go forward, understanding that the world was made for your knowledge, that you have the right to enter into and possess it.

And then besides, you need to train yourselves to sympathize with that which lies beyond you. It is easy to sympathize with that which lies within you. Many persons go through life sympathizing with themselves incessantly. What unhappy persons! How unfit for anything important! They are full of themselves and answer their own motion, while there beyond them lies all the wealthy world in which they might be sharers. For sympathy is feeling with, — it is the identification of ourself with that which at present is not ourself. It is going forth and joining that which we behold, not standing aloof and merely observing, as I said at first. When we observe, the object we observe is alien to us; when we sympathize, we identify ourselves with it. You may go into a home and observe, and you will make every person in that home wretched. But go into a home and sympathize, find out what lies beyond you there, see how differently those persons are thinking and feeling from the ways in which you are accustomed to think and feel; yet notice how imperfect you are in yourself, and how important it is that persons should be fashioned thus different from you if even your own completion is to come; then, I say, you will find yourself becoming large in your own being, and a large benefactor of others.

Do not stunt sympathy, then. Do not allow walls to rise up and hem it in. Never say to yourself, "This is my way; I don't do so and so. I know only this and that; I don't want to know anything else. You other people may have that habit, but these are my habits, and I always do thus and thus." Do not say that. Nothing is more immoral than moral psychology. You should have no interest in yourself as you stand; because a larger selfhood lies beyond you, and you should be going forth and claiming your heritage there. Do not stand apart from the movements of the country,—the political, charitable, religious, scientific, literary movements,—however distastefully they may strike you. Identify yourself with them, sympathize with them. They all have a noble side; seek it out and claim it as your own. Throw yourself into all life and make it nobly yours.

But I am afraid it would be impossible for you thus to observe, thus to sympathize, unless you bring within your imperfect self just grounds of self-respect. You must contribute to things if you would draw from things. You must already have acquired some sort of excellence in order to detect larger excellence elsewhere. You should therefore have made yourself the master of something which you can do, and do on the whole better than anybody else. That is the moral aspect of competition, that one person can do a certain thing best and so it is given him to do. Some of you who are going out into the world before long will, I fear, be astonished to find that the world is already full. It has no place for you; it never anticipated your coming and it has reserved for you no corner. Your only means of gaining a corner will be by doing something better than the people who are already there. Then they will make you a place. And that is what you should be considering here. You should be training yourself to do something well, it really does not matter much what. Can you make dresses well? Can you cook a good loaf of bread? Can you write a poem or run a typewriter? Can you do anything well? Are you a master somewhere? If you are, the world will have a place for you; and more than that, you will have within yourself just grounds for self-respect.

To sum up, what I have been saying throughout this address merely amounts to this: that the imperfect thing—the one thing of genuine interest in all the world—gets its right to be respected only through its connection with the totality of things. Do not, then, when you leave college say to yourself, "I know Greek. That is a splendid thing to know. These people whom I am meeting do not know it and are obviously of a lower grade than I." That will not be self-respectful, because it shows that you have not understood your proper place. You should respect yourself as a part of all, and not as of independent worth. To call this wide world our own larger self is not too extravagant an expression. But if we are to count it so, then we must count the particular thing which we are capable of doing as merely our special contribution to the great self. And we must understand that many are making similar contributions. What I want you to feel, therefore, is the profound conception of mutual helpfulness and resulting individual dignity which St. Paul has set forth, according to which each of us is performing a special function in the common life, and that life of all is recognized as the divine life, the manifestation of the life of the Father. When you have come to that point, when you have seen in the imperfect a portion, an aspect, of the total, perfect, divine life, then I am not afraid life will be uninteresting. Indeed I would say to every one who goes from this college, you can count with confidence on a life which shall be vastly more interesting beyond the college walls than ever it has proved here, if you have once acquired the art of penetrating into the imperfect, and finding in limited, finite life the infinite life. "To apprehend thus, draws us a profit from all things we see."

II
HARVARD PAPERS

The following papers relate primarily to Harvard University and are chiefly of historic interest. But since out of that centre of investigation and criticism has come a large part of what is significant in American education, the story of its experiences will be found pretty generally instructive for whoever would teach or learn.

The first three papers were published in the Andover Review for 1885, 1886, and 1887, and are now printed without alteration. Time has changed most of the facts recorded in these papers, and the University is now a different place from the one depicted here. An educational revolution was then in progress, more influential than any which has ever visited our country before or since. Harvard was its leader, and had consequently become an object of suspicion through wide sections of the land. I was one of those who sought to allay those suspicions and to clear up some of the mental confusions in which they arose. To-day Harvard's cause is won. All courses leading to the Bachelor's degree throughout the country now recognize the importance of personal choice. But the history of the struggle exhibits with peculiar distinctness a conflict which perpetually goes on between two currents of human progress, a conflict whose opposing ideals are almost equally necessary and whose champions never fail alike to awaken sympathy. As a result of this struggle our children enjoy an ampler heritage than was open to us their fathers. Do they comprehend their added wealth and turn it to the high uses for which it was designed? In good measure they do. A brief consideration of the ethical aims which have shaped the modern college may enable them to do so still more.

Appended to these are two papers: one on college economics in 1887, describing the first attempt ever made, I believe, to ascertain from students themselves the cost of the higher education; the other setting forth a picturesque and noble figure who belonged to the days before the Flood, when the prescribed system was still supreme.

VIII

THE NEW EDUCATION

During the year 1884-85 the freshmen of Harvard College chose a majority of their studies. Up to that time no college, so far as I know, allowed its first year's men any choice whatever. Occasionally, one modern language has been permitted rather than another; and where colleges are organized by "schools,"—that is, with independent groups of studies each leading to a different degree,—the freshman by entering one school turns away from others, and so exercises a kind of selection. But with these possible exceptions, the same studies have always been required of all the members of a given freshman class. Under the new Harvard rules, but seven sixteenths of the work of the freshman year will be prescribed; the entire remainder of the college course, with the exception of a few exercises in English composition, will be elective. A fragment of prescribed work so inconsiderable is likely soon to disappear. At no distant day the Harvard student will mark out for himself his entire curriculum from entrance to graduation.

Even if this probable result should not follow, the present step toward it is too significant to be passed over in silence, for it indicates that after more than half a century of experiment the Harvard Faculty are convinced of the worth of the elective system. In their eyes, option is an engine of efficiency. People generally treat it as a concession. Freedom is confessedly agreeable; restive boys like it; let them have as much as will not harm them. But the Harvard authorities mean much more than this. They have thrown away that established principle of American education, that every head should contain a given kind of knowledge; and having already organized their college from the top almost to the bottom on a wholly different plan, they now declare that their new principle has been proved so safe and effective that it should supplant the older method, even in that year when students are acknowledged to be least capable of self-direction.

On what facts do they build such confidence? What do they mean by calling their elective principle a system? Does not the new method, while rendering education more agreeable, tend to lower its standard? Or, if it succeeds in stimulating technical scholarship, is it equally successful in fostering character and in forming vigorous and law-revering men? These questions I propose to answer, for they are questions which every friend of Harvard, and indeed of American education, wishes people pressingly to ask. Those most likely to ask them are quiet, God-fearing parents, who, having bred their sons to a sense of duty, expect college life to broaden and consolidate the discipline of the home. These are the parents every college wants to reach. Their sons, whether rich or poor, are the bone and sinew of the land. In my judgment the new education, once understood, will appeal to them more strongly than to any other class.

But it is not easy to understand it. My own understanding of it has been of slow growth. When, in 1870, I left Andover Seminary and came to teach at Harvard, I distrusted the more extreme developments of the elective system. Up to 1876 I opposed the introduction of voluntary attendance at recitations. Not until four years ago did I begin to favor the remission of Greek in the requisites for entrance. In all these cases my party was defeated; my fears proved groundless; what I wished to accomplish was effected by means which I had opposed. I am therefore that desirable persuader, the man who has himself been persuaded. The misconceptions through which I passed, I am sure beset others. I want to clear them away, and to present some of the reasons which have turned me from an adherent of the old to an apostle of the new faith.

An elementary misconception deserves a passing word. The new system is not a mere cutting of straps; it is a system. Its student is still under bonds, bonds more compulsive than the old, because fitted with nicer adjustment to each one's person. On H. M. S. Pinafore the desires of every sailor receive instant recognition. The new education will not agree to that. It remains authoritative. It will not subject its student to alien standards, nor treat his deliberate wishes as matters of no consequence; but it does insist on that authority which reveals to a man his own better purposes and makes them firmer and finer than they could have become if directed by himself alone. What the amount of a young man's study shall be, and what its grade of excellence, a body of experts decides. The student himself determines its specific topic.

Everybody knows how far this is from a prescribed system; not so many see that it is at a considerable remove from unregulated or nomadic study. An American at a German university, or at a summer school of languages, applies for no degree and is under no restraint. He chooses whatever studies he likes, ten courses or five or one; he works on them as much as suits his need or his caprice; he submits what he does to no test; he receives no mark; the time he wastes is purely his own concern. Study like this, roving study, is not systematic at all. It is advantageous to adult students,—to those alone whose wills are steady, and who know their own wants precisely. Most colleges draw a sharp distinction between the small but important body of students of this class—special students, as they are called—and the great company of regulars. These latter are candidates for a degree, are under constant inspection, and are moved along the line only as they attain a definite standard in both the quantity and quality of their work. After accomplishing the studies of the freshman year, partly prescribed and partly elective, a Harvard student must pass successfully four elective courses in each of his subsequent three years. By "a course" is understood a single line of study receiving three hours a week of instruction; fifty per cent of a maximum mark must be won in each year in order to pass. Throwing out the freshman year, the precise meaning of the Harvard B.A. degree is therefore this: its holder has presented twelve courses of study selected by himself, and has mastered them at least half perfectly.

Here, then, is the essence of the elective system,—fixed quantity and quality of study, variable topic. Work and moderate excellence are matters within everybody's reach. It is not unfair to demand them of all. If a man cannot show success somewhere, he is stamped *ipso facto* a worthless fellow. But into the specific topic of work an element of individuality enters. To succeed in a particular branch of study requires fitness, taste, volition,—incalculable factors, known to nobody but the man himself. Here, if anywhere, is the proper field for choice; and all American colleges are now substantially agreed in accepting the elective principle in this sense and applying it within the limits here marked out. It is an error to suppose that election is the hasty "craze" of a single college. Every senior class in New England elects a portion of its studies. Every important New England college allows election in the junior year. Amherst, Bowdoin, Yale, and Harvard allow it in the sophomore. Outside of New England the case is the same. It is true, all the colleges except Harvard retain a modicum of prescribed study even in the senior year; but election in some degree is admitted everywhere, and the tendency is steadily in the direction of a wider choice.

The truth is, Harvard has introduced the principle more slowly than other colleges. She was merely one of the earliest to begin. In 1825, on the recommendation of Judge Story, options were first allowed, in modern languages. Twenty years of experiment followed. In 1846 electives were finally established for seniors and juniors; in 1867 for sophomores; in 1884 for freshmen. But the old method was abandoned so slowly that as late as 1871 some prescribed study remained for seniors, till 1879 for juniors, and till 1884 for sophomores. During this long and unnoticed period, careful comparison was made between the new and old methods. A mass of facts was accumulated, which subsequently rendered possible an extremely rapid adoption of the system by other colleges. Public confidence was tested. Comparing the new Harvard with the old, it is plain enough that a revolution has taken place; but it is a revolution like that in the England of Victoria, wrought not by sudden shock, but quietly, considerately, conservatively, inevitably. Those who have watched the college have approved; the time of transition has been a time of unexampled prosperity. For the last fifteen years the gifts to the University have averaged $250,000 a year. The steady increase in students may be seen at a glance by dividing the last twenty-five years into five-year periods, and noting the average number of undergraduates in each: 1861-65, 423; 1866-70, 477; 1871-75, 657; 1876-80, 808; 1881-85, 873.

These facts are sufficient to show that Harvard has reached her present great prosperity by becoming the pioneer in a general educational movement. What made the movement general was the dread of flimsy study. Our world is larger than the one our grandfathers inhabited; it is more minutely subdivided, more finely related, more subtly and broadly known. The rise of physical science and the enlargement of humanistic interests oblige the college of to-day to teach elaborately many topics which formerly were not taught at all. Not so many years ago a liberal education prepared men almost exclusively for the four professions,—preaching, teaching, medicine, and law. In the first century of its existence one half the graduates of Harvard became ministers. Of the graduates of the last ten years a full third have entered none of the four professions. With a narrow field of knowledge, and with students who required no great variety of training, the task of a college was simple. A single programme decently covered the needs of all. But as the field of knowledge widened, and men began to notice a difference between its contents and those of the college curriculum, an effort was made to enlarge the latter by adding subjects from the former. Modern languages crept in, followed by sciences, political economy, new departments of history, literature, art, philosophy. For the most part, these were added to the studies already taught. But the length of college days is limited. The life of man has not extended with the extension of science. To multiply subjects was soon found equivalent to cheapening knowledge. Where three subjects are studied in place of one, each is pushed only one third as far. A crowded curriculum is a curriculum of superficialities, where men are forever occupied with alphabets and multiplication-tables,—elementary matters, containing little mental nutriment. Thoroughgoing discipline, the acquisition of habits of intellectual mastery, calls for acquaintance with knowledge in its higher ranges, and there is no way of reaching these remoter regions during the brief season of college life except by dividing the field and pressing along paths where personal friction is least. Accordingly, alternative options began to be allowed, at first between the new subjects introduced, then between these and the old ones. But in this inevitable admission of option a new principle was introduced whose germinal force could not afterwards be stayed. The old conception had been that there were certain matters a knowledge of which constituted a liberal education. Compared with the possession of these, the temper of the receiving mind was a secondary affair. This view became untenable. Under the new conditions, college faculties were forced to recognize personal aptitudes, and to stake intellectual gains upon them. In assessing the worth of studies, attention was thus withdrawn from their subject-matter and transferred to the response they called forth in the apprehender. Hence arose a new ideal of education, in which temper of mind had preëminence over *quæsita,* the guidance of the powers of knowing over the store of matters known. The new education has accordingly passed through two stages of development: first, in order to avoid superficiality when knowledge was coming in like a flood, it was found necessary to admit choice; secondly, in the very necessity of this admission was disclosed a more spiritual ideal of the relation of the mind of man to knowledge.

And this new ideal, I hold, should now commend itself not as a thing good enough if collateral, but as a principle, organic and exclusive. To justify its dominance a single compendious reason is sufficient: it uplifts character as no other training can, and through influence on character it ennobles all methods of teaching and discipline. We say to our student at Harvard, "Study Greek, German, history, or botany,—what you will; the one thing of consequence is that you should will to study something." The moral factor is thus put forward, where it belongs. The will is honored as of prime consequence. Other systems treat it as a merely concurrent and auxiliar force. They try to smuggle it into operation wrapped in a mass of matter-of-course performances. It is the distinctive merit of the elective system that it strips off disguises, places the great facts of the moral life in the foreground, forces the student to be conscious of what he is doing, permits him to become a partaker in his own work, and makes him perceive that gains and losses are immediately connected with a volitional attitude. When such a consciousness is aroused, every step in knowledge becomes a step toward maturity. There is no sudden transformation, but the boy comes gradually to perceive that in the determination of the will are found the promise and potency of every form of life. Many people seem to suppose that at some epoch in the life of a young man the capacity to choose starts up of itself, ready-made. It is not so. Choice, like other human powers, needs practice for strength. To learn how to choose, we must choose. Keep a boy from exercising his will during the formative period from eighteen to twenty-two, and you turn him into the world a child when by years he should be a man. To permit choice is dangerous; but not to permit it is more dangerous; for it renders dependency habitual, places outside the character those springs of action which should be set within it, treats personal adhesion as of little account, and through anxiety to shield a young life from evil cuts it off from opportunities of virile good. Even when successful, the directive process breeds an excellence not to be desired. Plants and stones commit no errors. They are under a prescribed system and follow given laws. Personal man is in continual danger, for to self-direction is attached the prerogative of sin. For building up a moral manhood, the very errors of choice are serviceable.

I am not describing theoretic advantages. A manlier type of character actually appears as the elective principle extends. The signs of the better life are not easy to communicate to those who have not lived in the peculiar world of a college. A greater ease in uprightness, a quicker response to studious appeal, a deeper seriousness, still keeping relish for merriment, a readier amenability to considerations of order, an increase of courtesy, a growing disregard of coarseness and vice, a decay of the boyish fancy that it is girlish to show enthusiasm,—tendencies in these directions, hardly perceptible to others, gladden the watchful heart of a teacher and assure him that his work is not returning to him void. Every company of young men has a notion of what it is "gentlemanly" to do. Into this current ideal the most artificial and incongruous elements enter. Perhaps it is counted "good form" to haze a freshman, to wear the correctest cut of trousers, to have a big biceps muscle, or to be reputed a man of brains. Whatever the notion, it is allegiance to some such blind ideal, rather than the acceptance of abstract principles of conduct, which guides a young man's life. To change ever so little these influential ideals is the ambition of the educator; but they are persistent things, held with the amazing conservatism of youth. When I say that a better tone prevails as the elective system takes root, I mean that I find the word "gentleman," as it drops from student mouths, enlarging and deepening its meaning from year to year, departing from its usage as a term of outward description and drawing to itself qualities more interior. Direct evidence on a matter so elusive can hardly be given, but I can throw a few sidelights upon it. Hazing, window-smashing, disturbing a lecture-room, are things of the past. The office of proctor—the literary policeman of the olden time—has become a sinecure. Several years ago the Faculty awarded Honorable Mention at graduation to students who attained a high rank in three or more courses of a single department. The honor was not an exalted one, but being well within the powers of all it soon became "not quite the thing" to graduate without it. In the last senior class 91 men out of 191 received Honorable Mention.

This last fact shows that a decent scholarship has become reputable. But more than this is true: the rank which is reckoned decent scholarship is steadily rising. I would not overstate the improvement. The scale of marking itself may have risen slightly. But taking the central scholar of each class during the last ten years,—the scholar, that is, who stands midway between the head and the foot,—this presumably average person has received the following marks, the maximum being 100:—

YEAR	1874-75	1875-76	1876-77	1877-78	1878-79	1879-80	1880-81	1881-82	1882-83	1883-84
Fresh.	59	55	57	56	62	62	65	67	64	63
Soph.	59	64	63	65	67	68	70	69	69	68
Jun.	67	65	66	67	70	68	72	75	72	72
Sen.	67	70	70	73	76	73	77	75	79	81

It will be observed that the marks in this table become higher as the student approaches the end of his course and reaches the years where the elective principle is least restricted. Let the eye pass from the left upper corner of the table to the right lower corner and take in the full significance of a change which has transformed freshmen, doomed to prescribed studies and half of them ranking below sixty per cent, into seniors so energetic that half of them win four fifths of a perfect mark in four electives. It is not only the poor who are affected in this way. About half the men who appear on the Rank List each year receive no pecuniary aid, and are probably not needy men.

But it may be suspected that high marks mean easy studies. The many different lines of work cannot be equally severe, and it is said that those which call for least exertion will be sure to prove the favorites. As this charge of "soft" courses is the stock objection to the elective system, I shall be obliged to examine it somewhat minutely. Like most of the popular objections, it rests on an *a priori* assumption that thus things must be. Statistics all run the other way. Yet I am not surprised that people believe it. I believed it once myself when I knew nothing but prescribed systems. Under these, it certainly is true that ease is the main factor in making a study popular. When choice is permitted, the factor of interest gets freer play, and exerts an influence that would not be anticipated by those who have never seen it in operation. Severe studies are often highly popular if the subject is attractive and the teaching clear. Here is a list of the fifteen courses which in 1883-84 (the last year for which returns are complete) contained the largest numbers of seniors and juniors, those classes being at that time the only ones which had no prescribed studies: Mill's political economy, 125 seniors and juniors; European history from the middle of the eighteenth century, 102; history of ancient art, 80; comparative zoölogy, 58; political and constitutional history of the United States, 56; psychology, 52; geology, 47; constitutional government of England and the United States, 45; advanced geology, with field work, 43; Homer, sixteen books, 40; ethics, 38; logic, and introduction to philosophy, 38; Shakespeare, six plays, 37; economic history, advanced course, 36; legal history of England to the sixteenth century,

35. In these years the senior and junior classes together contained 404 men, who chose four electives apiece. In all, therefore, 1616 choices were made. The above list shows 832; so that, as nearly as may be, one half of the total work of two years is here represented. The other half was devoted to interests more special, which were pursued in smaller companies.

Are these choices unwise? Are they not the studies which should largely occupy a young man's thoughts toward the close of his college life? They are the ones most frequently set for the senior and junior years by colleges which retain prescribed studies. From year to year choices differ a little. The courses at the lower end of the list may give place to others which do not appear here. I print the list simply to indicate the general character of the studies elected. In it appears only one out of all the modern languages, and that, too, a course in pure literature in which the marking is not reputed tender. Another year a course of French or German might come in; but ordinarily—except when chosen by specialists—the languages, modern and ancient, are elected most largely during the sophomore year. Following directly the prescribed linguistic studies of the freshman year, they are deservedly among the most popular, though not the easiest, courses. In nearly half the courses here shown no text-book is used, and the amount of reading necessary for getting an average mark is large. A shelf of books representing original authorities is reserved by the instructor at the Library, and the pupil is sent there to prepare his work.

How, it will be asked, are choices so judicious secured? Simply by making them deliberate. Last June studies were chosen for the coming year. During the previous month students were discussing with one another what their electives should be. How this or that course is conducted, what are the peculiarities of its teacher, what is the proportion in it between work given and gains had, are matters which then interest the inhabitants of Hollis and Holyoke as stocks interest Wall Street. Most students, too, have some intimacy with one or another member of the Faculty, to whom they are in the habit of referring perplexities. This advice is now sought, and often discreetly rejected. The Elective Pamphlet is for a time the best-read book in college. The perplexing question is, What courses to give up? All find too many which they wish to take. The pamphlet of this year offers 189 courses, divided among twenty departments. The five modern languages, for example, offer, all told, 34 different courses; Sanskrit, Persian, Assyrian, Hebrew, and Arabic, 14; Greek and Latin, 18 each; natural history, 19; physics and chemistry, 18; mathematics, 18; history and philosophy, 12 each; the fine arts, including music, 11; political economy, 7; Roman law, 2. These numbers will show the range of choice; on its extent a great deal of the efficiency of the system depends.[4] After the electives are chosen and reported in writing to the Dean, the long vacation begins, when plans of study come under the scrutiny of parents, of the parish minister, or of the college graduate who lives in the next street. Until September 21, any elective may be changed on notice sent to the Dean. During the first ten

[4] But a great deal of the expense also. How much larger the staff of teachers must be where everything is taught to anybody than where a few subjects are offered to all, may be seen by comparing the number of teachers at Harvard—146, instructing 1586 men—with those of Glasgow University in 1878—42, instructing 2018 men.

days of the term, no changes are allowed. This is a time of trial, when one sees for himself his chosen studies. Afterwards, for a short time, changes are easy, if the instructors consent. For the remainder of the year no change is possible, unless the reasons for change appear to the Dean important. Other restrictions on the freedom of choice will readily be understood without explanation. Advanced studies cannot be taken till preliminary ones are passed. Notices are published by the French and German departments that students who elect those languages must be placed where proficiency fits them to go. Courses especially technical in character are marked with a star in the Elective Pamphlet, and cannot be chosen till the instructor is consulted.

By means like these the Faculty try to prevent the wasting of time over unprofitable studies. Of course they do not succeed. I should roughly guess that a quarter, possibly a third, of the choices made might be improved. This estimate is based on the answers I have received to a question put to some fifty recent graduates: "In the light of your present experience, how many of your electives would you change?" I seldom find a man who would not change some; still more rarely one who would change one half. As I look back on my own college days, spent chiefly on prescribed studies, I see that to make these serve my needs more than half should have been different. There was Anglo-Saxon, for example, which was required of all, no English literature being permitted. A course in advanced chemical physics, serviceable no doubt to some of my classmates, came upon me prematurely, and stirred so intense an aversion to physical study that subsequent years were troubled to overcome it. One meagre meal of philosophy was perhaps as much as most of us seniors could digest, but I went away hungry for more. I loved Greek, but for two years I was subject to the instructions of a certain professor, now dead, who was one of the most learned scholars and unprofitable teachers I ever knew. Of the studies which brought me benefit, few did so in any vigorous fashion. Every reader will parallel my experience from his own. Prescribed studies may be ill-judged or ill-adapted, ill-timed or ill-taught, but none the less inexorably they fall on just and unjust. The wastes of choice chiefly affect the shiftless and the dull, men who cannot be harmed much by being wasted. The wastes of prescription ravage the energetic, the clear-sighted, the original,—the very classes who stand in greatest need of protection. What I would assert, therefore, is not that in the elective system we have discovered the secret of stopping educational waste. That will go on as long as men need teaching. I simply hold that the monstrous and peculiarly pernicious wastes of the old system are now being reduced to a minimum. Select your cloth discreetly, order the best tailor in town to make it up, and you will still require patience for many misfits; but they will be fewer, at any rate, than when garments are served out to you and the whole regiment by the government quartermaster.

Nobody who has taught both elective and prescribed studies need be told how the instruction in the two cases differs. With perfunctory students, a teacher is concerned with devices for forcing his pupils onward. Teaching becomes a secondary affair; the time for it is exhausted in questioning possible shirks. Information must be elicited, not imparted. The text-book, with its fixed lessons, is a thing of consequence. It is the teacher's business to watch his pupils, to see that they carry off the requisite knowledge; their business, then, it soon becomes to try to escape without it. Between teacher and scholar there goes on an ignoble game of matching wits, in which the teacher is smart if he can catch a boy, and the boy is smart if he can know nothing without being found out. Because of this supposed antagonism of interests American higher education seldom escapes an air of unreality. We seem to be at the opera bouffe. A boy appears at the learning-shop, purchases his parcel of knowledge, and then tries to toss it under the counter and dodge out of the door before the shopman can be quick enough to make him carry off the goods. Nothing can cure such folly except insistence that pupil's neglect is not teacher's injury. The elective system points out to a man that he has something at stake in a study, and so trains him to look upon time squandered as a personal loss. Where this consciousness can be presumed, a higher style of teaching becomes possible. Methods spring up unlike formal lectures, unlike humdrum recitations. The student acquires—what he will need in after life—the power to look up a single subject in many books. Theses are written; discussions held; in higher courses, problems of research supersede defined tasks. During 1860-61, fifty-six per cent of the Harvard undergraduates consulted the college library; during 1883-84, eighty-five per cent.

In a similar way governmental problems change their character. Formerly, it was assumed that a student who followed his own wishes would be indisposed to attend recitations. Penalties were accordingly established to compel him to come. At present, there is not one of his twelve recitations a week which a Harvard student might not "cut." Of course I do not mean that unlimited absence is allowed. Any one who did not appear for a week would be asked what he was doing. But for several years there has been no mechanical regulation,—so much absence, so much penalty. I had the curiosity to see how largely, under this system of trust, the last senior class had cared to stay away. I counted all absences, excused and unexcused. Some men had been sick for considerable periods; some had been worthless, and had shamelessly abused their freedom. Reckoning in all misdeeds and all misfortunes, I found that on the average each man had been absent a little less than twice a week.[5] The test of high character is the amount of freedom it will absorb without going to pieces. The elective system enlarges the capacity to absorb freedom undisturbed. But it would be unfair to imply that the new spirit is awakened in students alone. Professors are themselves instructed. The obstacles to their proper work, those severest of all obstacles which come from defective sympathy, are cleared away. A teacher draws near his class, and learns what he can do for it. Long ago it was said that among the Gentiles—people spiritually rude—great ones exercised authority, while in a state of righteousness this should not be so; there the leader would estimate his importance by his serviceability. It was a teacher who spoke, and he spoke to teachers. To-day teachers' dangers lie in

[5] Or sixteen per cent of his recitations. Readers may like to compare this result with the number of absences elsewhere. At a prominent New England college, one of the best of those which require attendance, a student is excused from ten per cent of his exercises. But this amount does not cover absences of necessity,—absences caused by sickness, by needs of family, and by the many other perfectly legitimate hindrances to attendance. The percentage given for the Harvard seniors includes all absences whatsoever.

the same direction. Always dealing with inferiors, isolated from criticism, by nature not less sluggish than others, through the honorable passion which they feel for their subject disposed to set the private investigation of it above its exposition, teachers are continually tempted to think of a class as if it existed for their sakes rather than they for its. Fasten pupils to the benches, and nothing counteracts this temptation except that individual conscience which in all of us is a faculty that will well bear strengthening. It may be just to condemn the dull, the intolerant, the self-absorbed teacher; but why not condemn also the system which perpetuates him? Nobody likes to be inefficient; slackness is largely a fault of inadvertence. That system is good which makes inadvertence difficult and opens the way for a teacher to discover whether his instructions hit. Give students choice, and a professor gets the power to see himself as others see him.

How this is accomplished appears by examining three possible cases. Suppose, in the first place, I become negligent this year, am busy with private affairs, and so content myself with imparting nothing, with calling off questions from a text-book, or with reading my old lectures; I shall find out my mistake plainly enough next June, when fewer men than usual elect my courses. Suppose, secondly, I give my class important matter, but put it in such a form that young minds cannot readily assimilate it; the same effect follows, only in this case I shall probably attract a small company of the hardier spirits,—in some subjects the very material a teacher desires. Or suppose, lastly, I seek popularity, aim at entertainment, and give my pupils little work to do; my elective becomes a kind of sink, into which are drained off the intellectual dregs of the college. Other teachers will get rid of their loafers; I shall take them in. But I am not likely to retain them. A teacher is known by the company he keeps. In a vigorous community a "soft" elective brings no honor to its founder. I shall be apt to introduce a little stiffening into my courses each year, till the appearance of the proper grade of student tells me I am proved to have a value. There is, therefore, in the new method a self-regulating adjustment. Teacher and taught are put on their good behavior. A spirit of faithfulness is infused into both, and by that very fact the friendliest relation is established between them.

I have left myself little room to explain why the elective system should be begun as early as the freshman year, and surely not much room is needed. A system proved to exert a happy influence over character, and thence over manners and scholarly disposition, is exactly the maturing agency needed by the freshman of eighteen. It is the better suited to him because the early years of college life are its least valuable portion, which can bear, therefore, most economically the disciplining losses sure to come when a student is learning to choose. More than this, the change from school methods to character methods is too grave a one to be passed over as an incident in the transition from year to year. A change of residence should mark it. It should stand at the entrance to a new career. Parents should be warned, and those who have brought up their sons to habits of luxurious ease should be made fully aware that a college which appeals to character has no place for children of theirs.

Every mode of training has its exclusions. I prefer the one which brings least profit to our dangerous classes,—the indolent rich. Leslie Stephen has said that the only argument rascals can understand is the hangman. The only inducement to study, for boys of loose early life, is compulsion. But for the plain democratic many, who have sound seed in themselves, who have known duty early, and who have found in worthy things their law and impulse, the elective system, even during the freshman year, gives an opportunity for moral and mental expansion such as no compulsory system can afford.

Perhaps in closing I ought to caution the reader that he has been listening to a description of tendencies merely, and not of completed attainment. In no college is the New Education fully embodied. It is an ideal, toward which all are moving, and a powerfully influential ideal. In explaining it, for the sake of simplicity I have confined myself to tracing the working of its central principle, and I have drawn my illustrations from that Harvard life with which I am most familiar. But simplicity distorts; the shadows disappear. I am afraid I may seem to have hinted that the Harvard training already comes pretty near perfection. It does not—let me say so distinctly. We have much to learn. Side by side with nobler tendencies to which I have directed attention, disheartening things appear. The examination paper still attacks learning on its intellectual side, the marking system on its moral. All I have sought to establish is this: there is a method which we and many other colleges in different degrees have adopted, which is demonstrably a sound method. Its soundness should by this time be generally acknowledged, and criticism should now turn to the important work of bettering its details of operation. May what I have written encourage such criticism and help to make it wise, penetrative, and friendly.

IX

ERRONEOUS LIMITATIONS OF THE ELECTIVE SYSTEM

In a paper published in the Andover Review a year ago, I called attention to the fact that a new principle is at work in American education. That principle, briefly stated, is this: the student now consciously shares in his own upbuilding. His studies are knitted closely to his personal life. Under this influence a new species of power is developed. Scholarship broadens and deepens, boyishness diminishes, teacher and pupil meet less artificially. The college, as an institution, wins fresh life. Public confidence awakens; pupils, benefactions, flow in. Over what I wrote an eager controversy has arisen, a controversy which must have proved instructive to those who need instruction most. In the last resort questions of education are decided by educators, as those of sanitation by sanitary engineers; but in both cases the decision has reference to public needs, and people require to be instructed in the working of appliances which are designed for their comfort. There is danger that such instruction may not be given. Professional men become absorbed in their art and content themselves with reticence, leaving the public ignorant of the devices by which its health is to be preserved. A great opportunity, therefore, comes to the common householder when these professional men fall foul of one another. In pressing arguments home they frequently take to ordinary speech, and anybody who then lends an ear learns of the mysteries. The present discussion, I am sure, has brought this informatory gain to every parent who reads the Andover Review and has a studious boy. The gain will have been greater because of the candor and courtesy with which the attacking party has delivered its assault. The contest has been earnest. Its issues have been rightly judged momentous. For good or for ill, the choice youth of the land are to be shaped by whatever educational policy finally wins. Yet, so far as I recall, no unkind word has slipped from the pen of one of my stout opponents; no disparagement of man or college has mixed with the energetic advocacy of principle; the discussion has set in well toward things. I cannot call this remarkable. Of course it is not easy to be fair and strong at once. Sweetness and light are often parted. Yet we rightly expect the scholar's life to civilize him who pursues it, and we anticipate from books a refinement of the spirit and the manners as well as the understanding. My opponents have been scholars, and have spoken as scholars speak. It is a pleasure to linger in their kindly contentious company. So I gladly accept the invitation of the editors of the Review to sum up our discussion and to add some explanatory last words.

The papers which have appeared fall into two easily distinguishable classes, the descriptive and the critical. To the former I devote but a brief space, so much more direct is the bearing of the latter on the main topic of debate—the question, namely, what course the higher education can and what it cannot now take. Yet the descriptive papers perform a service and deserve a welcome word. Suspecting that I was showing off Harvard rather favorably, professors planted elsewhere have attempted to make an equally favorable exhibit of their own colleges. In my manifesto they have seen "a coveted opportunity to bring forward corresponding statistics which have not been formed under the Harvard method." Perhaps this was to mistake my aim a little. I did intend to advance my college in public esteem; she deserves that of me in everything I write. But primarily I thought of myself as the expounder of an important policy, which happens to have been longer perceived and more elaborately studied at Harvard than elsewhere. I hope I did not imply that Harvard, having this excellence, has all others. She has many weaknesses, which should not be shielded from discerning discussion. Nor did I intend to commit the injustice to Harvard—an injustice as gross as it is frequent—of treating her as a mere embodiment of the elective system. Harvard is a complex and august institution, possessed of all the attractions which can be lent by age, tradition, learning, continually renewed resources, fortunate situation, widespread clientage, enthusiastic loyalty, and forceful guidance. She is the intellectual mother of us all, honored certainly by me, and I believe by thousands of others, for a multiplicity of subtle influences which stretch far outside her special modes of instruction. But for the last half-century Harvard has been developing a new and important policy of education. Coincident with this development she has attained enormous popular esteem and internal power. The value and limits of this policy, the sources of this esteem and power, I wish everybody, colleges and populace, to scrutinize. To make these things understood is to help the higher education everywhere.

In undertaking this *quasi* philosophical task, I count it a piece of good fortune to have provoked so many lucid accounts of what other colleges are doing. The more of these the better. The public cannot be too persistently reminded of the distinctive merits of this college and of that. Let each be as zealous as possible; gains made by one are gains for all. Depreciatory rivalry between colleges is as silly as it is when religious sects quarrel in the midst of a perishing world. Probably such rivalries have their rise in the dull supposition that a fixed constituency of pupils exists somewhere, which if not turned toward one college may be drawn to another. As the old political economists tell of a "wages fund," fixed and constant in each community, so college governors are apt to imagine a public pupil-hoard, not susceptible of much increase or diminution, which may by inadvertence fall into other hands than their own. In reality each college creates its constituency. Its students come, in the main, from the inert mass of the uncollegiate public. Only one in eight among Harvard students is a son of a Harvard graduate; and probably the small colleges beget afresh an even larger percentage of their students. On this account the small colleges have been a power in the land. To disparage them shall never be my office. In a larger degree than the great universities they spread the college idea among people who would not otherwise possess it. The boy who lives within fifty miles of one of them reflects whether he will or will not have a college training. Were there no college in the neighborhood, he might never consider the matter at all. It is natural enough for undergraduates to decry every college except their own; but those who love education generously, and who seek to spread it far and wide, cannot afford the luxury of envy. One common danger besetting us all should bind us together. In the allurements of commerce boys may forget that college is calling. They do forget it. According to my computations the number of persons in the New England colleges to-day is about the same as the number in the insane asylums; but little more than the number of idiots. Probably this number is not increasing in proportion to population. Professor Newton, of Oberlin, finds that the increase of students during the ten years between 1870 and 1880, in twenty of our oldest leading colleges, was less than three and a half per cent, the population of the United States increasing during the same period twenty-three per cent. In view of facts like these, careful study of the line along which college growth is still possible becomes a necessity. It will benefit all colleges alike. No one engaged in it has a side to maintain. We are all alike seekers. Whatever instructive experience any college can contribute to the common study, and whatever pupils she may thereby gain, will be matter for general rejoicing.

To such a study the second, or critical, class of papers furnishes important stimulus; for these have not confined themselves to describing institutions: they have gone on to discuss the value and limits of the principle which actuates the new education everywhere. In many respects their writers and I are in full accord. In moral aim we always are, and generally too in our estimate of the present status. We all confess that the conditions of college education have changed, that the field of knowledge has enlarged, that a liberal training nowadays must fit men for more than the four professions of preaching, teaching, medicine, and law. We agree that the prescribed systems of the past are outgrown. We do not want them. We doubt whether they were well suited to their own time; we are sure they will never fit ours. Readjustments of curricula, we all declare, must be undertaken if the higher education is to retain its hold on our people. Further still, we agree in the direction of this readjustment. My critics, no less than I, believe that a widely extended scope must be given to individual choice. With the possible exception of Professor Denison, about whose opinion I am uncertain, everybody who has taken part in the controversy recognizes the elective principle as a beneficial one and maintains that in some form or other it has come to stay, People generally are not aware what a consensus of opinion on this point late years have brought about. To rid ourselves once for all of further controversy let us weigh well the words of my opponents.

Mr. Brearley begins his criticism addressed to the New York Harvard Club thus: "We premise that every one accepts the elective principle. Some system based on that principle must be established. No one wants the old required systems back, or any new required system." Professor Howison says: "An elective system, in its proper place, and under its due conditions, is demonstrably sound." Professor Ladd does not express himself very fully on this point in the Andover Review, but his opinions may be learned from the New Englander for January, 1885. When, in 1884, Yale College reformed its curriculum and introduced elective studies, it became desirable to instruct the graduates about the reasons for a step which had been long resisted. After a brief trial of the new system, Professor Ladd published his impressions of it. I strongly commend his candid paper to the attention of those who still believe the old methods the safer. He asserts that "a perfect and final course of college study is, if not an unattainable ideal, at present an impossible achievement." The considerations which were "the definite and almost compulsory reasons for instituting a comprehensive change" he groups under the following heads: (1) the need of modern languages; (2) the crowding of studies in the senior year; (3) the heterogeneous and planless character of the total course; (4) the need of making allowance for the tastes, the contemplated pursuits, and the aptitudes of the individual student. Substantially, these are the evils of prescription which I pointed out; only, in my view, they are evils not confined to a single year. Stating his observation of the results of election, Professor Ladd says: "Increased willingness in study, and even a new and marked enthusiasm on the part of a considerable number of students, is another effect of the new course already realized. The entire body of students in the upper classes is more attentive, regular, interested, and even eager, than ever before." "More intimate and effective relations are secured in many cases between teachers and pupils."

These convictions in regard to the efficiency which the elective principle lends to education are not confined to my critics and myself. Let me cite testimony from representatives of other colleges. The last Amherst Catalogue records (page 24) that "excellent results have appeared from this [the elective] method. The special wants of the student are thus met, his zest and progress in his work are increased, and his association with his teachers becomes thus more close and intimate." President Robinson says, in his annual report for 1885 to the Corporation of Brown University: "There are advantages in a carefully guarded system of optional studies not otherwise obtainable. The saving of time in preparing for a special calling in life is something, and the cumulative zeal in given lines of study, where a gratified and growing taste is ever beckoning onward, is still more. But above all, some provision for choice among ever-multiplying courses of study has become a necessity." In addressing the American Institute of Instruction at Bar Harbor, July 7, 1886, Professor A. S. Hardy, of Dartmouth, is reported as saying: "Every educator now recognizes the fact that individual characteristics are always sufficiently marked to demand his earliest attention; and, furthermore, that there is a stage in the process of education where the choice, the responsibility, and the freedom of the individual should have a wide scope." President Adams, in his inaugural address at Cornell in 1885, asserted that "there are varieties of gifts, call them, if you will, fundamental differences, that make it impossible to train successfully all of a group of boys to the same standard. These differences are partly matters of sheer ability, and partly matters of taste; for if a boy has so great an aversion to a given study that he can never be brought to apply himself to it with some measure of fondness, he is as sure not to succeed in it as he would be if he were lacking the requisite mental capacity."

In determining, then, what the new education may wisely be, let this be considered settled: it must contain a large element of election. That is the opinion of these unbiased judges. They find personal choice necessary for promoting a wider range of topics in the college, a greater zeal on the part of the student, and more suitable relations between teacher and pupil. With this judgment I, of course, heartily agree, though I should make more prominent the moral reason of the facts. I should insist that a right character and temper in the receiving mind is always a prerequisite of worthy study.[6] But I misrepresent these gentlemen if I allow their testimony to stop here. They maintain that the elective principle as thus far carried out, though valuable, is still meagre and one-sided. They do not think it will be found self-sufficing and capable of guarding its own working. They see that it has dangers peculiar to itself, and believe that to escape them it will require to be restricted and furnished with supplemental influences. I believe so too. Choice is important, but it is also important that one should choose well. The individual is sacred, but only so far as he is capable of recognizing the sacredness of laws which he has had no part in making. Unrestricted arbitrary choice is indistinguishable from chaos; and undoubtedly every method of training which avoids mechanism and includes choice as a factor leaves a door open in the direction of chaos. Infinite Wisdom left that door open when man was created. To dangers from this source I am fully alive. I totally dissent from those advocates of the elective system who would identify it with a *laissez-faire* policy. The cry that we must let nature take care of itself is a familiar one in trade, in art, in medicine, in social relations, in the religious life, in education; but in the long run it always proves inadequate. Man is a personal spirit, a director, a being fitted to compare and to organize forces, not to take them as they rise, like a creature of nature. The future will certainly not tolerate an education less organic than that of the past; but just as certainly will it demand that the organic tie shall be a living one,—one whose bond may assist those whom it restricts to become spontaneous, forcible, and diverse. If I am offered only the alternative of absolutism or *laissez-faire*, I choose *laissez-faire*. Out of chaotic nature beautiful forms do continually come forth. But absolutism kills in the cradle. It cannot tolerate a life that is imperfect, and so it stifles what it should nourish.

Up to this point my critics and I have walked hand in hand. Henceforth we part company. I shall not follow out all our little divergencies. My object from the first has been to trace the line along which education may now proceed. It must, it seems, be a line including election; but election limited how? To disentangle an

[6] These conditions of intellectual nourishment were long ago recognized in other, less formal, departments of mental training. In his essays on *Books and Reading* President Porter wrote in 1871: "The person who asks. What shall I read? or, With what shall I begin? may have read for years in a mechanical routine, and with a listless spirit; with scarcely an independent thought, with no plans of self-improvement, and few aspirations for self-culture. To all these classes the advice is full of meaning: 'Read what will satisfy your wants and appease your desires, and you will comply with the first condition to reading with interest and profit.' Hunger and thirst are better than manifold appliances and directions, in respect to other than the bodily wants, towards a good appetite and a healthy digestion. If a man has any self-knowledge or any power of self-direction, he is surely competent to ask himself what is the subject or subjects in respect to which he stands most in need of knowledge or excitement from books. If he can answer this question, he has gone very far towards answering the question, 'What book or books can I read with satisfaction and profit?'" (Chap. iv, p. 39.)

answer to this vexed question, I pass by the many points in which my critics have shown that I am foolish, and the few others in which I might show them so, and turn to the fundamental issue between us, our judgment of what the supplemental influences are which will render personal initiative safe. Personal initiative is assured. The authoritative utterances I have just quoted show that it can never again be expelled from American colleges. But what checks are compatible with it? Accepting choice, what treatment will render it continually wiser? Here differences of judgment begin to appear, and here I had hoped to receive light from my critics. The question is one where coöperative experience is essential. But those who have written against me seem hardly to have realized its importance. They generally confine themselves to showing how bad my plans are, and merely hint at better ones which they themselves might offer. But what are these plans? Wise ways of training boys are of more consequence than Harvard misdeeds. We want to hear of a constructive policy which can take a young man of nineteen and so train him in self-direction that four years later he may venture out alone into a perplexing, and for the most part hostile, world. The thing to be done is to teach boys how to manage themselves. Admit that the Harvard discipline does not do this perfectly at present; what will do it better? Here we are at an educational crisis. We stand with this aim of self-guidance in our hands. What are we going to do with it? It is as dangerous as a bomb. But we cannot drop it. It is too late to objurgate. It is better to think calmly what possible modes of treatment are still open. When railroads were found dangerous, men did not take to stage-coaches again; they only studied railroading the more.

Now in the mass of negative criticism which the last year has produced I detect three positive suggestions, three ways in which it is thought limitation may be usefully applied to supplement the inevitable personal initiative. These modes of limitation, it is true, are not worked out with any fulness of practical detail, as if their advocates were convinced that the future was with them. Rather they are thrown out as hints of what might be desirable if facts and the public would not interfere. But as they seem to be the only conceivable modes of restricting the elective principle by any species of outside checkage, I propose to devote the remainder of this paper to an examination of their feasibility. In a subsequent paper I shall indicate what sort of corrective appears to me more likely to prove congruous and lasting.

I. The first suggestion is that the elective principle should be limited from beneath. Universities and schools are to advance their grade, so that finally the universities will secure three or four years of purely elective study, while the schools, in addition to their present labors, will take charge of the studies formerly prescribed by the college. The schools, in short, are to become German gymnasia, and the colleges to delay becoming universities until this regeneration of the schools is accomplished.[7] A certain "sum of topics" is said to be essential to the culture of

[7] In deference to certain writers I employ their favorite term "university" in contrast with the term "college," yet I must own I do not know what it means. An old signification is clear. A university is an assemblage of schools, as our government is an assemblage of states. In England, different corporations, giving substantially similar instruction, are brought together by a common body which confers the degrees. In this country, a group

the man and the citizen. In the interest of church and state, young minds must be provided with certain "fact forms," with a "common consciousness," a "common basis of humanism." Important as personal election is, to allow it to take place before this common basis is laid is "to strike a blow at the historic substance of civilization." How extensive this common consciousness is to be may be learned from Professor Howison's remark that "languages, classical and modern; mathematics, in all its general conceptions, thoroughly apprehended; physics, acquired in a similar manner, and the other natural sciences, though with much less of detail; history and politics; literature, especially of the mother tongue, but, indispensably, the masterpieces in other languages, particularly the classic; philosophy, in the thorough elements of psychology, logic, metaphysics, and ethics, each historically treated, and economics, in the history of elementary principles, must all enter into any education that can claim to be liberal."

The practical objections to this monarchical scheme are many. I call attention to three only.

In the first place, the argument on which it is based proves too much. If we suppose a common consciousness to be a matter of such importance, and that it cannot be secured except by sameness of studies, then that state is criminally careless which allows ninety-nine hundredths of its members to get an individual consciousness by the simple expedient of never entering college. The theory seems to demand that every male—and why not female?—between sixteen and twenty be indoctrinated in "the essential subject-matters," without regard to what he or she may personally need to know or do. This is the plan of religious teaching adopted by the Roman Church, which enforces its "fact forms" of doctrine on all alike; without securing, however, by this means, according to the judgment of the outside world, any special freshness of religious life. I do not believe the results would be better in the higher secular culture, and I should be sorry to see Roman methods applied there; but if they are to be applied, let them fall impartially on all members of the community. To put into swaddling clothes the man who is wise enough to seek an education, and to leave his duller brother to kick about as he pleases, seems a little arbitrary.

But secondly, there is no more prospect of persuading our high schools to accept the prescribed subjects of the colleges than there is of persuading our government to transform itself into the German. Already the high schools and the colleges are unhappily drawing apart. The only hope of their nearer approach is in the remission by the colleges of some of the more burdensome subjects at present exacted. Paid for by common taxation, these schools are called on to equip

of professional schools—law, medicine, theology, and science—are associated through one governing body with the college proper, that is, with the candidates for the B.A. degree. In this useful sense, Tufts and Bowdoin are universities; Amherst and Brown, colleges. But Germany, which has thrown so many parts of the world into confusion, has introduced exaltation and mystery here. A university now appears to mean "a college as good as it can be," a stimulating conception, but not a finished or precise one. I would not disparage it. It is a term of aspiration, good to conjure with. When we want to elevate men's ideas, or to obtain their dollars, it is well to talk about creating a true university: just as it is wise to bid the forward-reaching boy to become "a true gentleman."

the common man for his daily struggle. That they will one day devote themselves to laying the foundations of an ideally best education for men of leisure is grotesquely improbable. Although Harvard draws rather more than one-third of her students from states outside New England, the whole number of students who have come to her from the high schools of these states, during a period of the last ten years, is but sixty-six. Fitting for college is becoming an alarmingly technical matter, and is falling largely into the hands of private tutors and academies.

It may be said, however, thirdly, that it is just these academies which might advantageously take the present freshmen and sophomore studies. They would thus become the exclusive avenues to the university of the future, leaving it free to do its own proper work with elective studies. Considering the great expense which this lengthening of the curriculum of the academy implies, it is plain that the number of schools capable of fitting boys in this way would always be small. These few academies, with their monopoly of learned training, would lose their present character and be erected into little colleges,—colleges of a second grade. That any such thing is likely to occur, I do not believe; but if it were, would it aid the higher education and promote its wide dispersion? Precisely the contrary. Instead of going to the university from the academies, boys would content themselves with the tolerable education already received. For the most part they would decline to go farther. It is useless to say that this does not happen in Germany, where the numbers resorting to the university are so large as to have become the subject of complaint; for the German government, controlling as it does all access to the professions, is able to force through the gymnasia and through special courses at the university a body of young men who would otherwise be seeking their fortunes elsewhere. Whether such control would be desirable in this country, I will not consider. Some questions are not feasible even for discussion. But it is to English experience we must look to see what our case would be. The great public schools of England—Eton, Rugby, Harrow, Winchester, Westminster, Cheltenham—are of no higher order than under the proposed plan Andover and Exeter would become. From these two academies nearly ninety-five per cent of the senior classes now enter some college. But of the young men graduating from the English schools named, so far as I can ascertain, less than fifty per cent go to the university. With the greater pressure toward commercial life in this country, the number would certainly be less than in England. To build up colleges of a second grade, and to permit none but those who have passed them to enter colleges of the first, is to cut off the higher education from nearly all those who do not belong to the privileged classes; it is to make the "common consciousness" less common, and to turn it, even more effectually than at present, into the consciousness of a clique. He who must make a living for himself or for others cannot afford to reach his profession late. The age of entering college is already too high. With improved methods of teaching I hope it maybe somewhat reduced. At any rate, every study now added to the high schools or academies is a fresh barrier between education and the people.

II. If, then, by prescribing a large amount of study outside the university the elective principle is not likely to be successfully limited, is it not probable that within the college itself the two counter principles of election and prescription, mutually limiting, mutually supporting, will always be retained? This is the second suggestion; to bring studies of choice and studies commanded into juxtaposition. The backbone of the college is to be kept prescribed, the fleshy parts to be made elective. By a special modification of the plan, the later years are turned largely, perhaps wholly, toward election, and a line is drawn at the junior, or even the sophomore year, below which elective studies are forbidden to penetrate. Is not this the plan that will finally be judged safest? It certainly is the safest for a certain number of years. Before it can securely reach anything else, every college must pass through this intermediate state. After half a century of testing election Harvard still retains some prescribed studies. The Harvard juniors chose for nineteen years before the sophomores, and the sophomores seventeen years before the freshmen. In introducing electives a sober pace is commendable. A university is charged with the greatest of public trusts. The intelligence of the community is, to a large extent, in its keeping. It is bound to keep away from risky experiments, to disregard shifting popular fancies, and to be as conservative as clearness of sight will permit. I do not plead, therefore, that Harvard and Yale should abolish all prescription the coming year. They certainly should not. In my opinion most colleges are moving too fast in the elective direction already. I merely plead that we must see where we are going. As public guides, we must forecast the track of the future if we would avoid stumbling into paths which lead nowhere. That is all I am attempting here. I want to ascertain whether the dual system of limitation is a stable system, one in which we can put our trust, or whether it is a temporary convenience, likely to slip away a little year after year. What does history say? Let us examine the facts of the past. The following table shows at the left the fifteen New England colleges. In the next three parallel columns is printed the percentage of elective studies which existed in these colleges in 1875-76; in the last three, the percentage which exists to-day. To render the comparison more exact, I print the sophomore, junior, and senior years separately, reserving the problem of the freshman year for later discussion.

	1875-76			1885-86		
	Soph.	Jun.	Sen.	Soph.	Jun.	Sen.
Amherst	.04	.20	.08	.20	.75	.75
Bates	0	0	0	0	0	0
Boston	0	0	0	.35	.66	.82
Bowdoin	0	0	0	.15	.25	.25
Brown	0	.04	.04	.14	.37	.55
Colby	0	0	0	0	.08	.16
Dartmouth	0	0	0	0	.41	.36
Harvard	.50	.78	1.00	1.00	1.00	1.00
Middlebury	0	0	0	0	0	0
Trinity	0	0	0	0	.25	.25

Tufts	0	.17	.17	0	.28	.43
Vermont	0	0	0	0	0	0
Wesleyan	0	.47	.47	.16	.47	.64
Williams	0	0	0	0	0	.37
Yale	0	0	0	.13	.53	.80

This table yields four conclusions: (1) A rapid and fateful revolution is going on in the higher education of New England. We do not exaggerate the change when we speak of an old education and a new. (2) The spread of it is in tolerable proportion to the wealth of the college concerned. The new modes are expensive. It is not disapproval which is holding the colleges back; it is inability to meet the cost. I am sorry to point out this fact. To my mind one of the gravest perplexities of the new education is the query, What are the small colleges to do? They have a usefulness altogether peculiar; yet from the life-giving modern methods of training they are of necessity largely cut off. (3) The colleges which long ago foresaw their coming necessities have been able to proceed more cautiously than those which acknowledged them late. (4) The movement is one of steady advance. There is no going back. It must be remembered, too, that the stablest colleges have been proceeding with these changes many more years than the period shown in the table. Are we, then, prepared to dismiss prejudice from our minds and to recognize what steadiness of advance means? In other matters when a general tendency in a given direction is discovered, extending over a long series of years, visible in individuals widely unlike, and presenting no solitary case of backward turning, we are apt to conclude that there is a force in the movement which will carry it still further onward. We are not disposed to seize on some point in its path and to count that an ultimate holding-ground. This, I say, would be a natural conclusion unless we could detect in the movement tendencies at work in an opposite direction. Are there any such tendencies here? I cannot find them. Prescription invariably loses; election invariably gains.

But in order to make a rational prediction about the future we must know more than the bare facts of the past; we need to know why these particular facts have arisen. What are the reasons that whenever elective and prescribed studies are mixed, an extrusive force regularly appears in the elective? The reasons are not far to seek. Probably every professor in New England understands them. The two systems are so incongruous that each brings out the vices rather than the virtues of its incompatible brother. Prescribed studies, side by side with elective, appear a bondage; elective, side by side with prescribed, an indulgence. So long as all studies are prescribed, one may be set above another in the mind of the pupil on grounds of intrinsic worth; let certain studies express the pupil's wishes, and almost certainly the remainder, valuable as they may be in themselves, will express his disesteem. It is useless to say this should not be so. It always is. The zeal of work, the freshness of interest, which now appear in the chosen studies, are deducted from those which are forced. On the latter as little labor as possible is expended. They become perfunctory and mechanical, and soon restive pupils and dissatisfied teachers call for fresh extension of energizing choice. This is why the younger officers in all the colleges are eager to give increased scope to the elective studies. They cannot any longer get first-rate work done in the prescribed. Alarmed by the dangers of the new principle, as they often and justly are, they find that the presence of prescription, instead of diminishing the dangers, adds another and a peculiarly enfeebling one to those which existed before. So certain are these dangers, and so inevitable the expanding power of the elective principle, that it is questionable whether it would not be wise for a college to refuse to have anything to do with elective studies so soon as it knows itself too weak to allow them to spread.

For where will the spreading stop? It cannot stop till the causes of it stop. The table just given shows no likelihood of its stopping at all, and a little reflection will show that each enlargement increases the reasons for another enlargement still. If prescribed studies are ever exceptional, ineffective, and obnoxious, they certainly become more so as they diminish in number. A college which retains one of them is in a condition of unstable equilibrium. But is this true of the freshman year? Will not a special class of considerations keep prescription enduring and influential there, long after it has lost its usefulness in the later years? A boy of nineteen comes from home about as untrained in will as in intelligence. Will it not always be thought best to give him a year in which to acquaint himself with his surroundings and to learn what studies he may afterwards profitably select? Possibly it will. I incline to think not. The case of the freshman year is undoubtedly peculiar. Taking a large body of colleges, we have direct evidence that during their last three years the elective principle steadily wins and never loses. We have but a trifle of such evidence as regards the freshman year. There the struggle of the two forces has barely begun. It has begun at Harvard, and the usual result is already foreshadowed. The prescribed studies are disparaged studies; they are not worked at the best advantage. Still, I do not like to prophesy on evidence so narrow. I will merely say I see no reason to suppose that colleges will meet with permanent success in mingling incompatible kinds of study in their freshman year. But I can only surmise. Let any college that inclines to try the experiment do so.

It may be thought, however, a wiser course to keep the freshman year untouched by choice. A solid year of prescription is thus secured as a limitation on the election that is to follow. This plan is so often advised, especially by persons unacquainted with the practical working of colleges, that it requires a brief examination by itself.

Let us suppose the revolution which we have traced in the sophomore, junior, and senior years to have reached its natural terminus; let us suppose that in these years all studies have become elective, while the freshman year remains completely prescribed; the college will then fall into two parts, a preparatory department and a university department. In these two departments the character of the instruction, the methods of study, the consciousness of the students, will be altogether dissimilar. The freshmen will not be taken by upper classmen as companions; they will be looked down upon as children. Hazing will find abundant excuse. An abrupt line will be drawn, on whose farther side freedom will lie, on whose hither side, bondage. The sophomore, a being who at best has his peculiarities, will find his sense of self-sufficiency doubled. Whatever badly-bred boy parents incline to send to college will seem to them safe enough for a year, and they will suppose that during this period he will learn how to behave. Of course he will learn nothing of the sort. Manly discipline has not yet begun. At the end of the freshman year a boy will be only so much less a boy as increase of age may make him. Through being forced to study mathematics this year there comes no sustaining influence fitted to fortify the judgment when one is called the next year to choose between Greek and German. On the contrary, the change from school methods to maturing methods is rendered as dangerous as possible by allowing it to take place quite nakedly, by itself, unsupported by other changes, and at the mere dictation of the almanac. An emancipation so bare and sudden is not usual elsewhere. For boys who do not go to college, departure from home is commonly recognized as a fit occasion for putting on that dangerous garment, the *toga virilis*. Entrance to the university constitutes a similar epoch, when change of residence, new companions, altered conditions of living, a realization that the old supports are gone, and the presumption with which every one now meets the youth that he is to be treated as a man among men, become helpful influences coöperating to ease the hard and inevitable transition from parental control to personal self-direction. A safer time for beginning individual responsibility cannot be found. At any rate, whether my diagnosis of reasons is correct or not, the fact is clear,—self-respecting colleges do not tolerate preparatory departments. They do not work well. They are an element of weakness in the institution which harbors them. Even where at first they are judged necessary, so soon as the college grows strong they are dropped. When we attempt to plan an education for times to come, we must bear in mind established facts. Turn the freshman year into a preparatory department, fill it with studies antithetic in aim, method, and spirit to those of later years, and something is established which no sober college ever permitted to remain long within its borders. This is the teaching of the past without an exception. To suppose the future will be different is but the blind hope of a timid transitionalism.

III. The third suggestion for restricting election is the group system. This deserves a more respectful treatment than the methods hitherto discussed, for it is something more than a suggestion: it is a system, a constructive plan of education, thought out in all its parts, and directed toward an intended end. The definition which I have elsewhere offered of the elective system, that it demands a fixed quantity and quality of study with variable topic, would be applicable also to the group system. Accordingly it belongs to the new education rather than to the old. No less than the elective system it is opposed to the methods of restriction thus far described. These latter methods attempt to limit election by the ballast of an alien principle lodged beneath it or by its side. They put a weight of prescription into the preparatory schools, into the early college years, or into parallel lines of study extending throughout the college course. The source of their practical trouble lies here: the two principles, election and prescription, are nowhere united; they remain sundered and at war, unserviceable for each other's defects. The group system intertwines them. It permits choice in everything, but at the same time prescribes everything. This it effects by enlarging the unit of choice and prescribing its constituent factors. A group or block of studies is offered for choice, not a single study. All the studies of a group must be taken if any are, the "if" being the only matter left for the student to settle. The group may include all the studies open to a student at the university. One decision may determine his entire course. Or, as in the somewhat analogous arrangement of the English universities, one group may be selected at the beginning and another in the middle of the university life. The group itself is sometimes contrived so as to allow an individual variation; different students read different books; a special phase of philosophy, history, or science receives prominence. But the boundaries of the group cannot be crossed. All the studies selected by the college authorities to form a single group must be taken; no others can be.

In this method of limiting choice there is much that is attractive. I feel that attraction strongly. Under the exceptional conditions which exist at the Johns Hopkins University, a group system has done excellent work. Like all the rest of the world, I honor that work and admire its wise directors. But group systems seem to me to possess features too objectionable to permit them to become the prevalent type of the future, and I do not see how these features can be removed without abandoning what is distinctive, and changing the whole plan into the elective system, pure and simple. The objectionable features connect themselves with the size of the unit of choice, with difficulties in the construction of the groups, and with the attempt to enforce specialization. But these are enigmatic phrases; let me explain them.

Obviously, for the young, foresight is a hard matter. While disciplining them in the intricate art of looking ahead, I should think it wise to furnish frequently a means of repairing errors. Penalties for bad choices should not be too severe. Now plainly the larger the unit of choice, the graver the consequences of erroneous judgment. The group system takes a large unit, a body of studies; the simple elective system, a small unit, the single study. Errors of choice are consequently less reparable under the group system than under pure election. To meet this difficulty the college course at Baltimore has been reduced from four years to three; but even so, a student who selects a group for which he finds himself unfit cannot bring himself into proper adjustment without the loss of a year. If he does not discover his unfitness until the second year has begun, he loses two years. Under the elective system, the largest possible penalty for a single mistake is the loss of a single study, one quarter of a year's work. This necessary difference in ease of reparability appears to me to mark an inferiority in group systems, considered as methods of educating choice. To the public it may seem otherwise. I am often astonished to find people approving irreparable choices and condemning reparable ones. That youths between nineteen and twenty-three should select studies for themselves shocks many people who look kindly enough on marriages contracted during those years. Boys still unbearded have a large share in deciding whether they will go to college, to a scientific school, to a store, to sea, or to a cattle-ranch. Their lives are staked on the wisdom of the step taken. Yet the American mode of meeting these family problems seems to our community, on the whole, safer than the English way of regulating them by tradition and dictation. The choice with heavy stakes of the boy who does not go to college is frequently set off favorably against the choices with light stakes of the boy who goes. Perhaps a similarly lenient judgment will in the long run be passed on the great stakes involved in group systems. I doubt it. I think it will ultimately be judged less dangerous and more maturing to grant a young man, in his passage through a period of moral discipline, frequent opportunities of repair.

Again, the practical difficulties of deciding what groups shall be formed are enormous. What studies shall enter into each? How many groups shall there be? If but one, we have the old-fashioned college with no election. If two, we have the plan which Yale has just abandoned, a fixed undergraduate department maintained in parallel vigor with a fixed scientific school. But in conceding the claims of variety even to this degree, we have treated the fundamental differences between man and man as worthy, not reprehensible; and can we say that the proper differences are only two? Must we not acknowledge a world at least as complex as that they have in Baltimore, where there appear to be seven reputable species of mankind: "Those who wish a good classical training; those who look toward a course in medicine; those who prefer mathematical studies with reference to engineering, astronomy, and teaching; those who wish an education in scientific studies, not having chosen a specialty; those who expect to pursue a course in theology; those who propose to study law; those who wish a literary training not rigidly classical." Here a classification of human wishes is attempted, but one suspects that there are legitimate wishes which lie outside the scheme. It does not, for example, at once appear why a prospective chemist should be debarred from all regular study of mathematics. It seems hard that a youth of literary tastes should be cut off from Greek at entrance unless he will agree to take five exercises in it each week throughout his college course. One does not feel quite easy in allowing nobody but a lawyer or a devotee of modern languages to read a page of English or American history. The Johns Hopkins programme is the most ingenious and the most flexible contrivance for working a group system that I have ever seen. For this reason I mention it as the most favorable type of all. Considering its purposes, I do not believe it can be much improved. As applied to its little band of students, 116, it certainly works few hardships. Yet all the exclusions I have named, and many more besides, appear in it. I instance these simply to show what barriers to knowledge the best group system erects. Remove these, and others quite as great are introduced. Try to avoid them by allowing the student of one group to take certain studies in another, and the sole line which parts the group system from the elective is abandoned. In practice, it usually is abandoned. Confronted with the exigencies of operation, the so-called group system turns into an elective system, with highly specialized lines of study strongly recommended. With this more genial working I have nothing now to do. My point is this: a system of hard and fast groups presents difficulties of construction and maintenance too great to recommend it to the average college of the future as the best mode of limiting the elective principle.

Probably, however, this difficulty will chiefly be felt by persons engaged in the actual work of educational organization. The outer public will think it a more serious objection that grouped colleges are in reality professional schools carried down to the limits of boyhood. So far as they hold by their groups, they are nurseries of specialization. That this is necessarily so may not at first be apparent. A little consideration of the contrast in aim between group systems and prescribed will make the matter plain. Prescribed systems have gained their long hold on popular confidence by aiming at harmonious culture. They argue, justly enough, that each separate sort of knowledge furnishes something of its own to the making of a man. This particular "something," they say, can be had from no other source. The sum of these "somethings" constitutes a rounded whole. The man who has not experienced each of them in some degree, however small, is imperfectly planned. One who has been touched by all has laid the foundations of a liberal education. Degree of acquaintance with this subject or with that may subsequently enlarge. Scholarly interest may concentrate. But at the first, the proper aim is balanced knowledge, harmonious development of all essential powers, avoidance of one-sidedness.

On this aim the group system bestows but a secondary attention. Regarding primarily studies, not men, it attempts to organize single connected departments of knowledge. Accordingly it permits only those studies to be pursued together which immediately cohere. It lays out five, ten, any number of paths through the field of knowledge, and to one of these paths the pilgrim is confined. Each group constitutes a specialty,—a specialty intensified in character as, in order to escape the difficulties of maintenance just pointed out, the number of groups is allowed to increase. By insistence on specialization regard for general culture is driven into a subordinate place. The advocates of prescription maintain that there are not half a dozen ground-plans of perfected humanity. They say there is but one. If we introduce variety of design into a curriculum, we neglect that ideal man who resides alike in all. We trust, on the contrary, in our power to hit some line of study which may deservedly appeal to one human being while not so appealing to another. We simply note the studies which are most congruous with the special line selected, and by this congruity we shape our group. In the new aim, congruity of studies, adaptation to a professional purpose, takes precedence of harmonious development of powers.

I have no doubt that specialization is destined to become more marked in the American education of the future. It must become so if we are to produce the strong departmental scholars who illuminate learning in other countries; indeed, it must become so if we are to train competent experts for the affairs of daily life. The popular distrust of specializing is sure to grow less as our people become familiar with its effects and see how often narrow and thorough study, undertaken in early life, leads to ultimate breadth. It is a pretty dream that a man may start broad and then concentrate, but nine out of every ten strong men have taken the opposite course. They have begun in some one-sided way, and have added other sides as occasion required. Almost in his teens Shakespeare makes a specialty of the theatre, Napoleon of military science, Beethoven of music, Hunter of medicine, Faraday of chemistry, Hamilton of political science. The great body of painters, musicians, poets, novelists, theologians, politicians, are early specialists. In fact, self-made men are generally specialists. Something has aroused an interest, and they have followed it out until they have surveyed a wide horizon from a single point of view. In offering wider opportunities for specialization, colleges have merely been assimilating their own modes of training to those which prevail in the world at large.

It does not, therefore, seem to me objectionable that group systems set a high value on specialization. That is what every man does, and every clear-eyed college must do it too. What I object to is that group systems, so far as they adhere to their aim, *enforce* specialization. Among every half-dozen students, probably one will be injured if he cannot specialize largely; two or three more might wisely specialize in lower degree; but to force the remaining two or three into curricula shaped by professional bias is to do them serious damage. There are sober boys of little intrepidity or positive taste, boys who properly enough wish to know what others know. They will not make scholars. They were not born to enlarge the boundaries of knowledge. They have another function: they preserve and distribute such knowledge as already exists. Many of them are persons of wealth. To furnish them glimpses of varied learning is to save them from barbarism. Still another large class is composed of boys who develop late. They are boys who will one day acquire an interest of their own, if they are allowed to roam about somewhat aimlessly in the domain of wisdom until they are twenty-one. Both of these classes have their rights. The prescribed system was built to support them; the elective shelters and improves them; but a group system shuts them all out, if they will not on leaving school adopt professional courses. Whenever I can hear of a group system which like the old college has a place for the indistinct young man, and like the new elective college matures him annually by suggesting that he take part in shaping his own career, I will accept the group system. Then, too, the public will probably accept it. Until then, rigid groups will be thought by many to lay too great a strain on unseasoned powers of choice, to present too many practical difficulties of construction, and to show too doctrinaire a confidence that every youth will fit without pinching into a specialized class.

X

NECESSARY LIMITATIONS OF THE ELECTIVE SYSTEM

The preceding paper has sufficiently discussed the impossible limitations of the elective system, and has shown with some minuteness the grounds of their impossibility. The methods there examined are the only ones suggested by my critics. They all agree in this, that they seek to narrow the scope of choice. They try to combine with it a hostile factor, and they differ merely in their mode of combination. The first puts a restraining check before election; the second puts one by its side; the third makes the two inseparable by allowing nothing to be chosen which is not first prescribed. The general purpose of all these methods is mine also. Election must be limited. Unchartered choice is licentious and self-destructive. I quarrel with them only because the modes of effecting their purpose tend to produce results of a transient and inappropriate sort. The aim of education, as I conceive it, is to spiritualize the largest possible number of persons, that is, to teach them how to do their own thinking and willing and to do it well. But these methods effect something widely different. They either aristocratize where they should democratize, or they belittle where they should mature, or else they professionalize where they should humanize. A common trouble besets them all: the limiting authority is placed in external and arbitrary juxtaposition to the personal initiative which it professes to support. It should grow out of this initiative and be its interpreter and realization. By limitation of choice the proposers of these schemes appear to mean making choice less. I mean fortifying it, keeping it true to itself, making it more. Control that diminishes the quantity of choice is one thing; control that raises the quality, quite another. How important is this distinction and how frequently it is forgotten! Words like "limitation," "control," "authority," "obedience," are words of majesty, but words also of doubtful import. They carry a freight of wisdom or of folly, according to the end towards which they steer. In order to sanction or discard limitations which induce obedience, we must bear that end in mind. Let us stop a moment, and see that we have it in mind now.

Old educational systems are often said to have erred by excess of authority. I could not say so. The elective system, if it is to possess the future, must become as authoritative as they. More accurately we say that their authority was of a wrong sort. A father may exercise an authority over his child no less directive than that of the master over the slave; but the father is trying to accomplish something which the master disregards; the father hopes to make the will of another strong, the master to make it weak; the father commands what the child himself would wish, had he sufficient experience. The child's obedience accordingly enlightens, steadies, invigorates his independent will. Invigoration is the purpose of the command. The authority is akin—secretly akin—to the child's own desires. No alien power intervenes, as when a slave obeys. Here a foreign will thwarts the slave's proper motions. Over against his own legitimate desires, the desire of a totally different being appears and claims precedence. Obedience like this brings no ennoblement. The oftener a child obeys, the less of a child is he; the oftener a slave, the more completely he is a slave. Roughly to say, then, that submission to authority is healthy for a college boy, argues a mental confusion. There are two kinds of authority,—the authority of moral guidance, and the authority of repressive control: parental authority, respecting and vivifying the individual life and thus continually tending to supersede itself; and masterly authority, whose command, out of relation to the obeyer's wish, tends ever to bring the obedient into bondage. Which shall college authority be? Authority is necessary, ever-present authority. If the young man's choice is to become a thing of worth, it must be encompassed with limitations. But as the need of these limitations springs from the imperfections of choice, so should their aim be to perfect choice, not to repress it. To impose limitations which do not ultimately enlarge the youth they bind is to make the means of education "oblige against its main end."

This moral authority is what the new education seeks. To a casual eye, the colleges of to-day seem to be growing disorganized; a closer view shows construction taking place, but taking place along the lines of the vital distinction just pointed out. Men are striving to bring about a germane and ethical authority in the room of the baser mechanical authorities of the past. In this distinction, then, a clue is to be found which, if followed up, will lead us away from impossible limitations of the elective system, and conduct us at length to the possible, nay, to the inevitable ones. As the elective principle is essentially ethical, its limitations, if helpfully congruous, must be ethical too. They must be simply the means of bringing home to the young chooser the sacred conditions of choice; which conditions, if I rightly understand them, may compactly be entitled those of intentionality, information, and persistence. To secure these conditions, limitations exist. In the very nature of choice such conditions are implied. Choice is sound as they prevail, whimsical as they diminish. An education which lays stress on the elective principle is bound to lay stress on these conditions also. It cannot slip over into lazy ways of letting its students drift, and still look for credit as an elective system. People will distrust it. That is why they distrust Harvard to-day. The objections brought against the elective system of Harvard are in reality not levelled against the elective system at all. They are directed against its bastard brother, *laissez-faire*. Objectors suspect that the conditions of choice which I have named are not fulfilled. They are not fulfilled, I confess, or rather I stoutly maintain. To come anywhere near fulfilling them requires long time and study, and action unimpeded by a misconceiving community. Both time and study Harvard has given, has given largely. The records of scholarship and deportment which I exhibited in my first paper show in how high a degree Harvard has already been able to remove from choice the capricious, ignorant, and unsteadfast characteristics which rightly bring it into disrepute. But much remains to do, and in that doing we are hampered by the fact that a portion of the public is still looking in wrong directions. It cannot get over its hankering after the delusive modes of limitation which I have discussed. It does not persistently see that at present the proper work of education is the study of means by which self-direction may be rendered safe. Leaders of education themselves see this but dimly, as the papers of my critics naïvely show. Until choice was frankly accepted as the fit basis for the direction of a person by a person, its fortifying limitations could not be studied. Now they must be studied, now that the old methods of autocratic control are breaking down. As a moral will comes to be recognized as the best sort of steam power, the modes of generating that power acquire new claims to attention. Henceforth the training of the will must be undertaken by the elective system as an integral part of its discipline.

I am not so presumptuous as to attempt to prophesy the precise forms which methods of moral guidance will take. Moral guidance is a delicate affair. Its spirit is more important than its procedure. Flexibility is its strength. Methods final, rigid, and minute do not belong to it. Nor can it afford to forget the one great truth of *laissez-faire*, that wills which are to be kept fresh and vigorous will not bear much looking after. Time, too, is an important factor in the shaping of moral influences. Experiments now in progress at Harvard and elsewhere must discriminate safe from unsafe limitations. Leaving then to the future the task of showing how wide the scope of maturing discipline may become, I will merely try to sketch the main lines along which experiments are now proceeding, I will give a few illustrative examples of what is being done and why, and I will state somewhat at large how, in my judgment, more is yet to be accomplished. To make the matter clear, a free exposition shall be given of the puzzling headings already named; that is, I will first ramblingly discuss the limitations on choice which may deepen the student's intentionality of aim; secondly, those which increase his information in regard to means; and thirdly, those which may strengthen his persistence in a course once chosen.

I. That intentionality should be cultivated, I need not spend many words in explaining. Everybody acknowledges that without a certain degree of it choice is impossible. Many persons assert also that boys come to college with no clear intentions, not knowing what they want, waiting to be told; for such, it is said, an elective system is manifestly absurd. I admit the fact. It is true. The majority of the freshmen whom I have known in the last seventeen years have been, at entrance, deficient in serious aims. But from this fact I draw a conclusion quite opposite to the one suggested. It is election, systematized election, which these boys need; for when we say a young student has no definite aims, we imply that he has never become sufficiently interested in any given intellectual line to have acquired the wish to follow that line farther. Such a state of things is lamentable, and certainly shows that prescribed methods—the proper methods, in my judgment, for the school years—have in his case proved inadequate. It is useless to continue them into years confessedly less suited to their exercise. Perhaps it is about equally useless to abandon the ill-formed boy to unguided choice. Prescription says, "This person is unfit to choose, keep him so"; *laissez-faire* says, "If he is unfit to choose, let him perish"; but a watchful elective system must say, "Granting him to be unfit, if he is not spoiled, I will fit him." And can we fit him? I know well enough that indifferent teachers incline to shirk the task. They like to divide pupils into the deceptive classes of good and bad, meaning by the former those who intend to work, and by the latter those who intend not to. But we must get rid of indifferent teachers. Teachers with enthusiasm in them soon discover that the two classes of pupils I have named may as well be dismissed from consideration. Where aims have become definite, a teacher has little more to do. The boy who means to work will get learning under the poorest teacher and the worst system; while the boy who means not to work may be forced up to the Pierian spring, but will hardly be made to drink. A vigorous teacher does not assume intention to be ready-made. He counts it his continual office to help in making it. On the middle two quarters of a class he spends his hardest efforts, on students who are friendly to learning but not impassioned for it, on those who like the results of study but like tennis also, and popularity, and cigars, and slackness. The culture of these weak wills is the problem of every college. Here are unintentional boys waiting to be turned into intentional men. What limitations on intellectual and moral vagrancy will help them forward?

The chief limitation, the one underlying all others, the one which no clever contrivance can ever supersede, is vitalized teaching. Suitable subjects, attractively taught, awake lethargic intention as nothing else can. An elective system, as even its enemies confess, enormously stimulates the zeal of teachers. It consequently brings to bear on unawakened boys influences of a strangely quickening character. When I hear a man trained under the old methods of prescription say, "At the time I was in college I could not have chosen studies for myself, and I do not believe my son can," I see, and am not surprised to see, that he does not understand what forces the elective system sets astir. So powerful an influence have these forces over both teachers and pupils, that questions of hard and easy studies do not, as outsiders are apt to suppose, seriously disturb the formation of sound intentions. The many leaders in education whose opinions on election I quoted in my previous paper agree that the new modes tend to sobriety and intentionality of aim. When Professor Ladd speaks of "the unexpected wisdom and manliness of the choices already made" in the first year of election at New Haven, he well expresses the gratified surprise which every one experiences on perceiving in the very constitution of the elective system a sort of limitation on wayward choice. This limitation seems to me, as Professor Ladd says he found it,[8] a tolerable preventive of choices directly aimed at ease. In a community devoted to athletics, baseball is not played because it is "soft," and football avoided on account of its difficulty. A similar state of things must be brought about in studies. In a certain low degree it has come about already. As election breeds new life in teaching, the old slovenly habit of liking best what costs least begins to disappear. Easy courses will exist and ought to exist. Prescribed colleges, it is often forgotten, have more of them than elective colleges. The important matter is, to see that they fall to the right persons. Where

[8] Doubtless some have carried out the intention of making everything as soft as possible for themselves. But the choices, in fact, do not as yet show the existence of any such intention in any considerable number of cases; they show rather the very reverse.—Professor Ladd in *The New Englander*, January, 1885, p. 119.

everything is prescribed, students who do not wish easy studies are still obliged to take them. Under election, soft courses may often be pursued with advantage. A student whose other courses largely depend for their profit on the amount of private reading or of laboratory practice accomplished in connection with them is wise in choosing one or more in which the bulk of the work is taken by the teacher. I do not say that soft courses are always selected with these wise aims in view. Many I know are not. We have our proper share of hardened loafers—"tares in our sustaining corn"—who have an unerring instinct as to where they can most safely settle. But large numbers of the men in soft courses are there to good purpose; and I maintain that the superficial study of a subject, acquainting one with broad outlines, is not necessarily a worthless study. At Harvard to-day I believe we have too few such superficial courses. As I look over the Elective Pamphlet, and note the necessarily varying degrees of difficulty in the studies announced there, I count but six which can, with any justice, be entitled soft courses; and several of these must be reckoned by anybody an inspiration to the students who pursue them. There is a tendency in the elective system, as I have shown elsewhere, to reduce the number of soft courses somewhat below the desirable number.

I insist, therefore, that under a pretty loose elective system boys are little disposed to intentionally vicious choices. My fears look in a different direction. I do not expect depravity, but I want to head off aimless trifling. I agree with the opponents of election in thinking that there is danger, especially during the early years of college life, that righteous intention may not be distinct and energetic. Boys drift. Inadequate influences induce their decisions. The inclinations of the clique in which a young man finds himself are, without much thought, accepted as his own. Heedlessness is the young man's bane. It should not be mistaken for vice; the two are different. A boy who will enter a dormitory at twelve o'clock at night, and go to the third story whistling and beating time on the banisters, certainly seems a brutish person; but he is ordinarily a kind enough fellow, capable of a good deal of self-sacrifice when brought face to face with need. He simply does not think. So it is in study: there, too, he does not think. Now in college a boy should learn perpetually to think; and an excellent way of helping him to learn is to ask him often what he is thinking about. The object of the questioning should not be to thwart the boy's aims, rather to insure that they are in reality his own. Essentially his to the last they should remain, even though intrinsically they may not be the best. Young persons, much more than their elders, require to talk over plans from time to time with an experienced critic, in order to learn by degrees the difficult art of planning. By such talk intentionality is fortified. There is much of this talk already; talk of younger students with older, talk with wise persons at home, and more and more every year with the teachers of the courses left and the courses entered. All this is good. Haphazard modes breed an astonishing average of choices that possess a meaning. The waste of a *laissez-faire* system comes nowhere near the waste of a prescribed. But what is good when compared with a bad thing may be poor when compared with excellence itself. We must go on. A college, like a man, should always be saying, "Never was I so good as to-day, and never again will I be so bad." We must welcome criticisms more than praises, and seek after our weak points as after hid treasures. The elective system seems to me weak at present through lacking organized means of bringing the student and his intentions face to face. Intentions grow by being looked at. At the English universities a young man on entering a college is put in charge of a special tutor, without whose consent he can do little either in the way of study or of personal management.[9] Dependence so extreme is perhaps better suited to an infant school than to an American college; and even in England, where respectful subservience on the part of the young has been cultivated for generations, the system is losing ground. Since the tutors were allowed to marry and to leave the college home, tutorial influence has been changing. In most American colleges twenty-five years ago there were officers known as class tutors, to whom, in case of need, a student might turn. Petty permissions were received from these men, instead of from a mechanical central office. So far as this plan set personal supervision in the place of routine it was, in my eyes, good. But the relation of a class tutor to his boys was usually one of more awe than friendship. At the Johns Hopkins University there is a board of advisers, to some member of which each student is assigned at entrance. The adviser stands *in loco parentis* to his charges. The value of such adjustments depends on the nature of the parental tie. If the relation is worked so as to stimulate the student's independence, it is good; if so as to discharge him from responsibility, it unfits for the life that follows. At Harvard special students not candidates for a degree have recently been put in charge of a committee, to whom they are obliged to report their previous history and their plans of study for each succeeding year. The committee must know at all times what their charges are doing. Something of this sort, I am convinced, will be demanded at no distant day, as a means of steadying all students in elective colleges. Large personal supervision need not mean diminution of freedom. A young man may possess his freedom more solidly if he recognizes an obligation to state and defend the reasons which induce his choice. For myself, I should be willing to make the functions of such advisory committees somewhat broad. As a college grows, the old ways of bringing about acquaintance between officers and students become impracticable. But the need of personal acquaintance, unhappily, does not cease. New ways should be provided. A boy dropped into the middle of a large college must not be lost to sight; he must be looked after. To allow the teacher's work of instruction to become divorced from his pastoral, his priestly, function is to cheapen and externalize education. I would have every student in college supplied with somebody who might serve as a discretionary friend; and I should not think it a disadvantage that such an expectation of friendship would be as apt to better the instructor as the student.

Before leaving this part of my subject, I may mention a subordinate, but still valuable, means of limiting choice so as to increase its intentionality. The studies open to choice in the early years should be few and elementary. The significance of advanced courses cannot be understood till elementary ones are mastered, and immature choice should not be confused by many issues. At Harvard this mode of limitation is largely employed. Although the elective list for 1886-87 shows 172 courses, a freshman has hardly more than one eighth of these to choose from; in

[9] As the minute personal care given to individual students in the English universities is often and deservedly praised, I may as well say that it costs something. Oxford spends each year about $2,000,000 on 2500 men; Harvard, $650,000 on 1700.

any given case this number will probably be reduced about one half by insufficient preparation or conflict of hours. Seemingly about a third of the list is offered to the average sophomore; but this amount is again cut down nearly one half by the operation of similar causes. The practice of hedging electives with qualifications is a growing one. It may well grow more. It offers guidance precisely at the point where it is most needed. It protects rational choice, and guards against many of the dangers which the foes of election justly dread.

II. A second class of limitations of the elective system, possible and friendly, springs from the need of furnishing the young elector ample information about that which he is to choose. The best intentions require judicious aim. If studies are taken in the dark, without right anticipation of their subject-matter, or in ignorance of their relation to other studies, small results follow. Here, I think it will be generally agreed, prescribed systems are especially weak. Their pupils have little knowledge beforehand of what a course is designed to accomplish. Work is undertaken blindly, minds consenting as little as wills. An elective system is impossible under such conditions. Its student must know when he chooses, what he chooses. He must be able to estimate whether the choice of Greek 5 will further his designs better than the choice of Greek 8.

At Harvard, methods of furnishing information are pretty fully developed. In May an elective pamphlet is issued, which announces everything that is to be taught in the college during the following year. Most departments, also, issue additional pamphlets, describing with much detail the nature of their special courses, and the considerations which should lead a student to one rather than another. If the courses of a department are arranged properly, pursuing one gives the most needful knowledge about the available next. This knowledge is generally supplemented at the close of the year by explanations on the part of the instructor about the courses that follow. In the Elective Pamphlet a star, prefixed to courses of an advanced and especially technical character, indicates that the instructor must be privately consulted before these courses can be chosen. Consultations with instructors about all courses are frequent. That most effective means of distributing information, the talk of students, goes on unceasingly. With time, perhaps, means may be devised for informing a student more largely what he is choosing. The fullest information is desirable. That which is at present most needed is, I think, some rough indication of the relations of the several provinces of study to one another. Information of this sort is peculiarly hard to supply, because the knowledge on which it professes to rest cannot be precise and unimpeachable. We deal here with intricate problems, in regard to which experts are far from agreed, problems where the different point of view provided in the nature of each individual will rightly readjust whatever general conclusions are drawn. The old type of college had an easy way of settling these troublesome matters dogmatically, by voting, in open faculty-meeting, what should be counted the normal sequence of studies, and what their mixture. But as the votes of different colleges showed no uniformity, people have gradually come to perceive that the subject is one where only large outlines can distinctly be made out.[10] To these large outlines I think it important

[10] I may not have a better opportunity than this to clear up a petty difficulty which seems to agitate some of my critics. They say they want the degree of A.B. to mean some-

to direct the attention of undergraduates. In most German universities a course of *Encyclopädie* is offered, a course which gives in brief a survey of the sciences, and attempts to fix approximately the place of each in the total organization of knowledge. I am not aware that such a course exists in any American college. Indeed, there was hardly a place for it till dogmatic prescription was shaken. But if something of the kind were now established in the freshman year, our young men might be relieved of a certain intellectual short-sightedness, and the choices of one year might better keep in view those of the other three.

III. And now granting that a student has started with good intentions and is well informed about the direction where profit lies, still have we any assurance that he will push those intentions with a fair degree of tenacity through the distractions which beset his daily path? We need, indeed we must have, a third class of helpful limitations which may secure the persistent adhesion of our student to his chosen line of work. Probably this class of limitations is the most important and complex of all. To yield a paying return, study must be stuck to. A decision has little meaning unless the volition of to-day brings in its train a volition to-morrow. Self-direction implies such patient continuance in well-doing that only after persistence has become somewhat habitual can choice be called mature. To establish onward-leading habits, therefore, should be one of the chief objects in devising limitations of election. Only we must not mistake; we must look below the surface. Mechanical diligence often covers mental sloth. It is not habits of passive docility that are desirable, habits of timidity and uncriticising acceptance. Against forming these pernicious and easily acquired habits, it may be necessary even to erect barriers. The habit wanted is the habit of spontaneous attack. Prescription deadened this vital habit; it mechanized. His task removed, the student had little independent momentum. Election invigorates the springs of action. Formerly I did not see this, and I favored prescribed systems, thinking them systems of duty. That absence of an aggressive intellectual life which prescribed studies induce, I, like many others, mistook for faithfulness. Experience has instructed me. I no longer have any question that for the average man sound habits of steady endeavor

---

thing definite, while at present, under the elective system, it means one thing for John Doe, and something altogether different for his classmate, Richard Roe. That is true. Besides embodying the general signification that the bearer has been working four years in a way to satisfy college guardians, the stately letters do take on an individual variation of meaning for every man who wins them. They must do so as long as we are engaged in the formation of living persons. If the college were a factory, our case would be different. We might then offer a label which would keep its identity of meaning for all the articles turned out. Wherever education has been a living thing, the single degree has always contained this element of variety. The German degree is as diverse in meaning as ours. The degree of the English university is diverse, and more diverse for Honors men—the only ones who can properly be said to deserve it—than for inert Pass men. Degrees in this country have, from the first, had considerable diversity, college differing from college in requirement, and certainly student from student in attainment. That twenty-five years ago we were approaching too great uniformity in the signification of degrees, I suppose most educators now admit. That was a mechanical and stagnant period, and men have brought over from it to the more active days of the present ideals formed then. Precision of statement goes with figures, with etiquette, with military matters; but descriptions of the quality of persons must be stated in the round.

grow best in fields of choice. Emerson's words are words of soberness:—

He that worketh high and wise
Nor pauses in his plan,
Will take the sun out of the skies
Ere freedom out of man.

Furthermore, in attempting to stimulate persistence I believe we must ultimately rely on the rational interest in study which we can arouse and hold. Undoubtedly much can be done to save this interest from disturbance and to hold vacillating attention fixed upon it; but it, and it alone, is to be the driving force. Methods of college government must be reckoned wise as they push into the foreground the intrinsic charm of wisdom, mischievous as they hide it behind fidelity to technical demand. In other matters we readily acknowledge interest as an efficient force. We call it a force as broad as the worth of knowledge, and as deep as the curiosity of man. "Put your heart into your work," we say, "if you will make it excellent." A dozen proverbs tell that it is love that makes the world go round. Every employment of life springs from an underlying desire. The cricketer wants to win the game; the fisherman to catch fish; the farmer to gather crops; the merchant to make money; the physician to cure his patient; the student to become wise. Eliminate desire, put in its place allegiance to the rules of a game, and what, in any of these cases, would be the chance of persistent endeavor? It seems almost a truism to say that limitations of personal effort designed to strengthen persistency must be such as will heighten the wish and clear its path to its object.

Obvious as is the truth here presented, it seems in some degree to have escaped the attention of my critics. After showing that the grade of scholarship at Harvard steadily rises, that our students become more decorous and their methods of work less childish, I stated that, under an extremely loose mode of regulating attendance five sixths of the exercises were attended by all our men, worst and best, sick and well, most reckless and most discreet. Few portions of my obnoxious paper have occasioned a louder outcry. I am told of a neighboring college where the benches show but three per cent of absentees. I wonder what the percentage is in Charlestown State Prison. Nobody doubts that attendance will be closer if compelled. But the interesting question still remains, "Are students by such means learning habits of spontaneous regularity?" This question can be answered only when the concealing restraint is removed. It has been removed at Harvard,—in my judgment too largely removed,—and the great body of our students is seen to desire learning and to desire it all the time. Is it certain that the students of other colleges, if left with little or no restraint, would show a better record? The point of fidelity and regularity, it is said, is of supreme importance. So it is. But fidelity and regularity in study, not in attending recitations. If ever the Harvard system is perfected, so that students here are as eager for knowledge as the best class of German university men, I do not believe we shall see a lower rate of absence; only then, each absence will be used, as it is not at present, for a studious purpose. The modern teacher stimulates private reading, exacts theses, directs work in libraries. Pupils engaged in these things are not dependent on recitations as text-book schoolboys are. The grade of higher education cannot rise much so long as the present extreme stress is laid on appearance in the class-room.

In saying this I would not be understood to defend the method of dealing with absences which has for some years been practised at Harvard. I think the method bad. I have always thought it so, and have steadily favored a different system. The behavior of our students under a regulation so loose seems to me a striking testimony to the scholarly spirit prevalent here. As such I mentioned it in my first paper, and as such I would again call attention to it. But I am not satisfied with the present good results. I want to impress on every student that absence from the class-room can be justified by nothing short of illness or a scholarly purpose. For a gainful purpose the merchant is occasionally absent from his office; for a gainful purpose a scholar of mine may omit a recitation. But Smith can be absent profitably when Brown would meet with loss. I accordingly object to methods of limiting absence which exact the same numerical regularity of all. College records may look clean, yet students be learning little about duty. Limitation, in my judgment, should be so adjusted as to strengthen the man's personal adhesion to plans of daily study. Such limitations cannot be fixed by statute and worked by a single clerk. Moral discipline is not a thing to be supplied by wholesale. Professors must be individually charged with the oversight of their men. I would have excuses for occasional absence made to the instructor, and I should expect him to count it a part of his work to see that the better purposes of his scholars did not grow feeble. A professor who exercised such supervisory power slackly would make his course the resort of the indolent; one who was over-stringent would see himself deserted by indolent and earnest alike. My rule would be that no student be allowed to present himself at an examination who could not show his teacher's certificate that his attendance on daily work was satisfactory. Traditions in this country and in Germany are so different that I should have confidence in a method working well here though it worked ill there. At any rate, whenever it fell into decay, it could—a proviso necessary in all moral matters—be readjusted. A rule something like this the Harvard Faculty has recently adopted by voting that "any instructor, with the approval of the Dean, may at any time exclude from his course any student who in his judgment has neglected the work of the course." Probably the amount of absence which has hitherto occurred at Harvard will under this vote diminish.

Suppose, then, by these limitations on a student's caprice we have secured his persistence in outward endeavor, still one thing more is needed. We have brought him bodily to a recitation room; but his mind must be there too, his aroused and active mind. Limitations that will secure this slippery part of the person are difficult to devise. Nevertheless, they are worth studying. Their object is plain. They are to lead a student to do something every day; to aid him to overcome those tendencies to procrastination, self-confidence, and passive absorption which are the regular and calculable dangers of youth. They are to teach him how not to cram, to inspire him with respect for steady effort, and to enable him each year to find such effort more habitual to himself. These are hard tasks. The old education tried to meet them by the use of daily recitations, a plan not without advantages. The new education is preserving the valuable features of recitations by adopting and developing the *Seminar*. But recitations pure and simple have serious drawbacks.

They presuppose a text-book, which, while it brings definiteness, brings also narrowness of view. The learner masters a book, not a subject. After-life possesses nothing analogous to the text-book. A struggling man wins what he wants from many books, from his own thought, from frequent consultations. Why should not a student be disciplined in the ways he must afterwards employ? Moreover, recitations have the disadvantage that no large number of men can take part on any single day. The times of trial either become amenable to reckoning, or, in order to prevent reckoning, a teacher must resort to schemes which do not commend him to his class. Undoubtedly in recitation the reciter gains, but the gains of the rest of the class are small. The listeners would be more profited by instruction. An hour with an expert should carry students forward; to occupy it in ascertaining where they now stand is wasteful. For all these reasons there has been of late years a strong reaction against recitations. Lectures have been introduced, and the time formerly spent by a professor in hearing boys is now spent by boys in hearing a professor. Plainly in this there is a gain, but a gain which needs careful limitation if the student's persistence in work is to be retained. A pure lecture system is a broad road to ignorance. Students are entertained or bored, but at the end of a month they know little more than at the beginning. Lectures always seem to me an inheritance from the days when books were not. Learning—how often must it be said!—is not acceptance; it is criticism, it is attack, it is doing. An active element is everywhere involved in it. Personal sanction is wanted for every step. One who will grow wise must perform processes himself, not sit at ease and behold another's performance.

These simple truths are now tolerably understood at Harvard. There remain in the college few courses of pure recitations or of pure lectures. I wish all were forbidden by statute. In almost all courses, in one way or another, frequent opportunity is given the student to show what he is doing. In some, especially in elementary courses, lectures run parallel with a text-book. In some, theses, that is, written discussions, are exacted monthly, half-yearly, annually, in addition to examinations. In some, examinations are frequent. In some, a daily question, to be answered in writing on the spot, is offered to the whole class. Often, especially in philosophical subjects, the hour is occupied with debate between officer and students. More and more, physical subjects are taught by the laboratory, linguistic and historical by the library. In a living university a great variety of methods spring up, according to the nature of the subject and the personality of the teacher. Variety should exist. In constantly diversified ways each student should be assured that he is expected to be doing something all the time, and that somebody besides himself knows what he is doing. As yet this assurance is not attained; we can only claim to be working toward it. Every year we discover some fresh limitation which will make persistence more natural, neglect more strange. I believe study at Harvard is to-day more interested, energetic, and persistent than it has ever been before. But that is no ground for satisfaction. A powerful college must forever be dissatisfied. Each year it must address itself anew to strengthening the tenacity of its students in their zeal for knowledge.

By the side of these larger limitations in the interest of persistency, it may be well to mention one or two examples of smaller ones which have the same end in view. By some provision it must be made difficult to withdraw from a study once chosen. Choice should be deliberate and then be final. It probably will not be deliberate unless it is understood to be final. A few weeks may be allowed for an inspection of a chosen course, but at the close of the first month's teaching the Harvard Faculty tie up their students and allow change only on petition and for the most convincing cause. An elective college which did not make changes of electives difficult would be an engine for discouraging intentionality and persistence.

I incline to think, too, that a regulation forbidding elementary courses in the later years would render our education more coherent. In this matter elective colleges have an opportunity which prescribed ones miss. In order to be fair to all the sciences, college faculties are obliged to scatter fragments of them throughout the length and breadth of prescribed curricula. Twenty-five years ago every Harvard man waited till his senior year before beginning philosophy, acoustics, history, and political economy. To-day the fourteen other New England colleges, most of whom, like the Harvard of twenty-five years ago, offer a certain number of elective studies, still show senior years largely occupied with elementary studies. Five forbid philosophy before the senior year; eight, political economy; two, history; six, geology. Out of the seven colleges which offer some one of the eastern languages, all except Harvard oblige the alphabet to be learned in the senior year. Of the six which offer Italian or Spanish, Harvard alone permits a beginning to be made before the junior year, while two take up these languages for the first time in the senior year. In three New England colleges German cannot be begun till the junior year. In a majority, a physical subject is begun in the junior and another in the senior year. At Yale nobody but a senior can study chemistry. Such postponement, and by consequence such fragmentary work, may be necessary where early college years are crowded with prescribed studies. But an elective system can employ its later years to better advantage. It can bring to a mature understanding the interests which freshmen and sophomores have already acquired. Elementary studies are not maturing studies; they do not make the fibre of a student firm. To studies of a solidifying sort the last years should be devoted. I should like to forbid seniors to take any elementary study whatever, and to forbid juniors all except philosophy, political economy, history, fine arts, Sanskrit, Hebrew, and law. Under such a rule we should graduate more men who would be first rate at something; and a man who is first rate at something is generally pretty good at anything.

Such, then, are a few examples of the ways in which choice may be limited so as to become strong. They are but examples, intended merely to draw attention to the three kinds of limitation still possible. Humble ways they may seem, not particularly interesting to hear about; business methods one might call them. But by means of these and such as these the young scholar becomes clearer in intention, larger in information, hardier in persistence. In urging such means I shall be seen to be no thick and thin advocate of election. That I have never been. Originally a doubter, I have come to regard the elective system, that is, election under such limitations as I have described, as the safest—indeed as the only possible—course which education can now take, I advocate it heartily as a system which need not carry us too fast or too far in any one direction, as a system so inherently flexible that its own great virtues readily unite with those of an alien type. Under its sheltering charge the worthier advantages of both grouped and prescribed systems are attainable. I proclaim it, therefore, not as a popular cry nor as an educational panacea, but as a sober opportunity for moral and intellectual training. Limited as it is at Harvard, I see that it works admirably with the studious, stimulatingly with those of weaker will, not unendurably with the depraved. These are great results. They cannot be set aside by calling them the outcome of "individualism." In a certain sense they are. But "individualism" is an uncertain term. In every one of us there is a contemptible individuality, grounded in what is ephemeral and capriciously personal. Systematic election, as I have shown, puts limitations on this. But there is a noble individuality which should be the object of our fostering care. Nothing that lends it strength and fineness can be counted trivial. To form a true individuality is, indeed, the ideal of the elective system. Let me briefly sketch my conception of that ideal.

George Herbert, praising God for the physical world which He has made, says that in it "all things have their will, yet none but thine." Such a free harmony between thinking man and a Lord of his thought it is the office of education to bring about. At the start it does not exist. The child is aware of his own will, and he is aware of little else. He imagines that one pleasing fancy may be willed as easily as another. As he matures, he discovers that his will is effective when it accords with the make of the world and ineffective when it does not. This discovery, bringing as it does increased respect for the make of the world and even for its Maker, degrades or ennobles according as the facts of the world are now viewed as restrictive finalities or as an apparatus for larger self-expression. Seeing the power of that which is not himself, a man may become passively receptive, and say, "Then I am to have no will of my own"; or he may become newly energetic, knowing that though he can have no will of his separate own, yet all the power of God is his if he will but understand. A man of the latter sort is spiritually educated. Much still remains to be done in understanding special laws; and with each fresh understanding, a fresh possibility of individual life is disclosed. The worth, however, of the whole process lies in the man's honoring his own will, but honoring it only as it grows strong through accordance with the will of God.

Now into our colleges comes a mixed multitude made up of all the three classes named: the childish, who imagine they can will anything; the docile, so passive in the presence of an ordered world that they have little individual will left; the spiritually-minded or original, who with strong interests of their own seek to develop these through living contact with truths which they have not made. Our educational modes must meet them all, respecting their wills wherever wise, and teaching the feeble to discriminate fanciful from righteous desires. For carrying forward such a training the elective system seems to me to have peculiar aptitudes. What I have called its limitations will be seen to be spiritual assistances. To the further invention of such there is no end. A watchful patience is the one great requisite, patience in directors, instructed criticism on the part of the public, and a brave expression of confidence when confidence is seen to have been earned.

XI

COLLEGE EXPENSES[11]

The subject of college expenses has been much debated lately. At our Commencement dinner, a year ago, attention was called to it. Our chairman on that occasion justly insisted that the ideal of the University should be plain living and high thinking. And certainly there is apt to be something vulgar, as well as vicious, in the man of books who turns away from winning intellectual wealth and indulges in tawdry extravagance. Yet every friend of Harvard is obliged to acknowledge with shame that the loose spender has a lodging in our yard. No clear-sighted observer can draw near and not perceive that in all his native hideousness the man of the club and the dog-cart is among us.

I do not think this strange. In fact, I regard it as inevitable. It is necessarily connected with our growth. The old College we might compare, for moral and intellectual range, with a country village; our present University is a great city, and we must accept the many-sided life, the temptations as well as the opportunities, of the great city. Probably nowhere on this planet can a thousand young men be found, between the ages of eighteen and twenty-four, who will not show examples of the heedless, the temptable, and the depraved. Let us not, then, shrink from acknowledging the ugly fact; extravagance is here,—shameless, coarse extravagance. I hope nothing I say may diminish our sense of its indecency. But how widespread is it? We must not lose sight of that important question. How largely does it infect the College? Are many students large spenders? Must a man of moderate means on coming here be put to shame? Will he find himself a disparaged person, out of accord with the spirit of the place, and unable to obtain its characteristic advantages? These are the weighty questions. Only after we have answered them can we determine the moral soundness of the University. Wherever we go on earth we shall find the insolently rich and wasteful. They, like the poor, are always with us; their qualities are cheap. But what we want to know is whether, side by side with them, we have a company of sober men, who care for higher things and who spend no more than the higher things require. Facts of proportion and degree form the firm basis of general judgments, and yet I am aware that these are the hardest facts to obtain. Hitherto nobody has known any such facts in regard to the expenses of Harvard. Assertions about the style of living here have only expressed the personal opinion of the assertor, or at best have been generalizations from a few chance cases. No systematic evidence on the subject has existed. It is

[11] Delivered in Memorial Hall, Cambridge, June 29, 1887. Since this date the scale of expenditure in college, as elsewhere, has been steadily rising.

time it did exist, and I have made an attempt to obtain it. To each member of the graduating class I sent a circular, a month ago, asking if he would be willing to tell me in confidence what his college course had cost. I desired him to include in his report all expenses whatever. He was to state not merely his tuition, board, and lodging, but also his furniture, books, clothing, travel, subscriptions, and amusements; in fact, every dollar he had spent during the four years of his study, except his charges for Class Day and the summer vacations; these times varying so widely, it seemed to me, in their cost to different men that they could not instructively enter into an average.

The reply has been very large indeed. To my surprise, out of a class of two hundred and thirty-five men actually in residence, two hundred and nineteen, or ninety-three per cent, have sent reports. Am I wrong in supposing that this very general "readiness to tell" is itself a sign of upright conduct? But I would not exaggerate the worth of the returns. They cannot be trusted to a figure. It has not been possible to obtain itemized statements. College boys, like other people, do not always keep accounts. But I requested my correspondents, in cases of uncertainty, always to name the larger figure; and though those who have lived freely probably have less knowledge about what they have spent than have their economical classmates, I think we may accept their reports in the rough. We can be reasonably sure whether they have exceeded or fallen below a certain medium line, and for purposes more precise I shall not attempt to use them. Anything like minute accuracy I wish expressly to repudiate. The evidence I offer only claims to be the best that exists at present; and I must say that the astonishing frankness and fulness of the reports give me strong personal assurance of the good faith of the writers. In these letters I have seen a vivid picture of the struggles, the hopes, the errors, and the repentings of the manly young lives that surround me.

What, then, are the results? Out of the two hundred and nineteen men who have replied, fifty-six, or about one quarter of the class, have spent between $450 and $650 in each of the four years of residence; fifty-four, or again about a quarter, have spent between $650 and $975; but sixty-one, hardly more than a quarter, have spent a larger sum than $1200. The smallest amount in any one year was $400; the largest, $4000.[12]

I ask you to consider these figures. They are not startling, but they seem to me to indicate that a soberly sensible average of expense prevails at Harvard. They

[12] Perhaps I had better mention the adjustments by which these results have been reached. When a man has been in college during only the closing years of the course, I assume that he would have lived at the same rate had he been here throughout it. I have added $150 for persons who board at home, and another hundred for those who lodge there. Though I asked to have the expenses of Class Day and the summer vacations omitted, in some instances I have reason to suspect that they are included; but of course I have been obliged to let the error remain, and I have never deducted the money which students often say they expect to recover at graduation by the sale of furniture and other goods. There is a noticeable tendency to larger outlay as the years advance. Some students attribute this to the greater cost of the studies of the later years, to the more expensive books and the laboratory charges; others, to societies and subscriptions; others, to enlarged acquaintance with opportunities for spending.

suggest that students are, after all, merely young men temporarily removed from homes, and that they are practising here, without violent change, the habits which the home has formed. Those who have been accustomed to large expenditure spend freely here; those of quiet and considerate habits do not lightly abandon them. I doubt if during the last twenty-five years luxury has increased in the colleges as rapidly as it has in the outside world.

There is no reason, either, to suppose that the addition of the sixteen men who have not replied would appreciably affect my results. The standing of these men on the last annual rank-list was sixty-eight per cent. They seem to me average persons. Their silence I attribute to mistakes of the mail, to business, to neglect, or to the very natural disinclination to disclose their private affairs. To refuse to answer my intrusive questions, or even to acknowledge that college days were costly, is not in itself evidence of wantonness. Small spenders are usually high scholars; but this is by no means always the case. In the most economical group I found seven who did not reach a rank of seventy per cent. last year; whereas out of the seven largest spenders of the class three passed seventy-five per cent. It would be rash to conclude that large sums cannot be honorably employed.

But it may seem that the smallest of the sums named is large for a poor man. It may be believed that even after restraint and wisdom are used, Harvard remains the college of the rich. There is much in our circumstances to make it so. An excellent education is unquestionably a costly thing, and to live where many men wish to live calls for a good deal of money. We have, it is true, this splendid hall, which lessens our expense for food and encompasses us with ennobling influences; but it costs $150 a year to board here. Our tuition bill each year is $150. The University owns 450 rooms; but not a third of them rent for less than $150 a year, the average rent being $146. These large charges for tuition and room-rent are made necessary by the smallness of the general fund which pays the running expenses of the college. Very few of the professorships are endowed, and so the tuition-fee and room-rent must mainly carry the expenses of teaching.

Still, there is another side to the story. Thus far I have figured out the expenses, and have said nothing about the means of meeting them. Perhaps to get the advantages of Harvard a student may need to spend largely; but a certain circumstance enables him to do so,—I mean the matchless benevolence of those who have preceded us here. The great sums intrusted to us for distribution in prizes, loan-funds, and scholarships make it possible for our students to offset the cost of their education to such a degree that the net output of a poor boy here is probably less than in most New England colleges. At any rate, I have asked a large number of poor students why they came to expensive Harvard, and again and again I have received the reply: "I could not afford to go elsewhere."

The magnitude of this beneficiary aid I doubt if people generally understand, and I have accordingly taken pains to ascertain what was the amount given away this year. I find that to undergraduates alone it was $36,000; to members of the graduate department, $11,000; and to the professional schools $6000: making in a single year a total of assistance to students of the University of more than $53,000. Next year this enormous sum will be increased $13,000 by the munificent bequest of Mr. Price Greenleaf. Fully to estimate the favorable position of the poor man at Harvard, we should take into account also the great opportunities for earning money through private tuition, through innumerable avenues of trade, and through writing for the public press. A large number of my correspondents tell of money earned outside their scholarships.[13]

These immense aids provided for our students maintain a balance of conditions here, and enable even the poorest to obtain a Harvard education. And what an education it is; how broad and deep and individually stimulating,—the most truly American education which the continent affords! But I have no need to eulogize it. It has already entered into the very structure of you who listen. Let me rather close with two pieces of advice.

The first shall be to parents. Give your son a competent allowance when you send him to Harvard, and oblige him to stick to it. To learn calculation will contribute as much to his equipment for life as any elective study he can pursue; and calculation he will not learn unless, after a little experience, you tell him precisely what sum he is to receive. If in a haphazard way you pour $2000 into his pocket, then in an equally haphazard way $2000 will come out. Whatever extravagance exists at Harvard to-day is the fault of you foolish parents. The college, as a college, cannot stop extravagance. It cannot take away a thousand dollars from your son and tell him—what would be perfectly true—that he will be better off with the remaining thousand; that you must do yourselves. And if you ask, "What is a competent allowance?" out of what my correspondents say I will frame you five answers. If your son is something of an artist in economy, he may live here on $600, or less; he will require to be an artist to accomplish it. If he will live closely, carefully, yet with full regard to all that is required, he may do so, with nearly half his class, on not more than $800. If you wish him to live at ease and to obtain the many refinements which money will purchase, give him $1000. Indeed, if I were a very rich man, and had a boy whose character I could trust, so that I could be sure that all he laid out would be laid out wisely, I might add $200 more, for the purchase of books and other appliances of delicate culture. But I should be sure that every dollar I gave him over $1200 would be a dollar of danger.

Let my second piece of advice be to all of you graduates. When you meet a poor boy, do not rashly urge him to come to Harvard. Estimate carefully his powers. If he is a good boy,—docile, worthy, commonplace,—advise him to go somewhere else. Here he will find himself borne down by large expense and by the crowd who stand above him. But whenever you encounter a poor boy of eager, aggressive mind, a youth of energy, one capable of feeling the enjoyment of struggling with a multitude and of making his merit known, say to him that Harvard College is expressly constituted for such as he. Here he will find the largest provision for his needs and the clearest field for his talents. Money is a power everywhere. It is a power here; but a power of far more restricted scope than in

[13] For the sake of lucidity, I keep the expense account and the income account distinct. For example, a man reports that he has spent $700 a year, winning each year a scholarship of $200, and earning by tutoring $100, and $50 by some other means. The balance against him is only $350 a year; but I have included him in the group of $700 spenders.

the world at large. In this magnificent hall rich and poor dine together daily. At the Union they debate together. At the clubs which foster special interests,—the Finance Club, the Philological Club, the Philosophical Club, the French Club, the Signet, and the O. K.—considerations of money have no place. If the poor man is a man of muscle, the athletic organizations will welcome him; if a man skilled in words, he will be made an editor of the college papers; and if he has the powers that fit him for such a place, the whole body of his classmates will elect him Orator, Ivy Orator, Odist, or Poet, without the slightest regard to whether his purse is full or empty. The poor man, it is true, will not be chosen for ornamental offices, for positions which imply an acquaintance with etiquette, and he may be cut off from intimacy with the frequenters of the ballroom and the opera; but as he will probably have little time or taste for these things, his loss will not be large. In short, if he has anything in him,—has he scholarship, brains, wit, companionability, stout moral purpose, or quiet Christian character,—his qualities will find as prompt a recognition at Harvard as anywhere on earth.

XII

A TEACHER OF THE OLDEN TIME

On the 14th of February, 1883, Evangelinus Apostolides Sophocles, Professor of Ancient, Byzantine, and Modern Greek in Harvard University, died at Cambridge, in the corner room of Holworthy Hall which he had occupied for nearly forty years. A past generation of American schoolboys knew him gratefully as the author of a compact and lucid Greek grammar. College students—probably as large a number as ever sat under an American professor—were introduced by him to the poets and historians of Greece. Scholars of a riper growth, both in Europe and America, have wondered at the precision and loving diligence with which, in his dictionary of the later and Bzyantine Greek, he assessed the corrupt literary coinage of his native land. His brief contributions to the Nation and other journals were always noticeable for exact knowledge and scrupulous literary honesty. As a great scholar, therefore, and one who through a long life labored to beget scholarship in others, Sophocles deserves well of America. At a time when Greek was usually studied as the schoolboy studies it, this strange Greek came among us, connected himself with our oldest university, and showed us an example of encyclopædic learning, and such familiar and living acquaintance with Homer and Æschylus—yes, even with Polybius, Lucian, and Athenæus—as we have with Tennyson and Shakespeare and Burke and Macaulay. More than this, he showed us how such learning is gathered. To a dozen generations of impressible college students he presented a type of an austere life directed to serene ends, a life sufficient for itself and filled with a never-hastening diligence which issued in vast mental stores.

It is not, however, the purpose of this paper to trace the influence over American scholarship of this hardly domesticated wise man of the East. Nor will there be any attempt to narrate the outward events of his life. These were never fully known; and could they be discovered, there would be a kind of impiety in reporting them. Few traits were so characteristic of him as his wish to conceal his history. His motto might have been that of Epicurus and Descartes: "Well hid is well lived." Yet in spite of his concealments, perhaps in part because of them, few persons connected with Harvard have ever left behind them an impression of such massive individuality. He was long a notable figure in university life, one of those picturesque characters who by their very being give impulse to aspiring mortals and check the ever-encroaching commonplace. It would be ungrateful to allow one formerly so stimulating and talked about to fall into oblivion. Now that a decent interval after death has passed, a memorial to this unusual man may be reverently set up. His likeness may be drawn by a fond though faithful hand. Or at least such stories about him may be kindly put into the record of print as will reflect some of those rugged, paradoxical, witty, and benignant aspects of his nature which marked him off from the humdrum herd of men.

My own first approach to Sophocles was at the end of my Junior year in college. It was necessary for me to be absent from his afternoon recitation. In those distant days absences were regarded by Harvard law as luxuries, and a small fixed quantity of them, a sort of sailor's grog, was credited with little charge each half-year to every student. I was already nearing the limit of the unenlargeable eight, and could not well venture to add another to my score. It seemed safer to try to win indulgence from my fierce-eyed instructor. Early one morning I went to Sophocles's room. "Professor Sophocles," I said, "I want to be excused from attending the Greek recitation this afternoon." "I have no power to excuse," uttered in the gruffest of tones, while he looked the other way. "But I cannot be here. I must be out of town at three o'clock." "I have no power. You had better see the president." Finding the situation desperate, I took a desperate leap. "But the president probably would not allow my excuse. At the play of the Hasty Pudding Club to-night I am to appear as leading lady. I must go to Brookline this afternoon and have my sister dress me." No muscle of the stern face moved; but he rose, walked to a table where his class lists lay, and, taking up a pencil, calmly said: "You had better say nothing to the president. You are here *now*. I will mark you so." He sniffed, he bowed, and, without smile or word from either of us, I left the room. As I came to know Sophocles afterwards, I found that in this trivial early interview I had come upon some of the most distinctive traits of his character; here was an epitome of his *brusquerie*, his dignity, his whimsical logic, and his kind heart.

Outwardly he was always brusque and repellent. A certain savagery marked his very face. He once observed that, in introducing a character, Homer is apt to draw attention to the eye. Certainly in himself this was the feature which first attracted notice; for his eye had uncommon alertness and intelligence. Those who knew him well detected in it a hidden sweetness; but against the stranger it burned and glared, and guarded all avenues of approach. Startled it was, like the eye of a wild animal, and penetrating, "peering through the portals of the brain like the brass cannon." Over it crouched bushy brows, and all around the great head bristled white hair, on forehead, cheeks, and lips, so that little flesh remained visible, and the life was settled in two fiery spots. This concentration of expression in the few elementary features of shape, hair, and eyes made the head a magnificent subject for painting. Rembrandt should have painted it. But he would never allow a portrait of himself to be drawn. Into his personality strangers must not intrude. Venturing once to try for memoranda of his face, I took an artist to his room. The courtesy of Sophocles was too stately to allow him to turn my friend away, but he seated himself in a shaded window, and kept his head in constant motion. When my frustrated friend had departed, Sophocles told me, though without direct reproach, of two sketches which had before been surreptitiously made,—one by the pencil of a student in his class, another in oils by a lady who had followed him on the street. Toward photography his aversion was weaker; perhaps because in that art a human being less openly meddled with him.

From this sense of personal dignity, which made him at all times determined to keep out of the grasp of others, much of his brusqueness sprang. On the morning after he returned from his visit to Greece a fellow professor saw him on the opposite side of the street, and, hastening across, greeted him warmly: "So you have been home, Mr. Sophocles; and how did you find your mother?" "She was up an apple-tree," said Sophocles, confining himself to the facts of the case. A boy who snowballed him on the street he prosecuted relentlessly, and he could not be appeased until a considerable fine was imposed; but he paid the fine himself. Many a bold push was made to ascertain his age; yet, however suddenly the question came, or however craftily one crept from date to date, there was a uniform lack of success. "I see Allibone's Dictionary says you were born in 1805," a gentleman remarked. "Some statements have been nearer, and some have been farther from the truth." One day, when a violent attack of illness fell on him, a physician was called for diagnosis. He felt the pulse, he examined the tongue, he heard the report of the symptoms, then suddenly asked, "How old are you, Mr. Sophocles?" With as ready presence of mind and as pretty ingenuity as if he were not lying at the point of death, Sophocles answered: "The Arabs, Dr. W., estimate age by several standards. The age of Hassan, the porter, is reckoned by his wrinkles; that of Abdallah, the physician, by the lives he has saved; that of Achmet, the sage, by his wisdom. I, all my life a scholar, am nearing my hundredth year." To those who had once come close to Sophocles these little reserves, never asserted with impatience, were characteristic and endearing. I happen to know his age; hot irons shall not draw it from me.

Closely connected with his repellent reserve was the stern independence of his modes of life. In his scheme, little things were kept small and great things large. What was the true reading in a passage of Aristophanes, what the usage of a certain word in Byzantine Greek,—these were matters on which a man might well reflect and labor. But of what consequence was it if the breakfast was slight or the coat worn? Accordingly, a single room, in which a light was seldom seen, sufficed him during his forty years of life in the college yard. It was totally bare of comforts. It contained no carpet, no stuffed furniture, no bookcase. The college library furnished the volumes he was at any time using, and these lay along the floor, beside his dictionary, his shoes, and the box that contained the sick chicken. A single bare table held the book he had just laid down, together with a Greek newspaper, a silver watch, a cravat, a paper package or two, and some scraps of bread. His simple meals were prepared by himself over a small open stove, which served at once for heat and cookery. Eating, however, was always treated as a subordinate and incidental business, deserving no fixed time, no dishes, nor the setting of a table. The peasants of the East, the monks of southern monasteries, live chiefly on bread and fruit, relished with a little wine; and Sophocles, in spite of Cambridge and America, was to the last a peasant and a monk. Such simple nutriments best fitted his constitution, for "they found their acquaintance there." The western world had come to him by accident, and was ignored; the East was in his blood, and ordered all his goings. Yet, as a grave man of the East might, he had his festivities, and could on occasion be gay. Among a few friends he could tell a capital story and enjoy a well-cooked dish. But his ordinary fare was meagre in the extreme. For one of his heartier meals he would cut a piece of meat into bits and roast it on a spit, as Homer's people roasted theirs. "Why not use a gridiron?" I once asked. "It is not the same," he said. "The juice then runs into the fire. But when I turn my spit it bastes itself." His taste was more than usually sensitive, kept fine and discriminating by the restraint in which he held it. Indeed, all his senses, except sight, were acute.

The wine he drank was the delicate unresinated Greek wine,—Corinthian, or Chian, or Cyprian; the amount of water to be mixed with each being carefully debated and employed. Each winter a cask was sent him from a special vineyard on the heights of Corinth, and occasioned something like a general rejoicing in Cambridge, so widely were its flavorous contents distributed. Whenever this cask arrived, or when there came a box from Mt. Sinai filled with potato-like sweetmeats,—a paste of figs, dates, and nuts, stuffed into sewed goatskins,—or when his hens had been laying a goodly number of eggs, then under the blue cloak a selection of bottles, or of sweetmeats, or of eggs would be borne to a friend's house, where for an hour the old man sat in dignity and calm, opening and closing his eyes and his jack-knife; uttering meanwhile detached remarks, wise, gruff, biting, yet seldom lacking a kernel of kindness, till bedtime came, nine o'clock, and he was gone, the gifts—if thanks were feared—left in a chair by the door. There were half a dozen houses and dinner tables in Cambridge to which he went with pleasure, houses where he seemed to find a solace in the neighborhood of his kind. But human beings were an exceptional luxury. He had never learned to expect them. They never became necessities of his daily life, and I doubt if he missed them when they were absent. As he slowly recovered strength, after one of his later illnesses, I urged him to spend a month with me. Refusing in a brief sentence, he added with unusual gentleness: "To be alone is not the same for me and for you. I have never known anything else."

Unquestionably much of his disposition to remain aloof and to resist the on-coming intruder was bred by the experiences of his early youth. His native place, Tsangarada, is a village of eastern Thessaly, far up among the slopes of the Pindus. Thither, several centuries ago, an ancestor led a migration from the west coast of Greece, and sought a refuge from Turkish oppression. From generation to generation his fathers continued to be shepherds of their people, the office of Proëstos, or governor, being hereditary in the house. Sturdy men those ancestors must have been, and picturesque their times. In late winter afternoons, at 3 Holworthy, when the dusk began to settle among the elms about the yard, legends of these heroes and their far-off days would loiter through the exile's mind. At such times bloody doings would be narrated with all the coolness that appears in Cæsar's Commentaries, and over the listener would come a sense of a fantastic world as different from our own as that of Bret Harte's Argonauts. "My great-grandfather was not easily disturbed. He was a young man and Proëstos. His stone house stood apart from the others. He was sitting in its great room one evening, and heard a noise. He looked around, and saw three men by the farther door. 'What are you here for?' 'We have come to assassinate you.' 'Who sent you?' 'Andreas.' It was a political enemy. 'How much did Andreas promise you?' 'A dollar.' 'I will promise you two dollars if you will go and assassinate Andreas.' So they turned, went, and assassinated Andreas. My great-grandfather went to Scyros the next day, and remained there five years. In five years these things are forgotten in Greece. Then he came back, and brought a wife from Scyros, and was Proëstos once more."

Another evening: "People said my grandfather died of leprosy. Perhaps he did. As Proëstos he gave a decision against a woman, and she hated him. One night she crept up behind the house, where his clothes lay on the ground, and spread over his clothes the clothes of a leper. After that he was not well. His hair fell off and he died. But perhaps it was not leprosy; perhaps he died of fear. The Knights of Malta were worrying the Turks. They sailed into the harbor of Volo, and threatened to bombard the town. The Turks seized the leading Greeks and shut them up in the mosque. When the first gun was fired by the frigate, the heads of the Greeks were to come off. My grandfather went into the mosque a young man. A quarter of an hour afterwards, the gun was heard, and my grandfather waited for the headsman. But the shot toppled down the minaret, and the Knights of Malta were so pleased that they sailed away, satisfied. The Turks, watching them, forgot about the prisoners. But two hours later, when my grandfather came out of the mosque, he was an old man. He could not walk well. His hair fell off, and he died."

Sometimes I caught glimpses of Turkish oppression in times of peace. "I remember the first time I saw the wedding gift given. No new-made bride must leave the house she visits without a gift. My mother's sister married, and came to see us. I was a boy. She stood at the door to go, and my mother remembered she had not had the gift. There was not much to give. The Turks had been worse than usual, and everything was buried. But my mother could not let her go without the gift. She searched the house, and found a saucer,—it was a beautiful saucer; and this she gave her sister, who took it and went away."

"How did you get the name of Sophocles?" I asked, one evening. "Is your family supposed to be connected with that of the poet?" "My name is not Sophocles. I have no family name. In Greece, when a child is born, it is carried to the grandfather to receive a name." (I thought how, in the Odyssey, the nurse puts the infant Odysseus in the arms of his mother's father, Autolycus, for naming.) "The grandfather gives him his own name. The father's name, of course, is different; and this he too gives when he becomes a grandfather. So in old Greek families two names alternate through generations. My grandfather's name was Evangelinos. This he gave to me; and I was distinguished from others of that name because I was the son of Apostolos, Apostolides. But my best schoolmaster was fond of the poet Sophocles, and he was fond of me. He used to call me his little Sophocles. The other boys heard it, and they began to call me so. It was a nickname. But when I left home people took it for my family name. They thought I must have a family name. I did not contradict them. It makes no difference. This is as good as any." One morning he received a telegram of congratulation from the monks in Cairo.

"It is my day," he said. "How did the monks know it was your birthday?" I asked. "It is not my birthday. Nobody thinks about that. It is forgotten. This is my saint's day. Coming into the world is of no consequence; coming under the charge of the saints is what we care for. My name puts me in the Virgin's charge, and the feast of the Annunciation is my day. The monks know my name."

To the Greek Church he was always loyal. Its faith had glorified his youth, and to it he turned for strength throughout his solitary years. Its conventual discipline was dear to him, and oftener than of his birthplace at the foot of Mt. Olympus he dreamed of Mt. Sinai. On Mt. Sinai the Emperor Justinian founded the most revered of all Greek monasteries. Standing remote on its sacred mountain, the monastery depends on Cairo for its supplies. In Cairo, accordingly, there is a branch or agency which during the boyhood of Sophocles was presided over by his Uncle Constantius. At twelve he joined this uncle in Cairo. In the agency there, in the parent monastery on Sinai itself, and in journeyings between the two, the happy years were spent which shaped his intellectual and religious constitution. Though he never outwardly became a monk, he largely became one within. His adored uncle Constantius was his spiritual father. Through him his ideals had been acquired,—his passion for learning, his hardihood in duty, his imperturbable patience, his brief speech which allowed only so many words as might scantily clothe his thought, his indifference to personal comfort. He never spoke the name of Constantius without some sign of reverence; and in his will, after making certain private bequests, and leaving to Harvard College all his printed books and stereotype plates, he adds this clause: "All the residue and remainder of my property and estate I devise and bequeath to the said President and Fellows of Harvard College in trust, to keep the same as a permanent fund, and to apply the income thereof in two equal parts: one part to the purchase of Greek and Latin books (meaning hereby the ancient classics) or of Arabic books, or of books illustrating or explaining such Greek, Latin, or Arabic books; and the other part to the Catalogue Department of the General Library.... My will is that the entire income of the said fund be expended in every year, and that the fund be kept forever unimpaired, and be called and known as the Constantius Fund, in memory of my paternal uncle, Constantius the Sinaite, Κωνσταντιος Σιναιτνης."

This man, then, by birth, training, and temper a solitary; whose heritage was Mt. Olympus, and the monastery of Justinian, and the Greek quarter of Cairo, and the isles of Greece; whose intimates were Hesiod and Pindar and Arrian and Basilides,—this man it was who, from 1842 onward, was deputed to interpret to American college boys the hallowed writings of his race. Thirty years ago too, at the period when I sat on the green bench in front of the long-legged desk, college boys were boys indeed. They had no more knowledge than the high-school boy of to-day, and they were kept in order by much the same methods. Thus it happened, by some jocose perversity in the arrangement of human affairs, that throughout our Sophomore and Junior years we sportive youngsters were obliged to endure Sophocles, and Sophocles was obliged to endure us. No wonder if he treated us with a good deal of contempt. No wonder that his power of scorn, originally splendid, enriched itself from year to year. We learned, it is true, something about everything except Greek; and the best thing we learned was a new type of human nature. Who that was ever his pupil will forget the calm bearing, the occasional pinch of snuff, the averted eye, the murmur of the interior voice, and the stocky little figure with the lion's head? There in the corner he stood, as stranded and solitary as the Egyptian obelisk in the hurrying Place de la Concorde. In a curious sort of fashion he was faithful to what he must have felt an obnoxious duty. He was never absent from his post, nor did he cut short the hours, but he gave us only such attention as was nominated in the bond; he appeared to hurry past, as by set purpose, the beauties of what we read, and he took pleasure in snubbing expectancy and aspiration.

"When I entered college," says an eminent Greek scholar, "I was full of the notion, which I probably could not have justified, that the Greeks were the greatest people that had ever lived. My enthusiasm was fanned into a warmer glow when I learned that my teacher was himself a Greek, and that our first lesson was to be the story of Thermopylæ. After the passage of Herodotus had been duly read, Sophocles began: 'You must not suppose these men stayed in the Pass because they were brave; they were afraid to run away.' A shiver went down my back. Even if what he said had been true, it ought never to have been told to a Freshman."

The universal custom of those days was the hearing of recitations, and to this Sophocles conformed so far as to set a lesson and to call for its translation bit by bit. But when a student had read his suitable ten lines, he was stopped by the raised finger; and Sophocles, fixing his eyes on vacancy and taking his start from some casual suggestion of the passage, began a monologue,—a monologue not unlike one of Browning's in its caprices, its involvement, its adaptation to the speaker's mind rather than to the hearer's, and its ease in glancing from heaven to earth, from earth to heaven. During these intervals the sluggish slumbered, the industrious devoted themselves to books and papers brought in the pocket for the purpose, the dreamy enjoyed the opportunity of wondering what the strange words and their still stranger utterer might mean. The monologue was sometimes long and sometimes short, according as the theme which had been struck kindled the rhapsodist and enabled him, with greater or less completeness, to forget his class. When some subtlety was approached, a smile—the only smile ever seen on his face by strangers—lifted for a moment the corner of the mouth. The student who had been reciting stood meanwhile, but sat when the voice stopped, the white head nodded, the pencil made a record, and a new name was called.

There were perils, of course, in records of this sort. Reasons for the figures which subsequently appeared on the college books were not easy to find. Some of us accounted for our marks by the fact that we had red hair or long noses; others preferred the explanation that our professor's pencil happened to move more readily to the right hand or to the left. For the most part we took good-naturedly whatever was given us, though questionings would sometimes arise. A little before my time there entered an ambitious young fellow, who cherished large purposes in Greek. At the end of the first month under his queer instructor he went to the regent and inquired for his mark in Plato. It was three, the maximum being eight. Horror-stricken, he penetrated Sophocles's room. "Professor Sophocles," he said. "I find my mark is only three. There must be some mistake. There is another Jones in the class, you know, J. S. Jones" (a lump of flesh), "and may it not be that our marks have been confused?" An unmoved countenance, a little wave of the hand, accompanied the answer: "You must take your chance,—you must take your chance." In my own section, when anybody was absent from a certain bench, poor Prindle was always obliged to go forward and say, "I was here to-day, Professor Sophocles," or else the gap on the bench where six men should sit was charged to Prindle's account. In those easy-going days, when men were examined for entrance to college orally and in squads, there was a good deal of eagerness among the knowing ones to get into the squad of Sophocles; for it was believed that he admitted everybody, on the ground that none of us knew any Greek, and it was consequently unfair to discriminate. Fantastic stories were attributed to him, for whose truth or error none could vouch, and were handed on from class to class. "What does Philadelphia mean?" "Brotherly love," the student answers. "Yes! It is to remind us of Ptolemy Philadelphus, who killed his brother." A German commentator had somewhere mentioned lions in connection with the Peloponnesus, and Sophocles inquires of Brown if he knows the date when lions first appeared in the Peloponnesus. He does not, nor does Smith nor Robinson. At length Green, driven to bay, declares in desperation that he doesn't believe there ever were lions in the Peloponnesus. To whom Sophocles: "You are right. There were none." "Do you read your examination books?" he once asked a fellow instructor. "If they are better than you expect, the writers cheat; if they are no better, time is wasted." "Is to-day story day or contradiction day?" he is reported to have said to one who, in the war time, eagerly handed him a newspaper, and asked if he had seen the morning's news.

How much of this cynicism of conduct and of speech was genuine perhaps he knew as little as the rest of us; but certainly it imparted a pessimistic tinge to all he did and said. To hear him talk, one would suppose the world was ruled by accident or by an utterly irrational fate; for in his mind the two conceptions seemed closely to coincide. His words were never abusive; they were deliberate, peaceful even; but they made it very plain that so long as one lived there was no use in expecting anything. Paradoxes were a little more probable than ordered calculations; but even paradoxes would fail. Human beings were altogether impotent, though they fussed and strutted as if they could accomplish great things. How silly was trust in men's goodness and power, even in one's own! Most men were bad and stupid,—Germans especially so. The Americans knew nothing, and never could know. A wise man would not try to teach them. Yet some persons dreamed of establishing a university in America! Did they expect scholarship where there were politicians and business men? Evil influences were far too strong. They always were. The good were made expressly to suffer, the evil to succeed. Better leave the world alone, and keep one's self true. "Put a drop of milk into a gallon of ink; it will make no difference. Put a drop of ink into a gallon of milk; the whole is spoiled."

I have felt compelled to dwell at some length on these cynical, illogical, and austere aspects of Sophocles's character, and even to point out the circumstances of his life which may have shaped them, because these were the features by which the world commonly judged him, and was misled. One meeting him casually had little more to judge by. So entire was his reserve, so little did he permit close conversation, so seldom did he raise his eye in his slow walks on the street, so rarely might a stranger pass within the bolted door of his chamber, that to the last he bore to the average college student the character of a sphinx, marvellous in self-sufficiency, amazing in erudition, romantic in his suggestion of distant lands and customs, and forever piquing curiosity by his eccentric and sarcastic sayings. All this whimsicality and pessimism would have been cheap enough, and little worth recording, had it stood alone. What lent it price and beauty was that it was the utterance of a singularly self-denying and tender soul. The incongruity between his bitter speech and his kind heart endeared both to those who knew him. Like his venerable cloak, his grotesque language often hid a bounty underneath. How many students have received his surly benefactions! In how many small tradesmen's shops did he have his appointed chair! His room was bare: but in his native town an aqueduct was built; his importunate and ungrateful relatives were pensioned; the monks of Mt. Sinai were protected against want; the children and grand-children of those who had befriended his early years in America were watched over with a father's love; and by care for helpless creatures wherever they crossed his path he kept himself clean of selfishness.

One winter night, at nearly ten o'clock, I was called to my door. There stood Sophocles. When I asked him why he was not in bed an hour ago, "A. has gone home," he said. "I know it," I answered; for A. was a young instructor dear to me. "He is sick," he went on. "Yes." "He has no money." "Well, we will see how he will get along." "But you must get him some money, and I must know about it." And he would not go back into the storm—this graybeard professor, solicitous for an overworked tutor—till I assured him that arrangements had been made for continuing A.'s salary during his absence. I declare, in telling the tale I am ashamed. Am I wronging the good man by disclosing his secret, and saying that he was not the cynical curmudgeon for which he tried to pass? But already before he was in his grave the secret had been discovered, and many gave him persistently the love which he still tried to wave away.

Toward dumb and immature creatures his tenderness was more frank, for these could not thank him. Children always recognized in him their friend. A group of curly-heads usually appeared in his window on Class Day. A stray cat knew him at once, and, though he seldom stroked her, would quickly accommodate herself near his legs. By him spiders were watched, and their thin wants supplied. But his solitary heart went out most unreservedly and with the most pathetic devotion toward fragile chickens; and out of these uninteresting little birds he elicited a degree of responsive intelligence which was startling to see. One of his dearest friends, coming home from a journey, brought him a couple of bantam eggs. When hatched and grown, they developed into a little five-inch burnished cock, which shone like a jewel or a bird of paradise, and a more sober but exquisite hen. These two, Frank and Nina, and all their numerous progeny for many years, Sophocles trained to the hand. Each knew its name, and would run from the flock when its white-haired keeper called, and, sitting upon his hand or shoulder, would show queer signs of affection, not hesitating even to crow. The same generous friend who gave the eggs gave shelter also to the winged consequences. And thus it happened that three times a day, so long as he was able to leave his room, Sophocles went to that house where Radcliffe College is now sheltered to attend his pets. White grapes were carried there, and the choicest of corn and clamshell; and endless study was given to devising conveniences for housing, nesting, and the promenade. But he did not demand too much from his chickens. In their case, as in dealing with human beings, he felt it wise to bear in mind the limit and to respect the foreordained. When Nina was laying badly, one springtime, I suggested a special food as a good egg-producer. But Sophocles declined to use it. "You may hasten matters," he said, "but you cannot change them. A hen is born with just so many eggs to lay. You cannot increase the number." The eggs, as soon as laid, were pencilled with the date and the name of the mother, and were then distributed among his friends, or sparingly eaten at his own meals. To eat a chicken itself was a kind of cannibalism from which his whole nature shrank. "I do not eat what I love," he said, rejecting the bowl of chicken broth I pressed upon him in his last sickness.

For protecting creatures naturally so helpless, sternness—or at least its outward seeming—became occasionally necessary. One day young Thornton's dog leaped into the hen-yard and caused a commotion there. Sophocles was prompt in defence. He drew a pistol and fired, while the dog, perceiving his mistake, retreated as he had come. The following day Thornton Senior, walking down the street, was suddenly embarrassed by seeing Sophocles on the same sidewalk. Remembering, however, the old man's usually averted gaze, he hoped to pass unnoticed. But as the two came abreast, gruff words and a piercing eye signalled stoppage. "Mr. Thornton, you have a son." "Yes, Mr. Sophocles, a boy generally well-meaning but sometimes thoughtless." "Your son has a dog." "A nervous dog, rather difficult to regulate." "The dog worried my chickens." "So I heard, and was sorry enough to hear it." "I fired a pistol at him." "Very properly. A pity you didn't hit him." "The pistol was not loaded." And before Mr. Thornton could recover his wits for a suitable reply Sophocles had drawn from his pocket one of his long Sinaitic sweetmeats, had cut off a lump with his jack-knife, handed it to Mr. Thornton, and with the words, "This is for the boy who owns the dog," was gone. The incident well illustrates the sweetness and savagery of the man, his plainness, his readiness to right a wrong and protect the weak, his rejection of smooth and unnecessary words, his rugged exterior, and the underlying kindness which ever attended it.

If in ways so uncommon his clinging nature, cut off from domestic opportunity, went out to children and unresponsive creatures, it may be imagined how good cause of love he furnished to his few intimates among mankind. They found in him sweet courtesy, undemanding gentleness, an almost feminine tact in adapting what he could give to what they might receive. To their eyes the great scholar, the austere monk, the bizarre professor, the pessimist, were hidden by the large and lovable man. Even strangers recognized him as no common person, so thoroughly was all he did and said purged of superfluity, so veracious was he, so free from apology. His everyday thoughts were worthy thoughts. He knew no shame or fear, and had small wish, I think, for any change. Always a devout Christian, he seldom used expressions of regret or hope. Probably he concerned himself little with these or other feelings. In the last days of his life, it is true, when his thoughts were oftener in Arabia than in Cambridge, he once or twice referred to "the ambition of learning" as the temptation which had drawn him out from the monastery, and had given him a life less holy than he might have led among the monks. But these were moods of humility rather than of regret. Habitually he maintained an elevation above circumstances,—was it Stoicism or Christianity?—which imparted to his behavior, even when most eccentric, an unshakable dignity. When I have found him in his room, curled up in shirt and drawers, reading the "Arabian Nights," the Greek service book, or the "Ladder of the Virtues" by John Klimakos, he has risen to receive me with the bearing of an Arab sheikh, and has laid by the Greek folio and motioned me to a chair with a stateliness not natural to our land or century. It would be clumsy to liken him to one of Plutarch's men; for though there was much of the heroic and extraordinary in his character and manners, nothing about him suggested a suspicion of being on show. The mould in which he was cast was formed earlier. In his bearing and speech, and in a certain large simplicity of mental structure, he was the most Homeric man I ever knew.

III
PAPERS BY ALICE FREEMAN PALMER

While Mrs. Palmer always avoided writing, and thought—generous prodigal!—that her work was best accomplished by spoken words, her complying spirit could not always resist the appeals of magazine editors. I could wish now that their requests had been even more urgent. And I believe that those who read these pages will regret that one possessed of such breadth of view, clearness, charm and cogency of style should have left a literary record so meagre. All these papers are printed precisely as she left them, without the change of a word. I have not even ventured on correction in the printed report of one of her addresses, that on going to college. Its looser structure well illustrates her mode of moving an audience and bringing its mothers to the course of conduct she approved.

XIII

THREE TYPES OF WOMEN'S COLLEGES[14]

American college education in the quarter-century since the Civil War has undergone more numerous and more fundamental changes than befell it in a hundred years before. These changes have not occurred unnoticed. A multitude of journals and associations are busy every year discussing the results of the experiments in teaching which go on with increasing daring and fruitfulness in nearly all our colleges and schools. There still exists a wide divergence of opinion among the directors of men's colleges in regard to a variety of important questions: the conditions and proper age for entrance; the length of the course of study; the elective system, both of government and instruction; the requirements for the bachelor's and master's degrees; the stress to be laid on graduate work—these, and many sequents of these, touching the physical, social, and religious life of the young men of the land, are undergoing sharp discussion.

The advanced education of young women is exposed to all the uncertainties which beset the education of men, but it has perplexities of its own in addition. After fifty years of argument and twenty-five of varied and costly experiment, it might be easy to suppose that we are still in chaos, almost as far from knowing the best way to train a woman as we were at the beginning. No educational convention meets without a session devoted to the difficulties in "the higher education of women," so important has the subject become, and so hard is it to satisfy in any one system the variety of its needs. Yet chaos may be thought more chaotic than it really is. In the din of discussion it would not be strange if the fair degree of concord already reached should sometimes be missed. We are certainly still far from having found the one best method of college training for girls. Some of us hope we may never find it, believing that in diversity, no less than in unity, there is strength. But already three tolerably clear, consistent, and accredited types of education appear, which it will be the purpose of this paper to explain. The nature of each, with its special strengths and weaknesses, will be set forth in no spirit of partisanship, but in the belief that a cool understanding of what is doing at present among fifty thousand college girls may make us wiser and more patient in our future growth. What, then, are the three types, and how have they arisen?

When to a few daring minds the conviction came that education was a right of personality rather than of sex, and when there was added to this growing sentiment the pressing demand for educated women as teachers and as leaders in philanthropy, the simplest means of equipping women with the needful prepara-

[14] Published in *The Forum* for September, 1891.

tion was found in the existing schools and colleges. Scattered all over the country were colleges for men, young for the most part and small, and greatly lacking anything like a proper endowment. In nearly every state west of the Alleghanies, "universities" had been founded by the voluntary tax of the whole population. Connected with all the more powerful religious denominations were schools and colleges which called upon their adherents for gifts and students. These democratic institutions had the vigor of youth, and were ambitious and struggling. "Why," asked the practical men of affairs who controlled them, "should not our daughters go on with our sons from the public schools to the university which we are sacrificing to equip and maintain? Why should we duplicate the enormously expensive appliances of education, when our existing colleges would be bettered by more students? By far the large majority of our boys and girls study together as children; they work together as men and women in all the important concerns of life; why should they be separated in the lecture room for only the four years between eighteen and twenty-two, when that separation means the doubling of an equipment already too poor by half?"

It is not strange that with this and much more practical reasoning of a similar kind, coeducation was established in some colleges at their beginning, in others after debate and by a radical change in policy. When once the chivalrous desire was aroused to give girls as good an education as their brothers, western men carried out the principle unflinchingly. From the kindergarten to the preparation for the doctorate of philosophy, educational opportunities are now practically alike for men and women. The total number of colleges of arts and sciences empowered by law to give degrees, reporting to Washington in 1888, was three hundred and eighty-nine. Of these two hundred and thirty-seven, or nearly two thirds, were coeducational. Among them are all the state universities, and nearly all the colleges under the patronage of the Protestant sects.

Hitherto I have spoken as if coeducation were a western movement; and in the West it certainly has had greater currency than elsewhere. But it originated, at least so far as concerns superior secondary training, in Massachusetts. Bradford Academy, chartered in 1804, is the oldest incorporated institution in the country to which boys and girls were from the first admitted; but it closed its department for boys in 1836, three years after the foundation of coeducational Oberlin, and in the very year when Mount Holyoke was opened by Mary Lyon, in the large hope of doing for young women what Harvard had been founded to do for young men just two hundred years before. Ipswich and Abbot Academies in Massachusetts had already been chartered to educate girls alone. It has been the dominant sentiment in the East that boys and girls should be educated separately. The older, more generously endowed, more conservative seats of learning, inheriting the complications of the dormitory system, have remained closed to women. The requirements for the two sexes are thought to be different. Girls are to be trained for private, boys for public life. Let every opportunity be given, it is said, for developing accomplished, yes, even learned women; but let the process of acquiring knowledge take place under careful guardianship, among the refinements of home life, with graceful women, their instructors, as companions, and with suitable opportunities for social life. Much stress is laid upon assisting girl students to attain balanced characters, charming manners, and ambitions that are not unwomanly. A powerful moral, often a deeply religious earnestness, shaped the discussion, and finally laid the foundations of woman's education in the East.

In the short period of the twenty years after the war the four women's colleges which are the richest in endowments and students of any in the world were founded and set in motion. These colleges—Vassar, opened in 1865, Wellesley and Smith in 1875, and Bryn Mawr in 1885—have received in gifts of every kind about $6,000,000, and are educating nearly two thousand students. For the whole country the Commissioner of Education reports two hundred and seven institutions for the superior instruction of women, with more than twenty-five thousand students. But these resources proved inadequate. There came an increasing demand, especially from teachers, for education of all sorts; more and more, too, for training in subjects of advanced research. For this, only the best equipped men's universities were thought sufficient, and women began to resort to the great universities of England and Germany. In an attempt to meet a demand of this sort the Harvard Annex began, twelve years ago, to provide women with instruction by members of the Harvard Faculty.

Where, in a great centre of education, for many years books have accumulated, and museums and laboratories have multiplied, where the prestige and associations of a venerable past have grown up, and cultivated surroundings assure a scholarly atmosphere; in short, in the shadow of all that goes to make up the gracious influences of an old and honorable university, it was to be expected that earnest women would gather to seek a share in the enthusiasm for scholarship, and the opportunities for acquiring it, which their brothers had enjoyed for two hundred and fifty years.

These, then—coeducation, the woman's college, and the annex—are the three great types of college in which the long agitation in behalf of women's education has thus far issued. Of course they are but types—that is, they do not always exist distinct and entire; they are rather the central forms to which many varieties approximate. The characteristic features of each I must now describe, and, as I promised at the beginning, point out their inherent strengths and weaknesses; for each, while having much to recommend it, still bears in itself the defects of its qualities. To explain dangers as well as promises is the business of the critic, as contrasted with that of the advocate. To this business I now turn, and I may naturally have most in mind the University of Michigan, my own Alma Mater, Wellesley College, with whose government I have been connected for a dozen years, and the Harvard Annex, whose neighbor I now am.

Coeducation involves, as its name implies, the education of a company of young men and women as a single body. To the two sexes alike are presented the same conditions of admission, of opportunities during the course, of requirements for the degrees, of guardianship, of discipline, of organization. The typical features are identical classrooms, libraries, and laboratories, occupied at the same time, under the same instructors; and the same honors for like work. Ordinarily all the instructors are men, although in a few universities professorships are held by women. Usually no dormitories or boarding-houses are provided for either the young men or women, and no more surveillance is kept over the one than over the other. This feature, however, is not essential. At Cornell, Oberlin, and elsewhere, often out of local necessity, buildings have been provided where the young women may—in some instances, must—live together under the ordinary regulations of home life, with a lady in charge. But in most of the higher coeducational institutions the principle has from the first been assumed that students of both sexes become sufficiently matured by eighteen years of home, school, and social life—especially under the ample opportunities for learning the uses of freedom which our social habits afford—safely to undertake a college course, and advantageously to order their daily lives. Of course all have a moral support in the advice and example of their teachers, and they are held to good intellectual work by the perpetual demand of the classroom, the laboratory, and the thesis.

The girl who goes to the University of Michigan to-day, just as when I entered there in 1872, finds her own boarding-place in one of the quiet homes of the pleasant little city whose interest centres in the two thousand five hundred students scattered within its borders. She makes the business arrangements for her winter's fuel and its storage; she finds her washerwoman or her laundry; she arranges her own hours of exercise, of study, and of sleep; she chooses her own society, clubs, and church. The advice she gets comes from another girl student of sophomoric dignity who chances to be in the same house, or possibly from a still more advanced young woman whom she met on the journey, or sat near in church on her first Sunday. Strong is the comradeship among these ambitious girls, who nurse one another in illness, admonish one another in health, and rival one another in study only less eagerly than they all rival the boys. In my time in college the little group of girls, suddenly introduced into the army of young men, felt that the fate of our sex hung upon proving that "lady Greek" involved the accents, and that women's minds were particularly absorptive of the calculus and metaphysics. And still in those sections where, with growing experience, the anxieties about coeducation have been allayed, a healthy and hearty relationship and honest rivalry between young men and women exists. It is a stimulating atmosphere, and develops in good stock a strength and independent balance which tell in after-life.

In estimating the worth of such a system as this, we may say at once that it does not meet every need of a woman's nature. No system can—no system that has yet been devised. A woman is an object of attraction to men, and also in herself so delicately organized as to be fitted peculiarly for the graces and domesticities of life. The exercise of her special function of motherhood demands sheltered circumstances and refined moral perceptions. But then, over and above all this, she is a human being—a person, that is, who has her own way in the world to make, and who will come to success or failure, in her home or outside it, according as her judgment is fortified, her observations and experiences are enlarged, her courage is rendered strong and calm, her moral estimates are trained to be accurate, broad, and swift. In a large tract of her character—is it the largest tract?—her own needs and those of the young man are identical. Both are rational persons, and the greater part of the young man's education is addressed to his rational personality rather than to the peculiarities of his sex. Why, the defenders of coeducation ask, may not the same principles apply to women? Why train a girl specifically to be a wife and mother, when no great need is felt for training a boy to be a husband and father? In education, as a public matter, the two sexes meet on common ground. The differences must be attended to privately.

At any rate, whatever may be thought of the relative importance of the two sides—the woman side and the human side—it will be generally agreed that the training of a young woman is apt to be peculiarly weak in agencies for bringing home to her the importance of direct and rational action. The artificialities of society, the enfeebling indulgence extended to pretty silliness, the gallantry of men glad ever to accept the hard things and leave to her the easy—by these influences any comfortably placed and pleasing girl is pretty sure to be surrounded in her early teens. The coeducationists think it wholesome that in her later teens and early twenties she should be subjected to an impartial judgment, ready to estimate her without swerving, and to tell her as freely when she is silly, ignorant, fussy, or indolent as her brother himself is told. Coeducation, as a system, must minimize the different needs of men and women; it appeals to them and provides for them alike, and then allows the natural tastes and instincts of each scope for individuality. The strengths of this system, accordingly, are to be found in its tendency to promote independence of judgment, individuality of tastes, common-sense and foresight in self-guidance, disinclination to claim favor, interest in learning for its own sake; friendly, natural, unromantic, non-sentimental relations with men. The early fear that coeducation would result in classroom romances has proved exaggerated. These young women do marry; so do others; so do young men. Marriage is not in itself an evil, and many happy homes have been founded in the belief that long and quiet acquaintance in intellectual work, and intimate interests of the same deeper sort, form as solid a basis for a successful marriage as ballroom intercourse or a summer at Bar Harbor.

The weaknesses of this system are merely the converse of its strengths. It does not usually provide for what is distinctively feminine. Refining home influences and social oversight are largely lacking; and if they are wanting in the home from which the student comes, it must not be expected that she will show, on graduation, the graces of manner, the niceties of speech and dress, and the shy delicacy which have been encouraged in her more tenderly nurtured sister.

The woman's college is organized under a different and far more complex conception. The chief business of the man's college, whether girls are admitted to it or not, is to give instruction of the best available quality in as many subjects as possible; to furnish every needed appliance for the acquirement of knowledge and the encouragement of special investigation. The woman's college aims to do all this, but it aims also to make for its students a home within its own walls and to develop other powers in them than the merely intellectual. At the outset this may seem a simple matter, but it quickly proves as complicated as life itself. When girls are gathered together by hundreds, isolated from the ordinary conditions of established communities, the college stands to them preëminently *in loco parentis*. It must provide resident physicians and trained nurses, be ready in case of illness and, to prevent illness, must direct exercise, sleep, hygiene and sanitation, accepting the responsibility not only of the present health of its students, but also in large degree of their physical power in the future. It generally furnishes them means of social access to the best men and women of their neighborhood; it draws to them leaders in moral and social reforms, to give inspiration in high ideals and generous self-sacrifice, and it undertakes religious instruction while seeking still to respect the varied faiths of its students. In short, the arrangements of the woman's college, as conceived by founders, trustees, and faculty, have usually aimed with conscious directness at building up character, inspiring to the service of others, cultivating manners, developing taste, and strengthening health, as well as providing the means of sound learning.

It may be said that a similar upbuilding of the personal life results from the training of every college that is worthy of the name; and fortunately it is impossible to enlarge knowledge without, to some extent, enlarging life. But the question is one of directness or indirectness of aim. The woman's college puts this aim in the foreground side by side with the acquisition of knowledge. By setting its students apart in homogeneous companies, it seeks to cultivate common ideals. Of its teaching force, a large number are women who live with the students in the college buildings, sit with them at table, join in their festivities, and in numberless intimate ways share and guide the common life. Every student, no matter how large the college, has friendly access at any time to several members of the faculty, quite apart from her relations with them in the classroom. In appointing these women to the faculty no board of trustees would consider it sufficient that a candidate was an accomplished specialist. She must be this, but she should be also a lady of unobjectionable manners and influential character; she should have amiability and a discreet temper, for she is to be a guiding force in a complex community, continually in the presence of her students, an officer of administration and government no less than of instruction. Harvard and Johns Hopkins can ask their pupils to attend the lectures of a great scholar, however brusque his bearing or unbrushed his hair. They will not question their geniuses too sharply, and will trust their students to look out for their own proprieties of dress, manners, and speech. But neither Wellesley nor any other woman's college could find a place in its faculty for a woman Sophocles or Sylvester. Learning alone is not enough for women.

Not only in the appointment of its teaching body, but in all its appliances the separate college aims at a rounded refinement, at cultivating a sense of beauty, at imparting simple tastes and generous sympathies. To effect this, pictures are hung on the walls, statues and flowers decorate the rooms, concerts bring music to the magnified home, and parties and receptions are paid for out of the college purse. The influence of hundreds of mentally eager girls upon the characters of one another, when they live for four years in the closest daily companionship, is most interesting to see. I have watched the ennobling process go on for many years among Wellesley students, and I am confident that no more healthy, generous, democratic, beauty-loving, serviceable society of people exists than the girls' college community affords. That choicest product of modern civilization, the American girl, is here in all her diverse colors. She comes from more than a dozen religious denominations and from every political party; from nearly every state and territory in the Union, and from the foreign lands into which English and American missionaries, merchants, or soldiers have penetrated. The farmer's daughter from the western prairies is beside the child whose father owns half a dozen mill towns of New England. The pride of a Southern senator's home rooms with an anxious girl who must borrow all the money for her college course because her father's life was given for the Union. Side by side in the boats, on the tennis-grounds, at the table, arm in arm on the long walks, debating in the societies, vigorous together in the gymnasium and the library, girls of every grade gather the rich experiences which will tincture their future toil, and make the world perpetually seem an interesting and friendly place. They here learn to "see great things large, and little things small."

This detailed explanation of the peculiarities of the girls' college renders unnecessary any long discussion of its strengths and weaknesses. According to the point of view of the critic these peculiarities themselves will be counted means of invigoration or of enfeeblement. Living so close to one another as girls here do, the sympathetic and altruistic virtues acquire great prominence. Petty selfishness retreats or becomes extinct. An earnest, high-minded spirit is easily cultivated, and the break between college life and the life from which the student comes is reduced to a minimum.

It is this very fact which is often alleged as the chief objection to the girls' college. It is said that its students never escape from themselves and their domestic standard, that they do not readily acquire a scientific spirit, and become individual in taste and conduct. Is it desirable that they should? That I shall not undertake to decide. I have merely tried to explain the kinds of human work which the different types of higher training-schools are best fitted to effect for women. Whether the one or the other kind of work needs most to be done is a question of social ethics which the future must answer. I have set forth a type, perhaps in the endeavor after clearness exaggerating a little its outlines, and contrasting it more sharply with its two neighbor types than individual cases would justify. There are colleges for women which closely approximate in aim and method the colleges for men. No doubt those which move furthest in the directions I have indicated are capable of modification. But I believe what I have said gives a substantially true account of an actually existing type—a type powerful in stirring the enthusiasm of those who are submitted to it, subtle in its penetrating influences over them, and effective in winning the confidence of a multitude of parents who would never send their daughters to colleges of a different type.

The third type is the "annex," a recent and interesting experiment in the education of girls, whose future it is yet difficult to predict. Only a few cases exist, and as the Harvard Annex is the most conspicuous, by reason of its dozen years of age and nearly two hundred students, I shall describe it as the typical example. In the Harvard Annex groups of young women undertake courses of study in classes whose instruction is furnished entirely by members of the Harvard Faculty. No college officer is obliged to give this instruction, and the Annex staff of teachers is, therefore, liable to considerable variation from year to year. Though the usual four classes appear in its curriculum, the large majority of its students devote themselves to special subjects. A wealthy girl turns from fashionable society to pursue a single course in history or economics; a hard-worked teacher draws inspiration during a few afternoons each week from a famous Greek or Latin professor; a woman who has been long familiar with French literature explores with a learned specialist some single period in the history of the language. Because the opportunities for advanced and detached study are so tempting, many ladies living in the neighborhood of the Annex enter one or more of its courses. There are consequently among its students women much older than the average of those who attend the colleges.

The business arrangements are taken charge of by a committee of ladies and gentlemen, who provide classrooms, suggest boarding-places, secure the instructors, solicit the interest of the public—in short, manage all the details of an independent institution; for the noteworthy feature of its relation to its powerful neighbor is this: that the two, while actively friendly, have no official or organic tie whatever. In the same city young men and young women of collegiate rank are studying the same subjects under the same instructors; but there are two colleges, not one. No detail in the management of Harvard College is changed by the presence in Cambridge of the Harvard Annex. If the corporation of Harvard should assume the financial responsibility, supervise the government, and give the girl graduates degrees, making no other changes whatever, the Annex would then become a school of the university, about as distinct from Harvard College as the medical, law, or divinity schools. The students of the medical school do not attend the same lectures or frequent the same buildings as the college undergraduates. The immediate governing boards of college and medical school are separate. But here comparison fails, for the students of the professional schools may elect courses in the college and make use of all its resources. This the young women cannot do. They have only the rights of all Cambridge ladies to attend the many public lectures and readings of the university.

The Harvard Annex is, then, to-day a woman's college, with no degrees, no dormitories, no women instructors, and with a staff of teachers made up from volunteers of another college. The Fay House, where offices, lecture and waiting rooms, library and laboratories are gathered, is in the heart of Old Cambridge, but at a little distance from the college buildings. This is the centre of the social and literary life of the students. Here they gather their friends at afternoon teas; here the various clubs which have sprung up, as numbers have increased, hold their meetings and give their entertainments. The students lodge in all parts of Cambridge and the neighboring towns, and are directly responsible for their conduct only to themselves. The ladies of the management are lavish in time and care to make the girls' lives happy and wholesome; the secretary is always at hand to give advice; but the personal life of the students is as separate and independent as in the typical coeducational college.

It is impossible to estimate either favorably or adversely the permanent worth of an undertaking still in its infancy. Manifestly, the opportunities for the very highest training are here superb, if they happen to exist at all. In this, however, is the incalculable feature of the system. The Annex lives by favor, not by right, and it is impossible to predict what the extent of favor may at any time be. A girl hears that an admirable course of lectures has been given on a topic in which she is greatly interested. She arranges to join the Annex and enter the course, but learns in the summer vacation that through pressure of other work the professor will be unable to teach in the Annex the following year. The fact that favor rules, and not rights, peculiarly hampers scientific and laboratory courses, and for its literary work obliges the Annex largely to depend on its own library. Yet when all these weaknesses are confessed—and by none are they confessed more frankly than by the wise and devoted managers of the Annex themselves—it should be said that hitherto they have not practically hindered the formation of a spirit of scholarship, eager, free and sane to an extraordinary degree. The Annex girl succeeds in remaining a private and unobserved gentlewoman, while still, in certain directions, pushing her studies to an advanced point seldom reached elsewhere.

A plan in some respects superficially analogous to the American annex has been in operation for many years at the English, and more recently at some of the Scotch universities, where a hall or college for women uses many of the resources of the university. But this plan is so complicated with the peculiar organization of English university life that it cannot usefully be discussed here. In the few colleges in this country where, very recently, the annex experiment is being tried, its methods vary markedly.

Barnard College in New York is an annex of Columbia only in a sense, for not all her instruction is given by Columbia's teaching force, though Columbia will confer degrees upon her graduates. The new Woman's College at Cleveland sustains temporarily the same relations to Adelbert College, though to a still greater extent she provides independent instruction.

In both Barnard and Cleveland women are engaged in instruction and in government. Indeed, the new annexes which have arisen in the last three years seem to promise independent colleges for women in the immediate neighborhood of, and in close relationship with, older and better equipped universities for men, whose resources they can to some extent use, whose standards they can apply, whose tests they can meet. When they possess a fixed staff of teachers they are not, of course, liable to the instabilities which at present beset the Harvard Annex. So far, however, as these teachers belong to the annex, and are not drawn from the neighboring university, the annex is assimilated to the type of the ordinary woman's college, and loses its distinctive merits. If the connection between it and the university should ever become so close that it had the same right to the professors as the university itself, it would become a question whether the barriers between the men's and the women's lecture rooms could be economically maintained.

The preceding survey has shown how in coeducation a woman's study is carried on inside a man's college, in the women's college outside it, in the annex beside it. Each of these situations has its advantage. But will the community be content to accept this; permanently to forego the counter advantages, and even after it fully realizes the powers and limitations of the different types, firmly to maintain them in their distinctive vigor? Present indications render this improbable. Already coeducational colleges incline to more careful leadership for their girls. The separate colleges, with growing wealth, are learning to value intrepidity, and are carrying their operations close up to the lands of the Ph.D. The annex swings in its middle air, sometimes inclining to the one side, sometimes to the other. And outside them all, the great body of men's colleges continually find it harder to maintain their isolation, and extend one privilege after another to the seeking sex.

The result of all these diversities is the most instructive body of experiment that the world has seen for determining the best ways of bringing woman to her powers. While the public mind is so uncertain, so liable to panic, and so doubtful whether, after all, it is not better for a girl to be a goose, the many methods of education assist one another mightily in their united warfare against ignorance, selfish privileges, and antiquated ideals. It is well that for a good while to come woman's higher education should be all things to all mothers, if by any means it may save girls. Those who are hardy enough may continue to mingle their girls with men; while a parent who would be shocked that her daughter should do anything so ambiguous as to enter a man's college may be persuaded to send her to a girls'. Those who find it easier to honor an old university than the eager life of a young college, may be tempted into an annex. The important thing is that the adherents of these differing types should not fall into jealousy, and belittle the value of those who are performing a work which they themselves cannot do so well. To understand one another kindly is the business of the hour—to understand and to wait.

XIV

WOMEN'S EDUCATION IN THE NINETEENTH CENTURY[15]

One of the most distinctive and far-reaching movements of the nineteenth century is that which has brought about the present large opportunities for the higher education of women. Confining itself to no country, this vast movement has advanced rapidly in some, slowly and timidly in others. In America three broad periods mark its progress: first, the period of quiescence, which ends about 1830; second, the period of agitation, ending with the civil war; the third, though far as yet from completion, may be called the period of accomplishment.

For the first two hundred years in the history of our country little importance was attached to the education of women, though before the nineteenth century began, twenty-four colleges had been founded for the education of men. In the early years of this century private schools for girls were expensive and short-lived. The common schools were the only grades of public instruction open to young women. In the cities of Massachusetts, where more was done for the education of boys than elsewhere, girls were allowed to go to school only a small part of the year, and in some places could even then use the schoolroom only in the early hours of the day, or on those afternoons when the boys had a half-holiday. Anything like a careful training of girls was not yet thought of.

This comparative neglect of women is less to be wondered at when we remember that the colleges which existed at the beginning of this century had been founded to fit men for the learned professions, chiefly for the ministry. Neither here nor elsewhere was it customary to give advanced education to boys destined for business. The country, too, was impoverished by the long struggle for independence. The Government was bankrupt, unable to pay its veteran soldiers. Irritation and unrest were everywhere prevalent until the ending of the second war with England, in 1815. Immediately succeeding this began that great migration to the West and South-west which carried thousands of the most ambitious young men and women from the East to push our frontiers farther and farther into the wilderness. Even in the older parts of the country the population was widely scattered. The people lived for the most part in villages and isolated farms. City life was uncommon. As late as 1840 only nine per cent of the population was living in cities of 8000 or more inhabitants. Under such conditions nothing more than the bare necessities of education could be regarded.

---

[15] Published in *The New York Evening Post*, 1900.

But this very isolation bred a kind of equality. In district schools it became natural for boys and girls to study together and to receive the same instruction from teachers who were often young and enthusiastic. These were as a rule college students, granted long winter vacations from their own studies that they might earn money by teaching village schools. Thus most young women shared with their brothers the best elementary training the country afforded, while college education was reserved for the few young men who were preparing for the ministry or for some other learned profession.

From the beginning it had been the general custom of this country to educate boys and girls together up to the college age. To-day in less than six per cent of all our cities is there any separate provision of schools for boys and girls. This habitual early start together has made it natural for our men and women subsequently to read the same books, to have the same tastes and interests, and jointly to approve a large social freedom. On the whole, women have usually had more leisure than men for the cultivating of scholarly tastes.

The first endowment of the higher education of women in this country was made by the Moravians in the seminary for girls which they founded at Bethlehem, Pennsylvania, in 1749. They founded another girls' seminary at Lititz in 1794. Though both of these honorable foundations continue in effective operation to-day, their influence has been for the most part confined to the religious communion of their founders. In 1804 an academy with wider connections was founded at Bradford, Massachusetts, at first open to boys and girls, since 1836 limited to girls. From that time academies and seminaries for girls increased rapidly. One of the most notable was Troy Seminary, founded by Emma Hart Willard and chartered in 1819. Miss Willard drew up broad and original plans for the higher education of girls, laid them before President Monroe, appealed to the New York Legislature for aid, and dreamed of establishing something like collegiate training. More than three hundred students entered her famous seminary, and for seventeen years she carried it on with growing reputation. Her address to the President in 1819 is still a strong statement of the importance to the republic of an enlightened and disciplined womanhood.

Even more influential was the life and work of Mary Lyon, who in 1837 founded Mount Holyoke Seminary, and labored for the education of women until her death, in 1849. Of strong religious nature, great courage and resource, she went up and down New England securing funds and pupils. Her rare gift of inspiring both men and women induced wide acceptance of her ideals of character and intelligence. Seminaries patterned after Mount Holyoke sprang up all over the land, and still remain as centres of powerful influence, particularly in the Middle West and on the Pacific Coast.

With this development, through the endowment of many excellent seminaries, of the primary education of girls into something like secondary or high-school opportunities, the period of quiescence comes to an end. There follows a period of agitation when the full privilege of college training side by side with men was demanded for women. This agitation was closely connected on the one hand with the antislavery movement and the general passion for moral reform at that time current; and, on the other, with the interest in teaching and that study of its methods which Horace Mann fostered. From 1830 to 1865 it was becoming evident that women were destined to have a large share in the instruction of children. For this work they sought to fit themselves, and the reformers aided them. Oberlin College, which began as a collegiate institute in 1833, was in 1850 chartered as a college. From the beginning it admitted women, and in 1841 three women took its diploma. Antioch College, under Horace Mann's leadership, opened in 1853, admitting women on equal terms with men. In 1855 Elmira College was founded, the first institution chartered as a separate college for women.

Even before the Civil War the commercial interests of the country had become so much extended that trade was rising into a dignity comparable to that of the learned professions. Men were more and more deserting teaching for the business life, and their places, at first chiefly in the lower grades, were being filled by women. During the five years of the war this supersession of men by women teachers advanced rapidly. It has since acquired such impetus that at present more than two thirds of the training of the young of both sexes below the college grade has fallen out of the hands of men. In the mean time, too, though in smaller numbers, women have invaded the other professions and have even entered into trade. These demonstrations of a previously unsuspected capacity have been both the cause and the effect of enlarged opportunities for mental equipment. The last thirty or forty years have seen the opening of that new era in women's education which I have ventured to call the period of accomplishment.

From the middle of the century the movement to open the state universities to women, to found colleges for men and women on equal terms, and to establish independent colleges for women spread rapidly. From their first organization the state universities of Utah (1850), Iowa (1856), Washington (1862), Kansas (1866), Minnesota (1868), Nebraska (1871) admitted women. Indiana, founded in 1820, opened its doors to women in 1868, and was followed in 1870 by Michigan, at that time the largest and far the most influential of all the state universities. From that time the movement became general. The example of Michigan was followed until at the present time all the colleges and universities of the West, excepting those under Catholic management, are open to women. The only state university in the East, that of Maine, admitted women in 1872. Virginia, Georgia, and Louisiana alone among all the state universities of the country remain closed to women. This sudden opening to women of practically all universities supported by public funds is not more extraordinary than the immense endowments which during the same period have been put into independent colleges for women, or into colleges which admit men and women on equal terms. Of these privately endowed colleges, Cornell, originally founded for men, led the way in 1872 in opening its doors to women. The West and South followed rapidly, the East more slowly. Of the 480 colleges which at the end of the century are reported by the Bureau of Education, 336 admit women; or, excluding the Catholic colleges, 80 per cent of all are open to women. Of the sixty leading colleges in the United States there are only ten in which women are not admitted to some department. These ten are all on the Atlantic seaboard and are all old foundations.

This substantial accomplishment during the last forty years of the right of women to a college education has not, however, resulted in fixing a single type of college in which that education shall be obtained. On the contrary, three clearly contrasted types now exist side by side. These are the independent college, the coeducational college, and the affiliated college.

To the independent college for women men are not admitted, though the grade, the organization, and the general aim are supposed to be the same as in the colleges exclusively for men. The first college of this type, Elmira (1855), has been already mentioned. The four largest women's colleges—Vassar, opened in 1861; Smith, in 1875; Wellesley, in 1875, and Bryn Mawr, in 1885—take rank among the sixty leading colleges of the country in wealth, equipment, teachers and students, and variety of studies offered. Wells College, chartered as a college in 1870, the Woman's College of Baltimore, opened in 1888, and Mt. Holyoke, reorganized as a college in 1893, have also large endowments and attendance. All the women's colleges are empowered to confer the same degrees as are given in the men's colleges.

The development of coeducation, the prevailing type of education in the United States for both men and women, has already been sufficiently described. In coeducational colleges men and women have the same instructors, recite in the same classes, and enjoy the same freedom in choice of studies. To the faculties of these colleges women are occasionally appointed, and, like their male colleagues, teach mixed classes of men and women. Many coeducational colleges are without halls of residence. Where these exist, special buildings are assigned to the women students.

The affiliated colleges, while exclusively for women, are closely connected with strong colleges for men, whose equipment and opportunities they are expected in some degree to share. At present there are five such: Radcliffe College, the originator of this type, connected with Harvard University, and opened in 1879; Sophie Newcomb Memorial College, at Tulane University, opened in 1886; the College for Women of Western Reserve University, 1888; Barnard College, at Columbia University, 1889; the Woman's College of Brown University, 1892. In all these colleges the standards for entrance and graduation are the same as those exacted from men in the universities with which they are affiliated. To a considerable extent the instructors also are the same.

During the last quarter-century many professional schools have been opened to women—schools of theology, law, medicine, dentistry, pharmacy, technology, agriculture. The number of women entering these professions is rapidly increasing. Since 1890 the increase of women students in medicine is 64 per cent, in dentistry 205 per cent, in pharmacy 190 per cent, in technology and agriculture 194 per cent.

While this great advance has been accomplished in America, women in England and on the Continent, especially during the last thirty years, have been demanding better education. Though much more slowly and in fewer numbers than in this country, they have everywhere succeeded in securing decided advantages. No country now refuses them a share in liberal study, in the instruction of young children, and in the profession of medicine. As might be expected, English-speaking women, far more than any others, have won and used the opportunities of university training. Since 1860 women have been studying at Cambridge, England, and since 1879 at Oxford. At these ancient seats of learning they have now every privilege except the formal degree. To all other English and Scotch universities, and to the universities of the British colonies, women are admitted, and from them they receive degrees.

In the most northern countries of Europe—in Iceland, Finland, Norway, Sweden, Denmark—the high schools and universities are freely open to women. In eastern Europe able women have made efforts to secure advanced study, and these efforts have been most persistent in Russia and since the Crimean war. When denied in their own land, Russian women have flocked to the Swiss and French universities, and have even gone in considerable numbers to Finland and to Italy. Now Russia is slowly responding to its women's entreaties. During the last ten years the universities of Rumania, Bulgaria, Hungary, and Greece have been open to women; while in Constantinople the American College for Girls offers the women of the East the systematic training of the New England type of college. In western, central, and southern Europe all university doors are open. In these countries, degrees and honors may everywhere be had by women, except in Germany and Austria. Even here, by special permission of the Minister of Education, or the professor in charge, women may hear lectures. Each year, too, more women are granted degrees by special vote and as exceptional cases.

In brief, it may be said that practically all European universities are now open to women. No American woman of scholarship, properly qualified for the work she undertakes, need fear refusal if she seeks the instruction of the greatest European scholars in her chosen field. Each year American women are taking with distinction the highest university degrees of the Continent. To aid them, many fellowships and graduate scholarships, ranging in value from $300 to $1000, are offered for foreign study by our colleges for women and by private associations of women who seek to promote scholarship. Large numbers of ambitious young women who are preparing themselves for teaching or for the higher fields of scientific research annually compete for this aid. Three years ago an association was formed for maintaining an American woman's table in the Zoölogical Station at Naples. By paying $500 a year they are thus able to grant to selected students the most favorable conditions for biological investigation. This association has also just offered a prize of $1000, to be granted two years hence, for the best piece of original scientific work done in the mean time by a woman. The American Schools of Classical Studies in Athens and Rome admit women on the same terms as men, and award their fellowships to men and women indifferently. One of these fellowships, amounting to $1000 a year, has just been won by a woman.

The experience, then, of the last thirty years shows a condition of women's education undreamed of at the beginning of the century. It shows that though still hampered here and there by timorous restrictions, women are in substantial possession of much the same opportunities as are available for men. It shows that they have both the capacity and the desire for college training, that they can make profitable and approved use of it when obtained, and that they are eager for that broader and more original study after college work is over which is at once the most novel and the most glorious feature of university education to-day. Indeed, women have taken more than their due proportion of the prizes, honors, and fellowships which have been accessible to them on the same terms as to men. Their resort to institutions of higher learning has increased far more than that of men. In 1872 the total number of college students in each million of population was 590. Last year it had risen to 1270, much more than doubling in twenty-seven years. During this time the number of men had risen from 540 to 947, or had not quite doubled. The women rose from 50 in 1872 to 323 in 1899, having increased their former proportional number more than six times, and this advance has also been maintained in graduate and professional schools.

The immensity of the change which the last century has wrought in women's education may best be seen by setting side by side the conditions at its beginning and at its close. In 1800 no colleges for women existed, and only two endowed schools for girls—these belonging to a small German sect. They had no high schools, and the best grammar schools in cities were open to them only under restrictions. The commoner grammar and district schools, and an occasional private school dedicated to "accomplishments," were their only avenues to learning. There was little hostility to their education, since it was generally assumed by men and by themselves that intellectual matters did not concern them. No profession was open to them, not even that of teaching, and only seven possible trades and occupations.

In 1900 a third of all the college students in the United States are women. Sixty per cent of the pupils in the secondary schools, both public and private, are girls—*i.e.* more girls are preparing for college than boys. Women having in general more leisure than men, there is reason to expect that there will soon be more women than men in our colleges and graduate schools. The time, too, has passed when girls went to college to prepare themselves solely for teaching or for other bread-winning occupations. In considerable numbers they now seek intellectual resources and the enrichment of their private lives. Thus far between 50 and 60 per cent of women college graduates have at some time taught. In the country at large more than 70 per cent of the teaching is done by women, in the North Atlantic portion over 80 per cent. Even in the secondary schools, public and private, more women than men are teaching, though in all other countries the advanced instruction of boys is exclusively in the hands of men. Never before has a nation intrusted all the school training of the vast majority of its future population, men as well as women, to women alone.

XV

WOMEN'S EDUCATION AT THE WORLD'S FAIR[16]

Few persons have stood in the Court of Honor at Chicago and felt the surpassing splendors gathered there, without a certain dismay over its swiftly approaching disappearance. Never in the world before has beauty been so lavish and so transient. Probably in all departments of the Fair a hundred million dollars have been spent. Now the nation's holiday is done, the little half-year is over, and the palaces with their widely gathered treasures vanish like a dream. Is all indeed gone? Will nothing remain? Wise observers perceive some permanent results of the merry-making. What these will be in the busy life of men, others may decide: I point out chiefly a few of the beneficial influences of the great Fair on the life of women.

The triumph of women in what may be called their detached existence, that is, in their guidance of themselves and the separated affairs of their sex, has been unexpectedly great. The Government appointed an independent Board of Lady Managers who, through many difficulties, gathered from every quarter of the globe interesting exhibits of feminine industry and skill. These they gracefully disposed in one of the most dignified buildings of the Fair, itself a woman's design. Here they attractively illustrated every aspect of the life of women, domestic, philanthropic, commercial, literary, artistic, and traced their historic advance. Close at hand, in another building also of their own erection, they appropriately appeared as the guardians and teachers of little children. Their halls were crowded, their dinners praised, their reception invitations coveted. Throughout they showed organizing ability on a huge scale; they developed noteworthy leaders; what is more, they followed them, and they have quarrelled no more, and have pulled wires less, than men in similar situations; their courage, their energy, their tact in the erection of a monument to woman were astonishing; and the efforts of their Central Board were efficiently seconded by similar companies in every state. As in the Sanitary and Christian Commissions and the hospital service of the war, in the multitude of women's clubs, the Woman's Christian Temperance Union, the King's Daughters, the associations for promoting women's suffrage, so once more here women found an opportunity to prove their ability as a banded sex; and it is clear that they awakened in the nation a deeper respect for their powers.

But the very triumph does away with its further necessity. Having amply proved what they can do when banded together, women may now the more easily cease to treat themselves as a peculiar people. Henceforth they are human beings.

[16] Published in *The Forum* for December, 1891.

Women's buildings, women's exhibits, may safely become things of the past. At any future fair no special treatment of women is likely to be called for. After what has been achieved, the self-consciousness of women will be lessened, and their sensitiveness about their own position, capacity, and rights will be naturally outgrown. The anthropologist may perhaps still assemble the work of a single sex, the work of people of a single color, or of those having blue eyes. But ordinary people will find less and less interest in these artificial classifications, and will more and more incline to measure men's and women's products by the same scale. Even at Chicago large numbers of women preferred to range their exhibits in the common halls rather than under feminine banners, and their demonstration of the needlessness of any special treatment of their sex must be reckoned as one of the most considerable of the permanent gains for women from the Fair.

If, then, women have demonstrated that they are more than isolated phenomena, that they should indeed be treated as integral members of the human family, in order to estimate rightly the lasting advantages they have derived from the Fair we must seek those advantages not in isolations but in conjunctions. In the common life of man there is a womanly side and a manly side. Both have profited by one splendid event. Manufactures and transportation and mining and agriculture will hereafter be different because of what has occurred at Chicago; but so will domestic science, the training of the young, the swift intellectual interest, the finer patriotism, the apprehension of beauty, the moral balance. It is by growth in these things that the emancipation of women is to come about, and the Fair has fostered them all in an extraordinary degree.

Although the Fair was officially known as a World's Fair, and it did contain honorable contributions from many foreign countries, it was, in a sense that no other exhibition has been before, a nation's fair. It was the climacteric expression of America's existence. It gathered together our past and our present, and indicated not uncertainly our future. Here were made visible our beginnings, our achievements, our hopes, our dreams. The nation became conscious of itself and was strong, beautiful, proud. All sections of the country not only contributed their most characteristic objects of use and beauty, but their inhabitants also came, and learned to know one another, and their land. During the last two years there has hardly been a village in the country which has not had its club or circle studying the history of the United States. No section has been too poor to subscribe money for maintaining national or state pride. In order to see the great result, men have mortgaged their farms, lonely women have taken heavy life insurance, stringent economy will gladly be practised for years. A friend tells me that she saw an old man, as he left the Court of Honor with tears in his eyes, turn to his gray-haired wife and say, "Well, Susan, it paid even if it did take all the burial money."

Once before, we reached a similar pitch of national consciousness,—in war. Young, unprepared, divided against ourselves, we found ourselves able to mass great armies, endure long strains, organize campaigns, commissariats, hospitals, in altogether independent ways, and on a scale greater than Europe had seen. Then men and women alike learned the value of mutual confidence, the strength of coöperation and organization. Once again now, but this time in the interest of beauty and of peace, we have studied the art of subordinating fragmentary interests to those of a whole. The training we have received as a nation in producing and studying the Fair, must result in a deeper national dignity, which will both free us from irritating sensitiveness over foreign criticism, and give us readiness to learn from other countries whatever lessons they can teach. Our own provinces too will become less provincial. With increased acquaintance, the East has begun to drop its toleration of the West, and to put friendliness and honor in its place. No more will it be believed along the Atlantic coast that the Mississippi Valley cares only for pork, grain and lumber. As such superstitions decay, a more trustful unity becomes possible. The entire nation knows itself a nation, possessed of common ideals. In this heightened national dignity, women will have a large and ennobling share.

But further, from the Fair men, and women with them, have acquired a new sense of the gains that come from minute obedience to law. Hitherto, "go as you please" has been pretty largely the principle of American life. In the training school of the last two years of preparation and the six months of the holding of the Fair, our people, particularly our women, have been solidly taught the hard and needful lesson that whims, waywardness, haste, inaccuracy, pettiness, personal considerations, do not make for strength. Wherever these have entered, they have flawed the beautiful whole, and flecked the honor of us all. Where they have been absent results have appeared which make us all rejoice. Never in so wide an undertaking was the unity of a single design so triumphant. As an unknown multitude coöperated in the building of a mediæval cathedral, so throughout our land multitudes have been daily ready to contribute their unmarked best for the erection of a common glory. We have thus learned to prize second thoughts above first thoughts, to league our lives and purposes with those of others, and to subordinate the assertion of ourselves to that of a universal reason. Hence has sprung a new trust in one another and a new confidence in our future. The friendliness of our people, already rendered natural by our democratic institutions, has received a deeper sanction. How distinctly it was marked on the faces of the visitors at the Fair! I was fortunate enough to spend several hours there on Chicago Day, when nearly seven hundred and fifty thousand people were admitted. The appearance of those plain, intelligent, happy, helpful thousands, all strangers and all kind, was the most encouraging sight one woman had at the Fair. It has been said that the moral education of a child consists in imparting to him the three qualities, obedience, sympathy, dignity. These all have been taught by the Fair, and women, more swiftly perceptive than men, have probably learned their lesson best.

One more profound effect of the Fair upon human character must be mentioned, on character in those features which are of especial importance to women. Our people have here gained a new sense of beauty, and of beauty at its highest and rarest, not the beauty of ornament and decoration, but that of proportion, balance, and ordered suitability of parts. Every girl likes pretty things, but the rational basis of beauty in the harmonious expression of use, and in furnishing to the eye the quiet satisfaction of its normal demands, seldom attracts attention. At Chicago these things became apparent. Each building outwardly announced its inner purpose. Each gained its effect mainly by outline and balance of masses rather than by richness of detail. Each was designed in reference to its site and to its neighbor buildings. Almost every one rested the eye which it still stimulated. Color, form, purpose, proportion, sculpture, vegetation, stretches of water, the brown earth, all coöperated toward the happy effect. What visitor could see it and not have begotten in him the demand for beauty in his own surroundings? It is said that the Centennial Exhibition affected the domestic architecture and the household decoration of the whole eastern seaboard. The Fair will do the same, but it will bring about a beauty of a higher, simpler sort. In people from every section, artistic taste has been developed, or even created; and not only in their houses, but in the architecture of their public buildings and streets shall we see the results of this vision of the White City by the Lake. Huddled houses in incongruous surroundings will become less common. At heart we Americans are idealists, and at a time when the general wealth is rapidly increasing, it is an indescribable gain to have had such a training of the æsthetic sense as days among the great buildings and nights on the lagoons have brought to millions of our people. The teachability of the common American is almost pathetic. One building was always crowded—the Fine Arts Building; yet great pictures were the one thing exhibited with which Americans have hitherto had little or no acquaintance. This beauty, connected essentially with the feminine side of life, will hereafter, through the influence of the Fair, become a more usual possession of us all.

If such are the permanent gains for character which women in common with men, yet even more than they, have derived from the Fair, there remain to be considered certain helps which have been brought to women in some of their most distinctive occupations. Of course they have had here an opportunity to compare the different kinds of sewing-machines, pianos, type-writers, telegraphs, clothes-wringers, stoves, and baby-carriages, and no doubt they will do their future work with these complicated engines more effectively because of such comparative study. But there are three departments which ancestral usage has especially consecrated to women, and to intelligent methods in each of these the Fair has given a mighty impulse. These three departments are the care of the home, the care of the young, and the care of the sick, the poor, and the depraved.

At Philadelphia in 1876 Vienna bread was made known, and the native article, sodden with saleratus, which up to that time had desolated the country, began to disappear. The results in cookery from the Chicago Exhibition will be wider. They touch the kitchen with intelligence at more points. Where tradition has reigned unquestioned, science is beginning to penetrate, and we are no longer allowed to eat without asking why and what. This new "domestic science"—threatening word—was set forth admirably in the Rumford Kitchen, where a capital thirty-cent luncheon was served every day, compounded of just those ingredients which the human frame could be demonstrated to require. The health-food companies, too, arrayed their appetizing wares. Workingmen's homes showed on how small a sum a family could live, and live well. Arrangements for sterilizing water and milk were there, Atkinson cookers, gas and kerosene stoves. The proper sanitation of the home was taught, and boards of health turned out to the plain gaze of the world their inquisitorial processes. Numberless means of increasing the health, ease, and happiness of the household with the least expenditure of time and money were here studied by crowds of despairing housekeepers. Many, no doubt, were bewildered; but many, too, went away convinced that the most ancient employment of women was rising to the dignity and attractiveness of a learned profession.

When it is remembered that nine tenths of the teachers of elementary schools are women, it can be seen how important for them was the magnificent educational exhibit. Here could be studied all that the age counts best in kindergarten, primary, grammar, high and normal schools, and in all the varieties of training in cookery, sewing, dressmaking, manual training, drawing, painting, carving. Many of the exhibitors showed great skill in making their methods apprehensible to the stranger.

And then there were the modes of bodily training, and the lamentable image of the misformed average girl; and in the children's building classes could actually be seen engaged in happy exercise, and close at hand appliances for the nursery and the playground. Nor in the enlarged appliances for woman's domestic life must those be omitted which tell how cheaply and richly the girl may now obtain a college training like her brother, and become as intelligent as he. No woman went away from the educational exhibits of the Fair in the belief that woman's sphere was necessarily narrow.

There is no need to dilate on the light shed by the Fair upon problems of sickness, poverty, and crime. Everybody knows that nothing so complete had been seen before. The Anthropological Building was a museum of these subjects, and scattered in other parts of the Fair was much to interest the puzzled and sympathetic soul. One could find out what an ideal hospital was like, and how its service and appliances should be ordered. One studied under competent teachers the care of the dependent and delinquent classes. One learned to distinguish surface charity from sound. As men grow busier and women more competent, the guidance of philanthropy passes continually more and more into the gentler hands. Women serve largely on boards of hospitals, prisons, charities, and reforms, and urgently feel the need of ampler knowledge. The Fair did much to show them ways of obtaining it.

Such are the permanent results of the Fair most likely to affect women. They fall into three classes: the proofs women have given of their independent power, their ability to organize and to work toward a distant, difficult, and complex end; the enlargement of their outlook, manifesting itself in a new sense of membership in a nation, a more willing obedience to law, and a higher appreciation of beauty; and, lastly, the direct assistance given to women in their more characteristic employments of housekeeping, teaching, and ministering to the afflicted. That these are all, or even the most important, results which each woman will judge she has obtained, is not pretended. Everybody saw at the Fair something which brought to individual him or her a gain incomparable.

And, after all, the greatest thing was the total, glittering, murmurous, restful, magical, evanescent Fair itself, seated by the blue waters, wearing the five crowns, served by novel boatmen, and with the lap so full of treasure that as piece by piece it was held up, it shone, was wondered at, and was lost again in the pile. This amazing spectacle will flash for years upon the inward eye of our people, and be a joy of their solitude.

XVI

WHY GO TO COLLEGE?

To a largely increasing number of young girls college doors are opening every year. Every year adds to the number of men who feel as a friend of mine, a successful lawyer in a great city, felt when in talking of the future of his four little children he said, "For the two boys it is not so serious, but I lie down at night afraid to die and leave my daughters only a bank account." Year by year, too, the experiences of life are teaching mothers that happiness does not necessarily come to their daughters when accounts are large and banks are sound, but that on the contrary they take grave risks when they trust everything to accumulated wealth and the chance of a happy marriage. Our American girls themselves are becoming aware that they need the stimulus, the discipline, the knowledge, the interests of the college in addition to the school, if they are to prepare themselves for the most serviceable lives.

But there are still parents who say, "There is no need that my daughter should teach; then why should she go to college?" I will not reply that college training is a life insurance for a girl, a pledge that she possesses the disciplined ability to earn a living for herself and others in case of need; for I prefer to insist on the importance of giving every girl, no matter what her present circumstances, a special training in some one thing by which she can render society service, not of amateur but of expert sort, and service too for which it will be willing to pay a price. The number of families will surely increase who will follow the example of an eminent banker whose daughters have been given each her specialty. One has chosen music, and has gone far with the best masters in this country and in Europe, so far that she now holds a high rank among musicians at home and abroad. Another has taken art; and has not been content to paint pretty gifts for her friends, but in the studios of New York, Munich, and Paris she has won the right to be called an artist, and in her studio at home to paint portraits which have a market value. A third has proved that she can earn her living, if need be, by her exquisite jellies, preserves, and sweetmeats. Yet the house in the mountains, the house by the sea, and the friends in the city are not neglected, nor are these young women found less attractive because of their special accomplishments.

While it is not true that all girls should go to college any more than that all boys should go, it is nevertheless true that they should go in greater numbers than at present. They fail to go because they, their parents, and their teachers, do not see clearly the personal benefits distinct from the commercial value of a college training. I wish here to discuss these benefits, these larger gifts of the college life,—what they may be, and for whom they are waiting.

It is undoubtedly true that many girls are totally unfitted by home and school life for a valuable college course. These joys and successes, these high interests and friendships, are not for the self-conscious and nervous invalid, nor for her who in the exuberance of youth recklessly ignores the laws of a healthy life. The good society of scholars and of libraries and laboratories has no place and no attraction for her who finds no message in Plato, no beauty in mathematical order, and who never longs to know the meaning of the stars over her head or the flowers under her feet. Neither will the finer opportunities of college life appeal to one who, until she is eighteen (is there such a girl in this country?), has felt no passion for the service of others, no desire to know if through history, or philosophy, or any study of the laws of society, she can learn why the world is so sad, so hard, so selfish as she finds it, even when she looks upon it from the most sheltered life. No, the college cannot be, should not try to be, a substitute for the hospital, reformatory, or kindergarten. To do its best work it should be organized for the strong, not for the weak; for the high-minded, self-controlled, generous, and courageous spirits, not for the indifferent, the dull, the idle, or those who are already forming their characters on the amusement theory of life. All these perverted young people may, and often do, get large benefit and invigoration, new ideals, and unselfish purposes from their four years' companionship with teachers and comrades of a higher physical, mental, and moral stature than their own. I have seen girls change so much in college that I have wondered if their friends at home would know them,—the voice, the carriage, the unconscious manner, all telling a story of new tastes and habits and loves and interests, that had wrought out in very truth a new creature. Yet in spite of this I have sometimes thought that in college more than elsewhere the old law holds, "To him that hath shall be given and he shall have abundance, but from him who hath not shall be taken away even that which he seemeth to have." For it is the young life which is open and prepared to receive which obtains the gracious and uplifting influences of college days. What, then, for such persons are the rich and abiding rewards of study in college or university?

Preëminently the college is a place of education. That is the ground of its being. We go to college to know, assured that knowledge is sweet and powerful, that a good education emancipates the mind and makes us citizens of the world. No college which does not thoroughly educate can be called good, no matter what else it does. No student who fails to get a little knowledge on many subjects, and much knowledge on some, can be said to have succeeded, whatever other advantages she may have found by the way. It is a beautiful and significant fact that in all times the years of learning have been also the years of romance. Those who love girls and boys pray that our colleges may be homes of sound learning, for knowledge is the condition of every college blessing. "Let no man incapable of mathematics enter here," Plato is reported to have inscribed over his Academy door. "Let no one to whom hard study is repulsive hope for anything from us," American colleges might paraphrase. Accordingly in my talk to-day I shall say little of the direct benefits of knowledge which the college affords. These may be assumed. It is on their account that one knocks at the college door. But seeking this first, a good many other things are added. I want to point out some of these collateral advantages of going to college, or rather to draw attention to some of the many forms in which the winning of knowledge presents itself.

The first of these is happiness. Everybody wants "a good time," especially every girl in her teens. A good time, it is true, does not always in these years mean what it will mean by and by, any more than the girl of eighteen plays with the doll which entranced the child of eight. It takes some time to discover that work is the best sort of play, and some people never discover it at all. But when mothers ask such questions as these: "How can I make my daughter happy?" "How can I give her the best society?" "How can she have a good time?" the answer in most cases is simple. Send her to college—to almost any college. Send her because there is no other place where between eighteen and twenty-two she is so likely to have a genuinely good time. Merely for good times, for romance, for society, college life offers unequalled opportunities. Of course no idle person can possibly be happy, even for a day, nor she who makes a business of trying to amuse herself. For full happiness, though its springs are within, we want health and friends and work and objects of aspiration. "We live by admiration, hope, and love," says Wordsworth. The college abounds in all three. In the college time new powers are sprouting, and intelligence, merriment, truthfulness, and generosity are more natural than the opposite qualities often become in later years. An exhilarating atmosphere pervades the place. We who are in it all the time feel that we live at the fountain of perpetual youth, and those who take but a four years' bath in it become more cheerful, strong, and full of promise than they are ever likely to find themselves again; for a college is a kind of compendium of the things that most men long for. It is usually planted in a beautiful spot, the charm of trees and water being added to stately buildings and stimulating works of art. Venerable associations of the past hallow its halls. Leaders in the stirring world of to-day return at each Commencement to share the fresh life of the new class. Books, pictures, music, collections, appliances in every field, learned teachers, mirthful friends, athletics for holidays, the best words of the best men for holy days,—all are here. No wonder that men look back upon their college life as upon halcyon days, the romantic period of youth. No wonder that Dr. Holmes's poems to his Harvard classmates find an echo in college reunions everywhere; and gray-haired men, who outside the narrowing circle of home have not heard their first names for years, remain Bill and Joe and John and George to college comrades, even if unseen for more than a generation.

Yet a girl should go to college not merely to obtain four happy years, but to make a second gain, which is often overlooked, and is little understood even when perceived; I mean a gain in health. The old notion that low vitality is a matter of course with women; that to be delicate is a mark of superior refinement, especially in well-to-do families; that sickness is a dispensation of Providence,—these notions meet with no acceptance in college. Years ago I saw in the mirror frame of a college freshman's room this little formula: "Sickness is carelessness, carelessness is selfishness, and selfishness is sin." And I have often noticed among college girls an air of humiliation and shame when obliged to confess a lack of physical vigor, as if they were convicted of managing life with bad judgment, or of some moral delinquency. With the spreading scientific conviction that health is a matter largely under each person's control, that even inherited tendencies to disease need not be allowed to run their riotous course unchecked, there comes an earnest purpose to be strong and free. Fascinating fields of knowledge are waiting to be explored; possibilities of doing, as well as of knowing, are on every side; new and dear friendships enlarge and sweeten dreams of future study and work, and the young student cannot afford quivering nerves or small lungs or an aching head any more than bad taste, rough manners, or a weak will. Handicapped by inheritance or bad training, she finds the plan of college life itself her supporter and friend. The steady, long-continued routine of mental work, physical exercise, recreation, and sleep, the simple and wholesome food, in place of irregular and unstudied diet, work out salvation for her. Instead of being left to go out of doors when she feels like it, the regular training of the gymnasium, the boats on lake and river, the tennis court, the golf links, the basket ball, the bicycle, the long walk among the woods in search of botanical or geological specimens,—all these and many more call to the busy student, until she realizes that they have their rightful place in every well-ordered day of every month. So she learns, little by little, that buoyant health is a precious possession to be won and kept.

It is significant that already statistical investigation in this country and in England shows that the standard of health is higher among the women who hold college degrees than among any other equal number of the same age and class. And it is interesting also to observe to what sort of questions our recent girl graduates have been inclined to devote attention. They have been largely the neglected problems of little children and their health, of home sanitation, of food and its choice and preparation, of domestic service, of the cleanliness of schools and public buildings. Colleges for girls are pledged by their very constitution to make persistent war on the water cure, the nervine retreat, the insane asylum, the hospital,—those bitter fruits of the emotional lives of thousands of women. "I can never afford a sick headache again, life is so interesting and there is so much to do," a delicate girl said to me at the end of her first college year. And while her mother was in a far-off invalid retreat, she undertook the battle against fate with the same intelligence and courage which she put into her calculus problems and her translations of Sophocles. Her beautiful home and her rosy and happy children prove the measure of her hard-won success. Formerly the majority of physicians had but one question for the mother of the nervous and delicate girl, "Does she go to school?" And only one prescription, "Take her out of school." Never a suggestion as to suppers of pickles and pound-cake, never a hint about midnight dancing and hurried daytime ways. But now the sensible doctor asks, "What are her interests? What are her tastes? What are her habits?" And he finds new interests for her, and urges the formation of out-of-door tastes and steady occupation for the mind, in order to draw the morbid girl from herself into the invigorating world outside. This the college does largely through its third gift of friendship.

Until a girl goes away from home to school or college, her friends are chiefly chosen for her by circumstances. Her young relatives, her neighbors in the same street, those who happen to go to the same school or church,—these she makes her girlish intimates. She goes to college with the entire conviction, half unknown to herself, that her father's political party contains all the honest men, her mother's social circle all the true ladies, her church all the real saints of the community. And the smaller the town, the more absolute is her belief. But in college she finds that the girl who earned her scholarship in the village school sits beside the banker's daughter; the New England farmer's child rooms next the heiress of a Hawaiian sugar plantation; the daughters of the opposing candidates in a sharply fought election have grown great friends in college boats and laboratories; and before her diploma is won she realizes how much richer a world she lives in than she ever dreamed of at home. The wealth that lies in differences has dawned upon her vision. It is only when the rich and poor sit down together that either can understand how the Lord is the Maker of them all.

To-day above all things we need the influence of men and women of friendliness, of generous nature, of hospitality to new ideas, in short, of social imagination. But instead, we find each political party bitterly calling the other dishonest, each class suspicious of the intentions of the other, and in social life the pettiest standards of conduct. Is it not well for us that the colleges all over the country still offer to their fortunate students a society of the most democratic sort,—one in which a father's money, a mother's social position, can assure no distinction and make no close friends? Here capacity of every kind counts for its full value. Here enthusiasm waits to make heroes of those who can lead. Here charming manners, noble character, amiable temper, scholarly power, find their full opportunity and inspire such friendships as are seldom made afterward. I have forgotten my chemistry, and my classical philology cannot bear examination; but all round the world there are men and women at work, my intimates of college days, who have made the wide earth a friendly place to me. Of every creed, of every party, in far-away places and in near, the thought of them makes me more courageous in duty and more faithful to opportunity, though for many years we may not have had time to write each other a letter. The basis of all valuable and enduring friendships is not accident or juxtaposition, but tastes, interests, habits, work, ambitions. It is for this reason that to college friendship clings a romance entirely its own. One of the friends may spend her days in the laboratory, eagerly chasing the shy facts that hide beyond the microscope's fine vision, and the other may fill her hours and her heart with the poets and the philosophers; one may steadfastly pursue her way toward the command of a hospital, and the other toward the world of letters and of art; these divergences constitute no barrier, but rather an aid to the fulness of friendship. And the fact that one goes in a simple gown which she has earned and made herself, and the other lives when at home in a merchant's modern palace—what has that to do with the things the girls care about and the dreams they talk over in the walk by the river or the bicycle ride through country roads? If any young man to-day goes through Harvard lonely, neglected, unfriended, if any girl lives solitary and wretched in her life at Wellesley, it is their own fault. It must be because they are suspicious, unfriendly, or disagreeable themselves. Certainly it is true that in the associations of college life, more than in any other that the country can show, what is extraneous, artificial, and temporary falls away, and the every-day relations of life and work take on a character that is simple, natural, genuine. And so it comes about that the fourth gift of college life is ideals of personal character.

To some people the shaping ideals of what character should be, often held unconsciously, come from the books they read; but to the majority they are given by the persons whom they most admire before they are twenty years old. The greatest thing any friend or teacher, either in school or college, can do for a student is to furnish him with a personal ideal. The college professors who transformed me through my acquaintance with them—ah, they were few, and I am sure I did not have a dozen conversations with them outside their classrooms—gave me, each in his different way, an ideal of character, of conduct, of the scholar, the leader, of which they and I were totally unconscious at the time. For many years I have known that my study with them, no matter whether of philosophy or of Greek, of mathematics or history or English, enlarged my notions of life, uplifted my standards of culture, and so inspired me with new possibilities of usefulness and of happiness. Not the facts and theories that I learned so much as the men who taught me, gave this inspiration. The community at large is right in saying that it wants the personal influence of professors on students, but it is wholly wrong in assuming that this precious influence comes from frequent meetings or talks on miscellaneous subjects. There is quite as likely to be a quickening force in the somewhat remote and mysterious power of the teacher who devotes himself to amassing treasures of scholarship, or to patiently working out the best methods of teaching; who standing somewhat apart, still remains an ideal of the Christian scholar, the just, the courteous man or woman. To come under the influence of one such teacher is enough to make college life worth while. A young man who came to Harvard with eighty cents in his pocket, and worked his way through, never a high scholar, and now in a business which looks very commonplace, told me the other day that he would not care to be alive if he had not gone to college. His face flushed as he explained how different his days would have been if he had not known two of his professors. "Do you use your college studies in your business?" I asked. "Oh, no!" he answered. "But I am another man in doing the business; and when the day's work is done I live another life because of my college experiences. The business and I are both the better for it every day." How many a young girl has had her whole horizon extended by the changed ideals she gained in college! Yet this is largely because the associations and studies there are likely to give her permanent interests—the fifth and perhaps the greatest gift of college life of which I shall speak.

The old fairy story which charmed us in childhood ended with "And they were married and lived happy ever after." It conducted to the altar, having brought the happy pair through innumerable difficulties, and left us with the contented sense that all the mistakes and problems would now vanish and life be one long day of unclouded bliss. I have seen devoted and intelligent mothers arrange their young daughters' education and companionships precisely on this basis. They planned as if these pretty and charming girls were going to live only twenty or twenty-five years at the utmost, and had consequently no need of the wealthy interests that should round out the fullgrown woman's stature, making her younger in feeling at forty than at twenty, and more lovely and admired at eighty than at either.

Emerson in writing of beauty declares that "the secret of ugliness consists not in irregular outline, but in being uninteresting. We love any forms, however ugly, from which great qualities shine. If command, eloquence, art, or invention exists in the most deformed person, all the accidents that usually displease, please, and raise esteem and wonder higher. Beauty without grace is the head without the body. Beauty without expression tires." Of course such considerations can hardly come with full force to the young girl herself, who feels aged at eighteen, and imagines that the troubles and problems of life and thought are hers already. "Oh, tell me to-night," cried a college freshman once to her president, "which is the right side and which is the wrong side of this Andover question about eschatology?" The young girl is impatient of open questions, and irritated at her inability to answer them. Neither can she believe that the first headlong zest with which she throws herself into society, athletics, into everything which comes in her way, can ever fail. But her elders know, looking on, that our American girl, the comrade of her parents and of her brothers and their friends, brought up from babyhood in the eager talk of politics and society, of religious belief, of public action, of social responsibility—that this typical girl, with her quick sympathies, her clear head, her warm heart, her outreaching hands, will not permanently be satisfied or self-respecting, though she have the prettiest dresses and hats in town, or the most charming of dinners, dances, and teas. Unless there comes to her, and comes early, the one chief happiness of life,—a marriage of comradeship,—she must face for herself the question, "What shall I do with my life?"

I recall a superb girl of twenty as I overtook her one winter morning hurrying along Commonwealth Avenue. She spoke of a brilliant party at a friend's the previous evening. "But, oh!" she cried, throwing up her hands in a kind of hopeless impatience, "tell me what to do. My dancing days are over!" I laughed at her, "Have you sprained your ankle?" But I saw I had made a mistake when she added, "It is no laughing matter. I have been out three years. I have not done what they expected of me," with a flush and a shrug, "and there is a crowd of nice girls coming on this winter; and anyway, I am so tired of going to teas and ball-games and assemblies! I don't care the least in the world for foreign missions, and," with a stamp, "I am not going slumming among the Italians. I have too much respect for the Italians. And what shall I do with the rest of my life?" That was a frank statement of what any girl of brains or conscience feels, with more or less bitter distinctness, unless she marries early, or has some pressing work for which she is well trained.

Yet even if that which is the profession of woman *par excellence* be hers, how can she be perennially so interesting a companion to her husband and children as if she had keen personal tastes, long her own, and growing with her growth? Indeed, in that respect the condition of men is almost the same as that of women. It would be quite the same were it not for the fact that a man's business or profession is generally in itself a means of growth, of education, of dignity. He leans his life against it. He builds his home in the shadow of it. It binds his days together in a kind of natural piety, and makes him advance in strength and nobility as he "fulfils the common round, the daily task." And that is the reason why men in the past, if they have been honorable men, have grown old better than women. Men usually retain their ability longer, their mental alertness and hospitality. They add fine quality to fine quality, passing from strength to strength and preserving in old age whatever has been best in youth. It was a sudden recognition of this fact which made a young friend of mine say last winter, "I am not going to parties any more; the men best worth talking with are too old to dance."

Even with the help of a permanent business or profession, however, the most interesting men I know are those who have an avocation as well as a vocation. I mean a taste or work quite apart from the business of life. This revives, inspires, and cultivates them perpetually. It matters little what it is, if only it is real and personal, is large enough to last, and possesses the power of growth. A young sea-captain from a New England village on a long and lonely voyage falls upon a copy of Shelley. Appeal is made to his fine but untrained mind, and the book of the boy poet becomes the seaman's university. The wide world of poetry and of the other fine arts is opened, and the Shelleyian specialist becomes a cultivated, original, and charming man. A busy merchant loves flowers, and in all his free hours studies them. Each new spring adds knowledge to his knowledge, and his friends continually bring him their strange discoveries. With growing wealth he cultivates rare and beautiful plants, and shares them with his fortunate acquaintances. Happy the companion invited to a walk or a drive with such observant eyes, such vivid talk! Because of this cheerful interest in flowers, and this ingenious skill in dealing with them, the man himself is interesting. All his powers are alert, and his judgment is valued in public life and in private business. Or is it more exact to say that because he is the kind of man who would insist upon having such interests outside his daily work, he is still fresh and young and capable of growth at an age when many other men are dull and old and certain that the time of decay is at hand?

There are two reasons why women need to cultivate these large and abiding interests even more persistently than men. In the first place, they have more leisure. They are indeed the only leisured class in the country, the only large body of persons who are not called upon to win their daily bread in direct, wage-earning ways. As yet, fortunately, few men among us have so little self-respect as to idle about our streets and drawing-rooms because their fathers are rich enough to support them. We are not without our unemployed poor; but roving tramps and idle clubmen are after all not of large consequence. Our serious non-producing classes are chiefly women. It is the regular ambition of the chivalrous American to make all the women who depend on him so comfortable that they need do nothing for themselves. Machinery has taken nearly all the former occupations of women out of the home into the shop and factory. Widespread wealth and comfort, and the inherited theory that it is not well for the woman to earn money so long as father or brothers can support her, have brought about a condition of things in which there is social danger, unless with the larger leisure are given high and enduring interests. To health especially there is great danger, for nothing breaks down a woman's health like idleness and its resulting ennui. More people, I am sure, are broken down nervously because they are bored, than because they are overworked; and more still go to pieces through fussiness, unwholesome living, worry over petty details, and the daily disappointments which result from small and superficial training. And then, besides the danger to health, there is the danger to character. I need not dwell on the undermining influence which men also feel when occupation is taken away and no absorbing private interest fills the vacancy. The vices of luxurious city life are perhaps hardly more destructive to character than is the slow deterioration of barren country life. Though the conditions in the two cases are exactly opposite, the trouble is often the same,—absence of noble interests. In the city restless idleness organizes amusement; in the country deadly dulness succeeds daily toil.

But there is a second reason why a girl should acquire for herself strong and worthy interests. The regular occupations of women in their homes are generally disconnected and of little educational value, at least as those homes are at present conducted. Given the best will in the world, the daily doing of household details becomes a wearisome monotony if the mere performance of them is all. To make drudgery divine a woman must have a brain to plan and eyes to see how to "sweep a room as to God's laws." Imagination and knowledge should be the hourly companions of her who would make a fine art of each detail in kitchen and nursery. Too long has the pin been the appropriate symbol of the average woman's life—the pin, which only temporarily holds together things which may or may not have any organic connection with one another. While undoubtedly most women must spend the larger part of life in this modest pin-work, holding together the little things of home and school and society and church, it is also true, that cohesive work itself cannot be done well, even in humble circumstances, except by the refined, the trained, the growing woman. The smallest village, the plainest home, give ample space for the resources of the trained college woman. And the reason why such homes and such villages are so often barren of grace and variety is just because these fine qualities have not ruled them. The higher graces of civilization halt among us; dainty and finished ways of living give place to common ways, while vulgar tastes, slatternly habits, clouds and despondency reign in the house. Little children under five years of age die in needless thousands because of the dull, unimaginative women on whom they depend. Such women have been satisfied with just getting along, instead of packing everything they do with brains, instead of studying the best possible way of doing everything small or large; for there is always a best way, whether of setting a table, of trimming a hat, or teaching a child to read. And this taste for perfection can be cultivated; indeed, it must be cultivated, if our standards of living are to be raised. There is now scientific knowledge enough, there is money enough, to prevent the vast majority of the evils which afflict our social organism, if mere knowledge or wealth could avail; but the greater difficulty is to make intelligence, character, good taste, unselfishness prevail.

What, then, are the interests which powerfully appeal to mind and heart, and so are fitted to become the strengthening companions of a woman's life? I shall mention only three, all of them such as are elaborately fostered by college life. The first is the love of great literature. I do not mean that use of books by which a man may get what is called a good education and so be better qualified for the battle of life, nor do I mention books in their character as reservoirs of knowledge, books which we need for special purposes, and which are no longer of consequence when our purpose with them is served. I have in mind the great books, especially the great poets, books to be adopted as a resource and a solace. The chief reason why so many people do not know how to make comrades of such books is because they have come to them too late. We have in this country enormous numbers of readers,—probably a larger number who read, and who read many hours in the week, than has ever been known elsewhere in the world. But what do these millions read besides the newspapers? Possibly a denominational religious weekly and another journal of fashion or business. Then come the thousands who read the best magazines, and whatever else is for the moment popular in novels and poetry—the last dialect story, the fashionable poem, the questionable but talked-of novel. Let a violent attack be made on the decency of a new story, and instantly, if only it is clever, its author becomes famous.

But the fashions in reading of a restless race—the women too idle, the men too heavily worked—I will not discuss here. Let light literature be devoured by our populace as his drug is taken by the opium-eater, and with a similar narcotic effect. We can only seek out the children, and hope by giving them from babyhood bits of the noblest literature, to prepare them for the great opportunities of mature life. I urge, therefore, reading as a mental stimulus, as a solace in trouble, a perpetual source of delight; and I would point out that we must not delay to make the great friendships that await us on the library shelves until sickness shuts the door on the outer world, or death enters the home and silences the voices that once helped to make these friendships sweet. If Homer and Shakespeare and Wordsworth and Browning are to have meaning for us when we need them most, it will be because they come to us as old familiar friends whose influences have permeated the glad and busy days before. The last time I heard James Russell Lowell talk to college girls, he said,—for he was too ill to say many words,—"I have only this one message to leave with you. In all your work in college never lose sight of the reason why you have come here. It is not that you may get something by which to earn your bread, but that every mouthful of bread may be the sweeter to your taste."

And this is the power possessed by the mighty dead,—men of every time and nation, whose voices death cannot silence, who are waiting even at the poor man's elbow, whose illuminating words may be had for the price of a day's work in the kitchen or the street, for lack of love of whom many a luxurious home is a dull and solitary spot, breeding misery and vice. Now the modern college is especially equipped to introduce its students to such literature. The library is at last understood to be the heart of the college. The modern librarian is not the keeper of books as was his predecessor, but the distributer of them, and the guide to their resources, proud when he increases the use of his treasures. Every language, ancient or modern, which contains a literature is now taught in college. Its history is examined, its philology, its masterpieces, and more than ever is English literature studied and loved. There is now every opportunity for the college student to become an expert in the use of his own tongue and pen. What other men painfully strive for he can enjoy to the full with comparatively little effort.

But there is a second invigorating interest to which college training introduces its student. I mean the study of nature, intimacy with the strange and beautiful world in which we live. "Nature never did betray the heart that loved her," sang her poet and high priest. When the world has been too much with us, nothing else is so refreshing to tired eyes and mind as woods and water, and an intelligent knowledge of the life within them. For a generation past there has been a well-nigh universal turning of the population toward the cities. In 1840 only nine per cent of our people lived in cities of eight thousand inhabitants or more. Now more than a third of us are found in cities. But the electric car, the telephone, the bicycle, still keep avenues to the country open. Certain it is that city people feel a growing hunger for the country, particularly when grass begins to grow. This is a healthy taste, and must increase the general knowledge and love of nature. Fortunate are the little children in those schools whose teachers know and love the world in which they live. Their young eyes are early opened to the beauty of birds and trees and plants. Not only should we expect our girls to have a feeling for the fine sunset or the wide-reaching panorama of field and water, but to know something also about the less obvious aspects of nature, its structure, its methods of work, and the endless diversity of its parts. No one can have read Matthew Arnold's letters to his wife, his mother, and his sister, without being struck by the immense enjoyment he took throughout his singularly simple and hard-working life in flowers and trees and rivers. The English lake country had given him this happy inheritance, with everywhere its sound of running water and its wealth of greenery. There is a close connection between the marvellous unbroken line of English song and the passionate love of the Englishman for a home in the midst of birds, trees, and green fields.

> The world is so full of a number of things,
> That I think we should all be as happy as kings,

is the opinion of everybody who knows nature as did Robert Louis Stevenson. And so our college student may begin to know it. Let her enter the laboratories and investigate for herself. Let her make her delicate experiments with the blowpipe or the balance; let her track mysterious life from one hiding-place to another; let her "name all the birds without a gun," and make intimates of flower and fish and butterfly—and she is dull indeed if breezy tastes do not follow her through life, and forbid any of her days to be empty of intelligent enjoyment. "Keep your years beautiful; make your own atmosphere," was the parting advice of my college president, himself a living illustration of what he said.

But it is a short step from the love of the complex and engaging world in which we live to the love of our comrades in it. Accordingly the third precious interest to be cultivated by the college student is an interest in people. The scholar to-day is not a being who dwells apart in his cloister, the monk's successor; he is a leader of the thoughts and conduct of men. So the new subjects which stand beside the classics and mathematics of mediæval culture are history, economics, ethics, and sociology. Although these subjects are as yet merely in the making, thousands of students are flocking to their investigation, and are going out to try their tentative knowledge in College Settlements and City Missions and Children's Aid Societies. The best instincts of generous youth are becoming enlisted in these living themes.

And why should our daughters remain aloof from the most absorbing work of modern city life, work quite as fascinating to young women as to young men? During many years of listening to college sermons and public lectures in Wellesley, I always noticed a quickened attention in the audience whenever the discussion touched politics or theology. These are, after all, the permanent and peremptory interests, and they should be given their full place in a healthy and vigorous life.

But if that life includes a love of books, of nature, of people, it will naturally turn to enlarged conceptions of religion—my sixth and last gift of college life. In his first sermon as Master of Balliol College, Dr. Jowett spoke of the college, "First as a place of education, secondly as a place of society, thirdly as a place of religion." He observed that "men of very great ability often fail in life because they are unable to play their part with effect. They are shy, awkward, self-conscious, deficient in manners, faults which are as ruinous as vices." The supreme end of college training, he said, "is usefulness in after life." Similarly, when the city of Cambridge celebrated in Harvard's Memorial Hall the life and death of the gallant young ex-Governor of Massachusetts, William E. Russell, men did well to hang above his portrait some wise words he had lately said, "Never forget the everlasting difference between making a living and making a life." That he himself never forgot; and it was well to remind citizens and students of it, as they stood there facing too the ancient words all Harvard men face when they take their college degrees and go out into the world, "They that be wise shall shine as the brightness of the firmament, and they that turn many to righteousness as the stars for ever and ever." Good words these to go out from college with. The girls of Wellesley gather every morning at chapel to bow their heads together for a moment before they scatter among the libraries and lecture rooms and begin the experiments of the new day. And always their college motto meets the eyes that are raised to its penetrating message, "Not to be ministered unto, but to minister." How many a young heart has loyally responded, "And to give life a ransom for many." That is the "Wellesley spirit"; and the same sweet spirit of devout service has gone forth from all our college halls. In any of them one may catch the echo of Whittier's noble psalm,—

> Our Lord and Master of us all!
> Whate'er our name or sign,
> We own Thy sway, we hear Thy call,
> We test our lives by Thine.

That is the supreme test of life,—its consecrated serviceableness. The Master of Balliol was right; the brave men and women who founded our schools and colleges were not wrong. "For Christ and the Church" universities were set up in the wilderness of New England; for the large service of the state they have been founded and maintained at public cost in every section of the country where men have settled, from the Alleghanies across the prairies and Rocky Mountains down to the Golden Gate. Founded primarily as seats of learning, their teachers have been not only scientists and linguists, philosophers and historians, but men and women of holy purposes, sound patriotism, courageous convictions, refined and noble tastes. Set as these teachers have been upon a hill, their light has at no period of our country's history been hid. They have formed a large factor in our civilization, and in their own beautiful characters have continually shown us how to combine religion and life, the ideal and practical, the human and the divine.

Such are some of the larger influences to be had from college life. It is true all the good gifts I have named may be secured without the aid of the college. We all know young men and women who have had no college training, who are as cultivated, rational, resourceful, and happy as any people we know, who excel in every one of these particulars the college graduates about them. I believe they often bitterly regret the lack of a college education. And we see young men and women going through college deaf and blind to their great chances there, and afterwards curiously careless and wasteful of the best things in life. While all this is true, it is true too that to the open-minded and ambitious boy or girl of moderate health, ability, self-control, and studiousness, a college course offers the most attractive, easy, and probable way of securing happiness and health, good friends and high ideals, permanent interests of a noble kind, and large capacity for usefulness in the world. It has been well said that the ability to see great things large and little things small is the final test of education. The foes of life, especially of women's lives, are caprice, wearisome incapacity, and petty judgments. From these oppressive foes we long to escape to the rule of right reason, where all things are possible, and life becomes a glory instead of a grind. No college, with the best teachers and collections in the world, can by its own power impart all this to any woman. But if one has set her face in that direction, where else can she find so many hands reached out to help, so many encouraging voices in the air, so many favoring influences filling the days and nights?

Printed by Libri Plureos GmbH in Hamburg,
Germany